As Long as the Rivers Run

Barbara Seaborn

As Long as the Rivers Run

Highlights From Columbia County's Past

Barbara Seaborn

With the Artistry of
Lynell Widener

Crown Point Publishing
Martinez, Georgia
2011

Published in the United States of America by
Crown Point Publishing
P.O. Box 204239
Martinez, Georgia 30917

Library of Congress Control Number: 2011902547

ISBN 978-0-615-39013-0 (hardcover)
ISBN 978-0-615-39014-7 (softcover)

Manufactured in the United States of America

To
the memories of those who paved the way,
and to those who now, or in the future,
call Columbia County "home"

CONTENTS

Contents

ILLUSTRATIONS

FOREWORD

More than a dozen years ago, when the issue of writing an account of Columbia County history was posed to me, I was asked who I thought could meet such a challenge. One name came to mind: Barbara Seaborn.

I met Barbara more than twenty-five years ago, after I had been publishing the *Columbia County News-Times* for about five years. We were experiencing a period of growth at the time, and I was considering expanding our writing staff. That's when Barbara appeared at my door and presented me with samples of her writing, including opinion pieces on a variety of topics. I told her I would like to begin publishing her columns in our newspaper, and she has continued to write for the *News-Times* ever since.

As we began working together, Barbara impressed me with her writing skills and her professionalism. In 1991, when a group of Columbia Countians traveled to Nowy Sącz, Poland, as part of a sister-city agreement with the county, Barbara and I were included. On that trip I had the opportunity to witness firsthand what a credit she is to her profession.

Readers of *As Long as the Rivers Run* will, no doubt, be both educated and entertained by Barbara's "Highlights From Columbia County's Past." She is a writer who takes research and accuracy to another level, and she has verified the content of these pages so the reader will be exposed to facts, not fiction. Accuracy and credibility often suffer when history books are written too hurriedly. Such is not the case with *As Long as the Rivers Run*.

Barbara Seaborn's commitment to this project has been unwavering, and the results are a credit to her dedication. Those who seek a thoughtful and accurate accounting of Columbia County's past will find it in this work.

Phil Blanchard
Publisher Emeritus
Columbia County News-Times

Preface

What began as a thumbnail sketch of Columbia County, Georgia, from 1750 to the twenty-first century soon evolved into a more detailed but select account of the people and events in county history from her first known inhabitants, circa 4,000 B.C. to the end of the nineteenth century, with an overview of the more recent years. Also, the more I learned, and the more I realized how quickly history in general is fading from our lives, the project acquired another purpose: relating Columbia County history to what was going on in the region and the world at the same time.

This is more than a county story, much less that of just one Georgia county. Columbia County's settling and settlers, challenges and achievements, are a microcosm of all settlements, her record part of the fabric of all places and the people who migrated there. It also is a specific story with outstanding players, including an abundance of state and national leaders, Georgia's only (two) signers of the U.S. Constitution, and the founders and first presidents of three major universities in the state: Emory, Mercer, and the University of Georgia.

But how could I, a Yankee author, write this Southern tale? How could I follow the advice of those who say, "You cannot write history as a spectator; you must become part of the story"? The answer came with time, thirteen years to be exact, and perhaps time enough to absorb the words of Georgia historian Charles C. Jones, Jr., that "Writing history is less a delay than a growth." However, there were pivotal moments during that growth when I realized that I, too, was part of that fabric of all places, even a county south of the Mason-Dixon Line. One moment stands above all the rest.

As a member of the Augusta Genealogical Society I had just attended a lecture about some of the early settlers of the very area I was researching. The program, held on a summer evening at the Augusta Museum of History, was especially interesting to the descendants of those settlers, but from the outset my spirits began to sag. Other than to gather information for this book, I had no connection to any of the stories I heard, no smile of recognition to match those around me who could say with pride, "That was my family; this is my heritage."

I left at dusk, drove west on Greene Street toward the Calhoun Expressway, and happened to glance to the right. There in the darkening sky loomed the unmistakable silhouette of a massive, 168-foot chimney towering over the Harrisburg section of the city, the only remaining structure of the expansive Confederate Powderworks Factory that lined both banks of the Augusta Canal during the Civil War—and I remembered.

Back in my hometown of Milo, Maine, in the front row of the town cemetery and facing another thoroughfare, stand three weathered gravestones bearing the names of my own ancestors who fought in the Civil War. They may not have fought for the Confederacy, and they were not among the 360,000 Union soldiers to die in battle, but they endured the same conflict, experienced similar horrors and hardships, and fought as hard for what they believed as did their temporary enemy to the south.

Suddenly I knew: This war—all wars—are uniters as much as dividers. The Confederate chimney, the Union graves, the passion of belief on both sides all scream to the passerby: "We were in this together!" And today as I pass that magnificent monument several times a week, I'd like to think we also say, "Let's not do this again." One story of many: war and peace, settling and upheaval, heartache and victory, the fabric of all stories, the substance of all times—including mine.

ACKNOWLEDGMENTS

I did not write this story alone; far from it. In addition to my friend and former neighbor, Lynell Widener, whose paintings not only illustrate this book but "write" chapters of county history without a single word, there are many more individuals and groups whose knowledge, encouragement, and, in some cases, financial support all contributed to this retelling of the Columbia County story. I offer the following names with some trepidation, fearing the list will be incomplete. Should that occur, please know that any omission is due only to faulty memory, not to any lack of gratitude for assistance given. Thanks to:

—Phil Blanchard, publisher of the *Columbia County News-Times*, who took a chance on a newcomer with few writing credentials twenty-five years ago and, later, suggested I also take on this writing project;

—Barry Paschal, current publisher of the *News-Times*, for his encouragement, knowledge of local history, and willingness to keep me as part of the newspaper staff;

—Dr. Edward Cashin, Jr., Augusta's premier historian, who, before his untimely death in 2007, took time from his demanding schedule as author, professor, and director of Augusta State University's Center for the Study of Georgia History to encourage, correct, and guide this neophyte historian through the research and writing process;

—Erick Montgomery, author and executive director of Historic Augusta, for correcting or filling in the gaps when my information was sparse or incorrect;

—Thomas Holley, author and Civil War expert, for his meticulous research into the lives of Columbia County residents who fought in that war;

—Graham Phillips, friend and photographer, for his publication-ready, photographic reproductions of Lynell Widener's paintings, including the cover of the book;

—earlier writers of Columbia County history—Pearl Baker, Janette Kelley, Patricia Moore, Michael White, Gerald Smith, Joseph Williams, Bette Sargent, and the prolific Grovetown historian, Charles Lord—each of whom supplied important pieces of the Columbia County story;

—retired middle school teacher, Marion Marshall, who loaned me the Columbia County portion of her Georgia History curriculum, an invaluable aid;

—G. B. "Jake" Pollard, Jr., former Georgia state senator, clerk of Columbia County, and lifelong resident of Appling who was always able to provide that last bit of information about his hometown and county;

—three wonderful ladies, all past ninety years of age, whose input greatly enhances the black history section of the book: educators Mary Sanders and Sarah Washington, and Zelean Pollard Quick, who, with very little education enthusiastically exclaimed, "I elevated myself all the way through" (sadly, Zelean passed away in November 2008);

—librarians galore at the main branch of the Augusta-Richmond County Public Library on Greene Street, the Augusta State University Library, the Georgia Historical Society in Savannah, the former Gibbs Library on Belair Road, and the new Columbia County Library in Evans, with special thanks to Sherryl James, former reference librarian at the Evans Library, who now is community services librarian at the main branch in Augusta;

—several community organizations, including the Columbia County Commission, for their generous stipend at the beginning of the project; the friends of the Columbia County Libraries, for constant encouragement and assistance; and the Columbia County Historical Society, who initiated the project and provided materials to get it started;

—a host of Columbia County residents who helped underwrite publication expenses through prepaid sales or outright donations, especially the committee who facilitated this process: Phil Blanchard, Cooper Cliatt, Vicki Proefrock, and Gale Dozier Sitton; and

—friends, family, encouragers all who helped more than they will ever know to see the project through from start to publication, including all the above individuals plus Jean Lewis Morris, Annelore Harrell, Jane Jacobson, Vern Gildhouse, Will Rogers, Pastor Jim McCollough and fellow members of Woodlawn United Methodist Church in Augusta, and kind readers of my columns in the *Columbia County News-Times*.

INTRODUCTION

Getting Started

We could begin the story of Columbia County, Georgia, or Anyplace, U.S.A., by citing statistics, dimensions, geographic location, and date of incorporation. We could add natural resources, population figures, key industries, and details of the men and women who settled there. We could even assemble an accurate story with a simple recitation of facts culled from a variety of reference books available to any interested reader. But to write such a skeletal story would miss so much, and there is so much to tell.

Compiling a history, unlike an almanac or a few pages in an encyclopedia, is similar to an archaeological expedition, a verbal "dig" perhaps, in which layers of information are retrieved, sifted, and ranked according to their importance or irrelevance to the discovery underway. Like any such excursion, however, the deeper we dig the more we find and the deeper we still want to go. In Columbia County, for example, we know about Euchee and Kiokee creeks, and Wrightsboro and Belair roads, but we wonder where these waterways and thoroughfares got their names. What happened to the Native-Americans, which the sounds of so many of these names remind us were here before our ancestors came?

Also, why was the southeastern part of America settled by the English instead of the Spanish, whose explorations retraced the voyages of Christopher Columbus more than two centuries before James Oglethorpe, the reputed founder of Georgia, claimed the last of the new world's thirteen colonies for the Crown? And why do so many current residents of Columbia County trace their latter seventeenth-century ancestry to Virginia, the Carolinas, and New England, when we imagine the rallying cry for those in search of greater, greener pastures at the time was to "go west?"

Though some disputes remain, all these questions have answers. Wanderlust or missionary zeal; a brilliant advertising campaign by the Georgia Colony Trustees or later offers of huge land tracts by the leaders of the State; and the promise of gold in the North Georgia hills drew settlers to the southernmost frontier faster than to any other state in the new, independent Union. Today, more than two centuries later, Georgia still attracts a large segment of the world's migrating population, and Columbia County ranks near the top of the growth charts throughout the state. On the following pages we will discover the reasons why.

County Government

The concept of county government emerged as part of the liberty-seeking process of English-speaking people long before the State of Georgia partitioned her parishes and organized her settled lands into eight subdivided regions. Smaller than a colony or state, but larger than the cities and towns clustered within its jurisdiction, the county grew among the stepping-stones where, in the words of the poet Alfred Lord Tennyson, "freedom broadened slowly down from precedent to precedent."[1]

Though unknown to the Romans or other empires in the ancient past, counties were communities of people with some common interest who were governed together under the English system of common law. These regions were not called counties at first, but "shires," from which we acquired the word "sheriff," a dominant figure who collected the King's taxes and carried out his justice.

In addition to the sheriff, each county or shire also had two other officers: a County Clerk to settle disputes between landlords and tenants, and a Judge Ordinarius, later shorted to Ordinary, to handle the common affairs of life and business. In Georgia, before the adoption of county boards of commissioners, the Ordinary managed the day-to-day affairs of the government. Later, as the role and responsibilities of the county commission grew, the scope of this office was gradually reduced and its name changed to "Judge of Probate."

There were many reasons to form a county, but the primary purpose was to serve the particular needs of her citizens. In the beginning Georgia counties offered their constituents little more assistance than scraping roads, choosing polling places, and counting votes. Still, county citizens banded together to address whatever need might arise, or to show their pride or rivalry to those who lived beyond their borders. As the state developed, the number of counties and the services they provided grew as well. Today the 159 county governments in Georgia oversee an ever-expanding list of benefits and regulations for both the more populous cities and the smaller towns or unincorporated countrysides.

County government, though less prominent in other parts of the country, remains strong in the South. It is the responsibility of the state legislature to establish or amend each county's geographic boundaries, governing bodies, and basic laws of operation, while county citizens elect representatives to the state legislature and choose leaders to govern local affairs. People in a specific area within a county may also create a further subdivision by obtaining a charter of incorporation as a city or town. These municipalities, while addressing still more localized needs of their citizens, remain subject to the laws of the county.

As population increases and spawns the need for more infrastructure, increased social concern, or greater levels of law enforcement, the responsibility for these added services shifts to the municipalities, thus reducing the administrative role county governments formerly held. Sometimes, as in nearby Richmond County, a county and city will consolidate and operate with only one government. Though Columbia County contains two small cities, Grovetown and Harlem, and talk of incorporating the larger communities of Evans and Martinez has been on the back burner for years, her government remains closer to the original county concept than does her neighbor to the southeast.

For whatever reason a county is formed, this level of government remains the most responsive of all political entities to the people it represents. Thus, the county becomes that stepping stone between a group of communities with common concerns, and the larger, more consumed state and national governments farther away.[2]

Columbia County

For 250 years the area known today as Columbia County has evolved from a sparsely settled, timber-covered frontier governed by a succession of immigrants who called the area "home," to the well-organized, part rural, part urban ring of communities she is today. Those who now call the county "home" owe much to the heroes, statesmen, planters, and religious enthusiasts who left already cleared and civilized lands behind and weathered war, disease, and the elements to clear and civilize a new land in our stead.

Our forebears weren't perfect. They fought for land and possession by any and many means. They fought against the Native-American and their neighbor, and for their independence and individual honor. They disregarded the rights of others and schemed for more land than they could use. They muddled through the organization process and nearly lost this southernmost colony back to the Crown as the other colonies were poised to become the first United States of America. But through a mixture of courage and fear, toil and indolence, honor and greed, and virtue and vice, they refined a land and bequeathed it to us—a people of courage and fear, toil and indolence, honor and greed, virtue and vice just like they were.

As Long as the Rivers Run

Part I

A Long, Long Time Ago

1

The Land, the Rivers, and the Sea

Like a giant clump of clay in the hands of a thousand sculptors, the land that one day would become Columbia County, Georgia, was formed, shaped, padded with rock, sand, and more clay, and shaped again. Not much has changed in the last ten million years or so, but if we were living 35–50 million years ago, we wouldn't have to travel 150 miles to the beach as we do now. The ocean was right here.

From the sandy soil that covers parts of the county today, we learn that a sweeping, prehistoric seashore cut across the present State of Georgia from Augusta to Columbus. But slowly, over millions of years, restless volcanic lava and rock changed the contours of the earth, merging continents and splitting them apart again with new dimensions. At the same time, air temperatures rose and fell, forming and melting glaciers, and altering the level of the seas. When the Appalachian Mountains rose from the earth in the southeastern section of the North American continent, rainfall and melting snow formed rivers in the crevices, and washed loose rock and sediment into the valleys below. Rising land levels around the mountains then pushed the sea farther away. Geologists call that exposed land between the foothills of Appalachia and the Atlantic Ocean the coastal plain. The foothills, borrowing a term from a similar land mass along Italy's border with France, are called the piedmont—literally, "the foot of a mountain."

Columbia County straddles the "fall line," an imaginary boundary following the Appalachian Mountain Range from New York to Alabama. In Georgia and South Carolina this fall line separates the piedmont from the coastal plain. The fall line is also where streams and rivers make a sudden descent, creating waterfalls or rapids before leveling off to mark the point where water navigation is possible. This border between piedmont and plain, coincidental with another boundary between water and dry ground, is a natural site for settlement and an ideal source of waterpower. Both the settlement, and enough power to fuel an industrial revolution, would someday take place on the banks of a river our predecessors called, "Savannah."

2

THE FIRST TO ARRIVE

About seventy-thousand years ago, long after the mountains, low-lands, and the streams that bisected them both were stabilized, a giant glacier that even today blankets the northern tip of the earth increased greatly in size. So much additional water froze during this "ice age" that sea levels dropped as much as thirty feet. Although not all scientists agree about when this extreme temperature change took place, most believe the lower sea level across the Bering Strait between present-day Siberia and Alaska exposed a land bridge that allowed animal and human migrations to cross into the new continent for the first time. That modern archeologists have found similar animal fossils on both sides of the now water-covered strait supports their claim.

Though it may seem incredulous to us that prehistoric mankind with little means of transportation except foot, beast, or crude watercraft could travel from northeastern Asia, across Canada, down both U.S. coastlines, and even into Central and South America, evidence points to the fact that they did. But it was a slow journey, a short distance or one generation at a time.

The Egyptian pyramids were in the planning stage 4,500–5,000 years ago, when some of those presumed Asian descendants reached the southeastern section of the North American continent, and settled on a small island in the Savannah River between Georgia and South Carolina just below the present Stevens Creek Dam. From research and relics unearthed on what is now called "Stallings Island," archaeologists have determined many things about the first residents of what would become Columbia County.

First, we know that the nomadic tradition that kept their ancestors on the move continued those many generations later. The concept of land possession, except as a kind of communal guarding of resources, would not come into being until much later. Food, shelter, and the means to secure them both were far more important. But whether provisions were more plentiful here or the climate and conditions better than what they had found before, this combination river-land location was no temporary home. It would be centuries until the last of a continuous line of prehistoric inhabitants disappeared from their island home as abruptly and mysteriously as they had come.

As migration repositioned the earth's people, changes in climate and other factors altered the animal population. Larger animals once natural to this area became extinct, causing meat-eating man to turn to smaller land animals and fish for food. From the abundance of shells discarded by the Stallings Island people, researchers have learned that their most plentiful food seems to have been the freshwater mussels and other shellfish that lay in the bed of the river.

Like backpackers today, ancient nomads lived simply and traveled light. Only the barest stone, wood, or earth furnishings complemented their crude but functional homes. Implements for housekeeping and cooking, especially as their diet changed, would develop as early man's ingenuity coincided with his need.

Fingers might have been the logical forerunners of forks and dinnerware for eating, but something more heat resistant than human hands was needed for preparing food over an open fire. Some foods were roasted by placing them on sticks or in a deerskin "hammock" held above the fire. Vegetables or other foods that could be cooked in water were likely "stone-boiled," using perhaps clay-lined baskets or wooden containers into which food, water, and heated stones were combined.

In all likelihood the sticks and deerskins burned through, or those who held them in place suffered from burns or arm fatigue. Also, the stones cooled quickly and had to be returned to the fire often to be reheated. Even the prehistoric housewife must have longed for "modern conveniences" with which to prepare her family's food.

So just as modern arrows sprung from supple bows were more effective than hand-held spears for bringing down smaller, faster moving deer and other game, new forms of "cookware" would be devised by the Stallings Island people during their sojourn here.

In place of written records and firsthand knowledge, those who study the past make educated guesses based on personal exploration and extensive research. The Stallings Islanders left a cache of clues about their lifestyle, including some of the oldest pottery fragments found in North America. We may wonder, "Why pottery, and why here?" The answer, in addition to searching for a more effective way to prepare food, is most likely found in the plentiful clay soil.

Again, we don't know for sure, but it seems possible that someone noticed the clay around the edge of the pit fires hardened with time. Perhaps someone tested a piece of the brittle substance, found it fireproof, and began molding clay that had not been near a fire into shapes suitable for cooking and storing food. Then they placed the finished product into the fire to harden.

Through continued experimentation, these early potters must have used varying amounts of clay, water, and sand until they found the right recipe for the greatest strength and durability. Some pottery found only on Stallings Island, however, is called "fiber-tempered" because of plant fibers, likely Spanish moss, which were added to the clay mixture. Though the fibers oxidized in the firing, the holes they left in the pottery provided better insulation and greater resistance to cracking than the solid clay mixture alone.

With so much land available along the river, we may wonder, too, why these early residents chose to settle on a less accessible island rather than on the riverbanks. But Stallings Island may not have been an island during prehistoric times. The grassy area surrounded by water today might have been closer to one side of the river or the other, and it is quite certain that the water was more shallow and, thus, more easy to ford then than it is now.

The Stallings name, like that of the river which nourished its land and people, would not be added until the early 1800's, long after Columbia County and the concept of land ownership both were born. Named for nearby plantation owner James Stallings, the island today belongs to the Archaeological Conservancy, a nonprofit New Mexico organization that acquires similar properties for the purpose of preservation and research. Stallings Island is also one of five Columbia County sites currently listed in the National Register of Historic Places.

Although the earliest inhabitants of the area left no names for themselves, we know them by the remnants of civilization they left behind. The next wave of settlers would have many names: Yuchi, Muscogee, Chickasaw, Cherokee, Creek, and more. An Italian explorer sailing under the flag of Spain, who mistakenly thought he had reached India instead of the offshore islands of a new continent, called the auburn-skinned natives he found there, "Indians." The Europeans who followed Christopher Columbus to the "New World" would also find them there.

3

CUSTODIANS OF THE LAND

They called themselves Muscogees, but when they settled beside rivers and streams the white man called them Creeks. For a while, they called each other friends.

There may have been a genetic link between the prehistoric, Stallings Island people and the Indians (now called Native Americans) who greeted the exploring Europeans, but they were two distinct groups of people separated at least by centuries, if not also by nationality or race. There was, however, a great similarity between the Indians and the Europeans—both equated prosperity with the land.

Lush, tall hardwoods filled the forests and covered much of the fertile, piedmont soil, while smaller, softwood pines were more common in the sandy, coastal plain. Various food and flowering plants stretched from the mountains to the sea, and adapted easily to cultivation in both kinds of soil. Animals, sheltered by the trees, nourished by the fruit, nuts, and berries from both plant and tree, and refreshed by wide rivers and clear, running streams, were plentiful too.

With no written language in any Indian tribe in America until 1825, when the Cherokee Chief Sequoia established the first alphabet compatible with his people's speech, exact dates and itineraries of the migrating American natives are impossible to know. Enough is known through archaeology and oral tradition, however, to suggest that after the Muscogees were driven from the Red River area of the American Southwest by neighboring, hostile tribes, they traveled east, crossed the Mississippi River, and searched for other rivers and lands to call their own.

When the Muscogees found what they were looking for in the American Southeast, they scattered, clustered into extended families or tribes, and either chose or were given new names. Among those who flourished in their new, southeastern surroundings were the Choctaws and Chickasaws, who halted their migration soon after they crossed the Mississippi; the Seminoles who veered south; the Cherokees, who sought higher elevations north and east of the Appalachian Mountains; and the Creeks, who settled most of what would become the interior of the Colony of Georgia.

The Creeks assimilated a number of smaller tribes as part of their own, including the Yuchis (also spelled Uchee, Ugee, or Euchee) and the Kiokees, both of whom settled along the western bank of the Savannah River a short distance above present-day Augusta.

Savannah is also an Indian name, likely a corruption of the French word for "Shawnee," and the name of a tribe living across the river on land future English settlers would call "South Carolina." Sometime during the mid 1600's those settlers enlisted the aid of the Savannah Indians to drive out the marauding Westo tribe, who dominated the river and plagued anyone else who plied their trade there. South Carolina rewarded the victors by giving them a village of their own called "Savannah Town," and renaming the former Westobou River after them.

By whatever name they were called, however, those who occupied the land before our ancestors crossed a sea to join them had already put down firm roots. The blend of tightly knit, communal people with a variety of names had settled here; planted beans, potatoes, pumpkins, squash, corn, and tobacco here; and reserved large tracts of their nearly limitless space for hunting the plentiful game that sustained them here.

From the Spaniard de Soto to an Englishman named Oglethorpe and those who would stream into Georgia after the colony was established, the Indian welcomed the white man to his land and taught the newcomer well. But the two races would not be co-custodians of the land for long. Soon the immigrants would need more land. The hunting grounds of the host nation were an obvious source, and the colonists would devise a plan to acquire it from them.

But before the Native Americans retraced their steps across the Mississippi, this time to lands they would not choose, the interaction between the races would alter the human landscape as visibly as the European settlers altered the forests and the fields. A remarkable era lay ahead: discovery, new arrivals, shifting loyalties, and war.

4

It All Began with Columbus

The Europeans were running out of room. Growing populations in small, neighboring nations crowded against each other like weeds in an untended garden, and land for expansion was scarce. The Europeans were also an adventurous people and unafraid to journey into the unknown, especially if they thought some kind of bounty lay at the end of a far-flung rainbow. Above all, the Europeans were zealous for a cause. Preserving national honor, competing with rival nations for greater wealth and landholdings, or persuading strangers to adopt their politics or religion were reasons enough for the stalwart to pack their saddlebags or sail across a sea.

With all Europe casting an envious eye at the older, more opulent Asian continent, a forty-ish, displaced Italian named Christopher Columbus also succumbed to the treasure hunter's lure. Settling briefly in Portugal before moving on to Spain, the restless sailor spent eight years trying to gain backing for an expedition to India, where he expected not only to gather riches for Spain and for himself, but to establish a new sea route between East and West.

Columbus' idea of traveling west to reach the East, however, was difficult to sell. Besides a lingering belief that the world was not round as Columbus believed, but flat as tradition assumed, earlier explorers had already reached India by sailing around the Cape of Good Hope at the southern tip of Africa. Though Columbus expected his route to be shorter, the African direction was the acknowledged travel route at the time.

Finally, in 1492, King Ferdinand and Queen Isabella of Spain, whose idea of the size of the ocean between their country and Columbus' destination was as flawed as his, agreed to sponsor the explorer's expedition. In addition to the bounty Columbus expected to find, perhaps the monarchs hoped he would return to Spain with rights to new land and an expansion of their kingdom. But even they could not know that, because of their faith in a curious Italian immigrant whose initial voyage inspired others to make similar journeys, Spain would become the first European nation to establish a stronghold in the New World.

Columbus never reached India, and he may never have known how far off course he really was. Still, he called the first land he saw "The West Indies" and its people "Indians," in the mistaken conclusion that the islands in the Caribbean Sea between the future continents of North and South America were part of the Asian country he thought he had found.

Columbus also never stepped foot on what would become American soil, not in 1492 or on three later voyages to the new, western world. But future American schoolchildren would always have reason to believe it was the adventurous Italian who "discovered America," and nearly three hundred years after that famous, fifteenth-century voyage, a small group of newly independent Americans in the Colony of Georgia would name their county, "Columbia," after him. Today many county residents believe this name was influenced by the Quaker community at Wrightsboro, who were opposed to war and, thus, to choosing such an honor for someone with a military connection. But perhaps it was the adventurous spirit shared by Columbus and the later Georgia pioneers that made them adopt the explorer's name as their own.

5

THE RACE TO THE NEW WORLD

It would be wrong to suggest excitement and competition were the only reasons residents of the Old World began flocking to the new. Deep-seated rivalries that divided one group from another in Europe also kindled the migration, even if the change of scene did little to heal the political and religious differences emigrants thought they were leaving behind. Two factors especially—Spain's domination of Europe at the time and the Protestant Reformation—extended those conflicts to the land across the sea.

Initially a succession of Spanish explorers followed Columbus to the New World, but the French and English were not far behind. Though sporadic, Old World expeditions had reached the New World's northeastern shore as much as five hundred years earlier. Spain's Juan Ponce de León was the first to set foot on what would become the American Southeast. The young man with a legendary fear of growing old didn't find the "fountain of youth" he was looking for, but on Easter Sunday, 1513, he did discover a new, unsettled land, which he called "Florida" and claimed for Spain.

Like Columbus who underestimated the size of the ocean he was about to cross, neither Ponce de León nor future Spanish explorers would realize the vastness of their New World for a long time. But, however mistakenly, Spain believed most of the land from the Atlantic Gulf Coast to the later English colony of Virginia belonged to Florida and, therefore, to them.

In 1539, with nearly a thousand men, two hundred horses, and what would turn out to be inadequate supplies, another treasure-seeking Spaniard entered Florida's Tampa Bay. For three years Hernando de Soto crisscrossed the interior of his country's presumed new land and became the first recorded white man to set foot on future Georgia soil. Exact routes are in dispute, but it is known that de Soto crossed the Savannah River somewhere near Silver Bluff, South Carolina, before circling north and west to the Mississippi River and beyond.

History does not treat de Soto nor, by association, the Spanish explorers well. Gold, jewels, and Indian slaves were the objects of that first expedition. Making friends with the natives they found there was not. De Soto gathered more slaves than gold, and scattered more ill will than kinship with those who already inhabited the land. At the end of three years, with most of the animals and many of his men dead, de Soto contracted a fever and died, too. Without fanfare, his remaining companions disposed of his body in the Mississippi River.

After de Soto, the Spanish would change their focus from exploration to mission work among the Indians and confine their settlements to the coast. With continued heavy-handedness, and as much emphasis on converting the natives to Spain as to Christianity, their efforts were met with diminishing success. Although they continued to claim much of the American Southeast as their own, Spain's dominion over the New World came to an end a scant century after it began.

With one eye on the Spanish, and another on the growing persecution of Protestants in Europe, the French followed a different course in their bid for a foothold in the New World. Except for a settlement at St. Augustine and mission compounds along the future Georgia coast, the Spanish had put down few roots across the land they claimed. The French, however, formed settlements flagrantly in Spain's shadow on Port Royal Sound and at the mouth of the St. Johns River almost as soon as they arrived. Other French explorers would travel north and inland, before moving down the Mississippi River and across the Gulf coast to establish New Orleans, Biloxi, and Mobile.

France and Spain continued to battle for New World sovereignty throughout much of the sixteenth and seventeenth centuries, all the while bouncing possession of the northern Florida settlements back and forth, and attempting to keep each other from crossing the self-determined boundaries each nation called its own.

But religion, which was just as important to the French as to the Spanish, would become as much a determining factor in their pursuit of the New World as possession of its land. As the Protestant Reformation swept across Europe, France became embroiled in a series of civil wars that were as religious as they were political. With their government in Catholic hands, French Protestants—also called Huguenots—attracted sympathy from England, Germany, and Switzerland to strengthen their side, while the government brought in reinforcements from Spain.

Outflanked and subject to continued persecution, large numbers of French Protestants fled to the more tolerant countries in Europe, or to the promise of religious freedom in the New World. For the latter group, memories of persecution would linger on, fueling their prejudice against Catholics in general and the Spanish in particular. In a ripple effect, this principle would later compel the Georgia founders to forbid Catholics from settling there. Should conflicts break out in the New World, they feared religious ties would loom stronger than national loyalty and tip the balance of power toward Spain.

England's entry into the New World fray began with a succession of small landings and isolated settlements along the eastern American seaboard, and culminated in the birth of a nation. Two knighted subjects of Queen Elizabeth I, Sir Francis Drake, who seemed more interested in plundering the Spanish than gaining new ground, and Sir Walter Raleigh, who returned home in 1587 with a new substance called "tobacco" but without planting English roots along the future North Carolina coast, were among the first to scout the New World for the Crown.

In 1607 Captain John Smith was credited with accomplishing what Raleigh failed to do twenty years before—establish the seed of the first successful English colony on American soil. The Jamestown settlement on the mid-Atlantic coast halted Spanish advancement to the north, and overcame famine, fire, and disease to become the forerunner and first capital of the Colony of Virginia. Thirteen years later and farther north, a group of religious freedom seekers called "Puritans" landed their sailing vessel, *Mayflower*, at Plymouth Rock, and founded the first permanent settlement in the future Colony of Massachusetts, the hub of the later New England States.

With Virginia pushing England's claims southward, France creeping in from the West, and Spain still trying to expand its territory northward, the struggle both for control of the land in between and for the loyalty of the ever-present Indians grew more intense.

Grants and treaties between England, Spain, and those who wished to join their countrymen in the New World continued throughout the seventeenth century. In 1663 King Charles II granted a stretch of land between Virginia and Spanish Florida to eight friends, who called them-selves "Lords Proprietors" and named their property "Carolina"; and in 1670 a new treaty recognized England's claims to all land adjoining the Atlantic coast from Massachusetts to "Charles Town," Carolina's largest settlement and namesake of the beneficent king.

The actual boundary between England and Spain, however, was never accurately determined, giving rise to the term "debatable lands" for the area between Charles Town (later renamed Charleston) and St. Augustine. Predictably, frequent skirmishes occurred as Spain, unhappy with the smaller share, attempted to annex this area for herself. At the same time, with the French still poised to move in from the West and Indian resent-ment mounting against all land-hungry Europeans, the natives began lay-ing down their peace pipes and conducting some skirmishes of their own.

Danger heightened in this friction quadrangle when the Carolina Colony began allowing traders to cross the Savannah River and exchange English goods for valuable Indian bounty, animal pelts and skins. The threat to their personal safety, and to this increasingly successful venture, alarmed the traders and drove them to the Lords Proprietors and the Crown for help.

The idea for an English "buffer colony," which had already occurred to the Lords Proprietors, pricked the ears of a scattering of lone Englishmen willing to rally to Carolina's defense. None succeeded, however, until a social dilemma taking place in England at the same time convinced a few members of Parliament that creating a thirteenth colony in the New World could solve their country's problems on both sides of the Atlantic.

James Edward Oglethorpe, one of those parliamentarians and member of the soon to be formed Trustees for Establishing the Colony of Georgia in America, would succeed where others failed. Before long the man with a tender heart and altruistic goals became the founder of Georgia, the last of the original English colonies in the New World, and the first since the founding of Pennsylvania fifty years before.

6

THE GEORGIA PLAN

It may be true, as the Bible claims, that "the poor will always be with you,"[1] but eighteenth-century England believed they had more of the unfortunate folks than their share. Few solutions existed for an Englishman who could not pay his debts, except to be labeled a criminal and thrown into debtors' prison. By the early 1700's, some four thousand debtors a year were crowded into England's substandard prisons—and charged seven shillings a day for room and board.[2]

In 1729, when his imprisoned friend died of smallpox, one member of Parliament led an investigation into the English prison system. James Edward Oglethorpe's findings saddened him and shocked his country. Jailers were fired, thousands of prisoners were set free, and Oglethorpe became a national hero. But the "hero" wanted more than praise for himself: he wanted a remedy for England's poor.

Consumed with his new cause, Oglethorpe assembled a group of sympathetic philanthropists to help solve their country's debtor problem. Today their solution might be called welfare; in 1729 it was called "Georgia."

An unenthusiastic King George II took nearly three years to grant a charter for the new colony. But the Georgia Trustees, as the philanthropists called themselves, were optimistic, and they used the delay to promote their ambitious plan.

What a propaganda campaign. Advertised in superlatives, England's newest colony in the New World promised prosperity—"A New Eden"—to the former poor; a resource for expensive goods such as silk, wine, and rice for the mother country; and social purity where, in the minds of many, the other New World colonies had failed. In theory this purity would occur through a series of prohibitions: no rum to incite drunkenness, no slaves to encourage laziness, no private land ownership to generate new debt, no Catholics to lure trouble with Spain, and no lawyers—called "the scum and scourge of the land"—to cause trouble with anyone.[3] In reality, all these taboos were soon ignored and gradually overturned. Within a generation Georgia's "Eden" would go the way of other "perfect societies," born in idealism but set against the backdrop of an imperfect world.

By the time the two hundred-ton ship *Ann* left Gravesend, England, for America in November 1732, there were few debtors among the thirty-five families and 114 passengers on board. Hundreds had applied for the trip to "Eden," but only those deemed the most worthy, or whose creditors had forgiven their debt, were allowed to go. The original purpose of the Georgia plan, to provide a new start for England's unfortunate poor, had slipped to last place. New products to increase the Mother Country's wealth, and greater defense for the other southern colonies, had become the main reasons to establish Colony 13. Those who arrived on Yamacraw Bluff overlooking the Savannah River in February 1733 would still receive their new start, but England the country, rather than her trailblazing citizens, had the most to gain.

The "buffer colony" was to be established on that portion of land lying between the Altamaha and Savannah Rivers. Although under existing treaties the king had authority to grant such land, a wise Oglethorpe also asked permission of the Yamacraw Indians he found there to settle on "their" land. Chief Tomochichi and his small, breakaway Creek tribe agreed to "share" that land between the rivers, and the first Georgia settlement was made more secure by diplomacy unmatched by the Spanish or the French.

With help from the Indians and grateful Carolinians, the first Georgians cleared land, built homes, planted crops for food and export, and renamed their bluff "Savannah," but not without great cost.

Not only were there few debtors among the willing migrants sailing to the New World, but there also were few planters to grow the anticipated, prolific crops on Georgia's "land so fertile it requires no manure."[4] Most of the early arrivals were artisans, who were more accustomed to plying skilled hands on wood or metal than applying rough hands to the sickle or plow. Their very survival, however, demanded that they also learn to till the land. Still, whether it was the warmer than expected climate, diseases from which they were not immune, or a mixture of homesickness and discouragement from the constant toil, by the end of that first summer nearly a third of those who arrived on the first voyage to the new "Eden" had died.

Eventually, thanks largely to those who climbed the bluff, learned new trades, and weathered early hardship, Savannah would blossom and become the heart of the "Lowcountry," as southeastern Georgia and South Carolina are still called today.

But the complete story of Georgia's beginning could never be told from the pinnacle of Yamacraw Bluff. A still unmeasured interior, stretching to the Mississippi River or, some would say, to the Pacific Ocean, remained to be explored, bargained for, settled upon, and given a distinctive, new name: "the Backcountry."

Those who entered the new colony by sea and settled near the mouth of the Savannah River were not the first Europeans to build communities to the north and west. Others were already there. Before long, those who were dissatisfied with the climate or conditions in the northern colonies would follow the Appalachian Mountain range southward and also settle there. Through continued wisdom and diplomacy, James Edward Oglethorpe would make certain the Backcountry became part of Georgia too.

7

A New Treaty of Friendship

and Commerce

Without James Oglethorpe and his fellow pioneers, and the founding of Georgia at Savannah, the Backcountry might have become an extension of Carolina—West Carolina, perhaps. In fact, early records refer to the new colony as "Georgia in Carolina." And had some intramural competition between the two southernmost English colonies not occurred, the Backcountry might not have been called Georgia at all.

As Lowcountry Georgians were putting down roots, the area that would become the Town and Fort of Augusta—and eventually Richmond and Columbia counties—lay outside the boundaries agreed upon by the Indians and the Crown. The given land between the Altamaha and Savannah rivers had its limits: Georgia would encompass only the tidewater region, or scarcely ten to fifteen miles from the coast. The Backcountry was a good 150 miles away.

But like all treaties between the incoming tide of white settlers and the Indians who still occupied the land, the Georgia agreement would change, sometimes by new treaties with the Indians, sometimes without their knowledge, and sometimes because those who lived on or near the land had a different perspective from that of the treaty makers back in England.

Carolina's perspective had been in place for years. Almost as soon as Englishmen began settling on the eastern side of the Savannah River, savvy settlers joined the Spanish, French, and prior English colonists in the lucrative business of Indian trade. The Indians carried deerskins and beaver pelts along Backcountry, fall-line trails to the primary transportation site, the river. (One day, the approximate route of two of those trails would be called Washington and Wrightsboro roads.) In return, the traders dazzled the Indians with guns, rum, blankets, and an array of trinkets that lured them easily into the white man's plan.

Guns replaced the bow and arrow, and benefited both sides. The Indians could kill more deer, supply more skins to the traders and choose more English goods in return; and the traders, could ship cargoes of skins to England for substantially more money than what their bartering goods had cost. Rum and trinkets had their benefits, too: the Indians enjoyed the "fire water"; the women reveled in their beads, baubles, and a new novelty—mirrors; and the traders watched their profits soar. If James Oglethorpe had only let things be, the traders might have prospered indefinitely with their mercenary upper hand.

Oglethorpe may have been the first to suggest the building of an outpost in the Backcountry, but since traders had long been encouraged to venture away from the Charles Town area and live as close to the Indians as possible, there already were a number of settlements on the Carolina side of the river. The more adventurous traders had even crossed the river and trespassed on forbidden Indian land, although the larger contingent stopped at the Carolina trading post, Savannah Town, about where Beech Island is today.

Closer to the river and near the present Sand Bar Ferry Bridge, the Carolina authorities had also built Fort Moore, which both provided storage space for ammunition and trading supplies, and offered protection from the occasional hostile Indians who still roamed the land. (Both Savannah Town and Fort Moore would eventually be called "New Windsor.") The idea to build a similar town and fort on the Georgia side of the river stemmed from a number of causes, most of which would please the Indians. Few would please the men from Carolina.

The traders had honed their trading skills to the maximum: let the rum flow freely, tempt the Indians with more and gaudier trinkets, alter weights and prices to benefit themselves, and extend the Indians' credit at the trading posts until their only means of payment were additional pelts and skins. (Soon Georgians would use the same strategy to acquire more Indian land.)

Though the traders fooled the Indians for a while, long before the first Georgians arrived the red men knew they were being cheated regularly by those who at first had seemed so kind. But the diplomacy Oglethorpe used with Chief Tomochichi at Yamacraw Bluff worked again. The Indians agreed to extend Georgia's northern boundary to allow for a trading post in the Backcountry, because they believed the close supervision and stricter trade regulations would benefit them. The traders, however, were angered to the same degree the Indians were pleased.

Carolina's trader-licensing policy was either loosely defined or largely ignored, because the traders tended to travel and trade wherever they wished on both sides of the Savannah. But soon the stricter "Indian Acts" enacted by the Georgia Trustees required that anyone trading in Georgia had to be licensed in Georgia as well. Also, all weights and prices would have to be carefully determined, and any land designated by the Indians as their hunting grounds or living quarters was off limits to anyone but them. And then there were those Georgia prohibitions against rum and slaves, both of which had always been allowed in Carolina.

In reality, Oglethorpe and the other Trustees had a higher motive for regulating the Indian trade than either punishing the Carolina traders or competing with them. Since few Savannah settlers would likely leave their homes and row the long distance upriver, the Georgia Backcountry would be settled first by Carolina residents anyway. The new regulations, the Trustees believed, would regain the Indians' trust and increase trade for the English. The French, and to some degree the Spanish, were still lurking by the edges of both colonies, and Oglethorpe knew it was to England's advantage to treat the Indians well or they would run to the arms of those who offered them more. Whoever gained the allegiance of the Indians and controlled the Indian trade, all three governments knew, would eventually control the much-desired Indian land.

By amending the "Treaty of Friendship and Commerce," which he had negotiated with Tomochichi soon after his arrival in Georgia, Oglethorpe secured his trading post; the Indians, at least temporarily, enjoyed fair trade; and the Backcountry land west of the Savannah River would never again be part of Carolina.

The Town and Fort of Augusta would also lay the groundwork for more boundary extension, including settlements farther upriver which, in less than sixty years, would be called "Columbia County."

8

Taming the Backcountry

Anything west of Savannah, Georgia, in 1735 could have been called "the Wild West." Except for small, native villages scattered across the wilderness monotony of the Backcountry, there were few towns, fewer roads, and hardly any civilization at all in the southeastern interior of the New World. But all that was about to change.

Nearly two years had passed since the Georgia-bound frigate *Ann* docked at Yamacraw Bluff. With Savannah now stable, James Oglethorpe and a small group of friendly Indians, including Chief Tomochichi and his family, sailed for England to confer with the Georgia Trustees. By the time Oglethorpe returned to Georgia, the decision to establish two additional settlements in the colony had been made.

With defense against the Spanish on his mind, and military experience in his past—the Georgia founder is often referred to as "General Oglethorpe"—Oglethorpe himself supervised the southern settlement on St. Simon's Island, while surveyor Noble Jones and planter Roger Lacy went north to lay out a trading post there. When the latter plans were complete, members of the Chickasaw Indian tribe from Carolina honored their part in the recent "friendship treaty" by crossing the river to help construct the Georgia town. To reward the Chickasaws for their loyalty and assistance, Lacy and Jones also laid out a town for them on the

Georgia side of the river. It wasn't long before "New Savannah," located near present-day Augusta Regional Airport, became the tribe's permanent home.

Although still unfinished, by 1736 the two developing outposts were united by colony and marriage when they were named for the Prince and Princess of Wales: "Fort Frederica" on St. Simon's Island for Prince Frederick, the eldest son of King George II, and the trading post "Augusta" for his new bride. Oglethorpe was careful to monitor the northern settlement, but it would be three more years before he came there for his first and only visit. He might not have come then had he not been on a peace mission to surrounding Indian tribes and needed a place to recover from a fever before returning to Frederica. A seventeen-gun salute from the newly completed Fort Augusta greeted the much admired Oglethorpe as he arrived.[5]

As expected, planters from Carolina crossed the river and began settling Augusta Town. Grants, including a generous house lot in town plus as much as five hundred acres of nearby farmland, became a powerful enticement to those who saw their wealth and future tied to the land.

Despite the prohibition, those who had owned slaves in Carolina brought them along when they moved to Georgia. Without slave labor, the planters believed, running a five hundred-acre farm was impossible. The Trustees may have known they would have difficulty forcing the men from Carolina to obey Georgia's laws. Or perhaps they were rethinking their slavery policy altogether, for not nearly as much effort was spent trying to enforce those original laws in Augusta as there had been in Savannah.

But for whatever reason the Augusta settlement was allowed to develop rules and traditions of her own, it did not take long for the Savannah residents to notice that not only were the rules more lax in Augusta, but the Backcountry settlement had begun to outpace the Lowcountry in every way: more people, more trade, and more crops from their fields. Before long, the Augusta way would become the Georgia way.

Augusta, however, was hardly problem-free. Traders and other newcomers who were unaccustomed to obeying laws in another colony were not likely to follow them in Georgia, especially if by skirting the regulations they could increase their trade and profits even more.

As settlers usurped more and more Indian land, and Indians continued to travel along accustomed trails now occupied by white men, cries of trespassing, boundary-breaking, and a host of annoyances angered both sides. The friendship between the races, which had dominated Georgia's beginnings, began to wane. There would be more treaties and much good will between succeeding generations of white men and the Indians whose land they were allowed to share, but there would also be tensions and, sometimes, bloodshed.

But those who would come to Augusta Town, fan out through a land yet untamed, and turn the wilderness into many more fields and towns would do more than subdue the Backcountry. They would settle it, shape it, govern it, and hold it against all internal and external threats. The men of the Georgia Backcountry, hardly more than illiterate pioneers with scant experience in farming, governing, or diplomacy, held on to the land they had grown to love through the birthing process, not only of a colony, but also of a nation.

Now that we have explored background information concerning the land, the prehistoric settlers, and Native Americans; learned why the English were more successful in the new world than the Spanish or the French; and determined how the western section of the Backcountry became part of Georgia instead of South Carolina, we will narrow our focus to the area which became Columbia County.

Still, because Columbia County history and that of surrounding counties and a developing nation inevitably overlap, much intertwining will continue. But for the remainder of our story we will transport ourselves back 250 years and watch the unfolding of a specific group of people whose contribution to this area extended far beyond their own generations. These earlier Columbia Countians are linked to some of us by birth, but to all of us who live by the same streams and on the same ground where they lived and labored before we came.

PART II
FROM COLONY TO COUNTY

Fury's Ferry Bridge over the Savannah River

9

LAND, LOTS OF LAND

The best-laid plans, as they say, often go awry. Or perhaps the vision the Georgia Trustees had for their utopian, new colony was not the best it could be after all—at least in the minds of the settlers. Try as they might, those generous Englishmen who had conceived a land free of social ills and financed her early days could not keep slaves or rum out of Georgia. Quite possibly a forbidden lawyer or Catholic slipped inside her borders, too.

So it was that in 1752, less than two decades after the first settlers planted the flag of England on Yamacraw Bluff, the Georgia Trustees released their hold over the colony and surrendered their charter back to the Crown. A succession of royal governors would head the colony now, until the men and women of Georgia joined their sister colonies in raising a flag of their own over all their bluffs and towns.

Had the difference between leadership by governor and trustee only been slaves and rum, however, the colonists might not have noticed the change. Both prohibitions were difficult to enforce and had been visible in the Backcountry all along. But it was the release of one, final restriction that changed the frontier forever. Gradually, as more and more settlers arrived, more and more land would be granted, willed, inherited, and the zenith of all conditions: privately owned. Only one obstacle stood in the way of taking possession of this bounty right away. All that land lying beyond the boundary set between the Indians and the Crown in 1733 still belonged to the Indians.

This is where our story gets fuzzy. By 1752 hundreds of settlers were already living in the Georgia Backcountry. Part of this influx coincided with James Oglethorpe's request for additional land for the trading post, Augusta. But as more and more people arrived, much more land began sprouting houses, farms, and pastureland than the Indians allowed or was needed by traders, merchants, and the garrison assigned to Fort Augusta.

So, if the land belonged to the Indians, and if there were treaties, agreements, or even handshakes and mutual faith between the Indians and the Europeans about where each could live, why do we find white men on the red man's land long before it was legal to be there?

To borrow a modern term, we could say these early Backcountry settlers, like pioneers throughout history, were living by "situation ethics." There was so much land, so few people, and so little obsession for following proper procedures, that it seemed logical to find a piece of property you liked and stake your claim. The proper folks called these people squatters, drifters or, especially in Georgia, "Crackers." History calls them illegal.

But perhaps for an expansive, new area like the Georgia Backcountry and a people whose initial need was survival, illegal is too harsh a term or, at least, only part of the story. Many laws, including title searches, zoning restrictions, and other safeguards for today's property owner, did not exist during Georgia's infancy, and the laws that did exist were often ignored. Laws made in London or Savannah were not necessarily respected in the Backcountry anyway. As historian Kenneth Coleman writes: "Land rules were harsh, but leniently enforced."[1]

Another reason for the discrepancy were the ill-equipped or inadequately trained surveyors who created further problems and left much of their work in dispute—if, in fact, it was done at all. Researchers trying to reconstruct this period estimate that only one in four grants ever had a plat of survey made, and sometimes a plat was made when the land was not granted. Accurate record keeping was rare, or rarely up-to-date.

There were no official records at all between the end of the Trustee period in 1752 and the arrival of Georgia's first Royal Governor, John Reynolds, in October 1754. Therefore, in an attempt to create order out of his chaotic new territory, the governor simply put out a request for land records from anyone who had them. So, in effect, all land records prior to 1755 depended on the memories of whoever turned them in.

We should also note that land rules during this period, even when observed, changed often. Initially, for those whose passage to Georgia was paid for by the Trustees, each male head of family was given fifty acres of land with the stipulation that a percentage of the property be cultivated within a prescribed length of time or the land would be withdrawn. In this system, called "in tail male," the property was not actually granted, but allotted or leased; the land never fully belonged to the occupant. More land might be allotted to those who paid their own way. In either case, the land could not be sold, subleased, or left to a female heir. The gender distinction, however, was not so much a discrimination against women as it was a means to keep as many men as possible on hand to take up arms in case of war.

During the colonial period, in conjunction with a series of treaties in which the Indians ceded more of their land to the Crown, the Governor could issue grants under the "Headright System" to anyone he assumed would make good use of the land. Under this plan, each head of household was entitled to two hundred acres of land, plus an additional fifty acres for his wife and each child or slave, up to a maximum of one thousand acres. Those who paid their own way to Georgia, brought indentured servants, or demonstrated what later Governor James Wright would call "the better sort" could receive larger grants. Larger groups like the Quakers who settled in Wrightsborough often requested and, at the Governor's discretion, received still more land.

But what of the Indians whose land was being granted away, acre-by-acre, before their eyes? One thing, at least, is certain—they did not just roll up their belongings and head west because the white man wanted their land. Ultimately they would leave, but not before resisting the gradual usurping of their land for nearly a hundred more years.

By now the early rapport James Oglethorpe had established with Chief Tomochichi at Yamacraw Bluff was little more than a distant memory. Coexistence still might have been possible, however, if both sides had obeyed the treaties they all signed, or respected the other man's culture and need. Land ownership, for example, meant something different to each side. Though the white man understood buying, selling, and individual ownership of as much land as he could afford, the Indian's idea of land possession, like that of the prehistoric occupants of Stallings Island, was communal. For him, the whole land belonged to the whole tribe, and no Indian had the right to sell or give away more than his share.

There also were differences in how important each group considered the pivotal words "bargain" and "boundary" to be. For the Indian, a bargain was a bargain and a boundary was a boundary. For the white man, a bargain was more like the initial stage of an agreement, a place to start until some way could be found to increase the bargaining power for his side; and a boundary included some movable partitions in those not so rigid creeks and stone walls.

But bargain they would, as we will learn when we discuss the important treaties of 1763 and 1773. For now we will search those scant and sometimes unreliable records and try to determine who lived in this area and where, while it was still called the Backcountry or, "a few miles above Augusta Town."

10

Moving up the River

Less than twenty years after the founding of Georgia, the Backcountry was the most populous section of the colony. Well-worn trails plus fertile land and navigable rivers and streams fed the normal stirrings of frontiersmen to claim new parcels of this abundant land as their own. Just as restless settlers from South Carolina had moved across the river to establish Augusta, now new arrivals from Europe and adventurers from the other colonies began trickling farther north and west of the trading post town than ever before. Soon that trickle would become a torrent.

But trying to establish 250 years later where in that new frontier a certain person lived is like putting together a jigsaw puzzle with half the pieces missing. Typically, land descriptions included the name of a road, creek, "the fallen tree," the neighbor whose property adjoined each side, or some other identifying detail known only to the people involved, and which became obsolete as soon as those who lived there died, moved, or transferred the land to someone else. It's fascinating, however, to study those records, as recorded by Augusta author Berry Fleming and try to fill in the missing details:

—Patrick Clark–300 acres "on a great swamp about 4 miles above Scott's Hole";

—Joseph and Sarah Day–500 acres "that had belonged to their father";

—Richard Johnston–500 acres "on an island in the river about 30 miles above Augusta";

—William McDonald–500 acres "about a mile above King Creek near a German settlement at Bryar [Brier] Creek";

—John McIntosh–300 acres "in addition to the 500 he already has."[2]

—And this example from the *Colonial Records of Georgia*: "Andrew Collins petitioned this Board for 300 acres of land upon the head of a marsh about two miles aback of lands granted to Peter MacHugh."[3]

Fortunately we do have more information about some of the early settlers of what would become Columbia County. Sometimes colorful, not always law-abiding, but industrious in his own way, each of the following pioneers placed a cornerstone in the bedrock north and west of Augusta, which remained long after they and their descendants were gone and, except by an interested few, forgotten.

William Bearfutt, Anthony Groobs, and Thomas Reed

Poor, overworked Captain Richard Kent, the Georgia Board of Trustees' Charge d'Affaires in the 1740's Backcountry, was no match for the impatient newcomers who poured into his territory and "settled in a very irregular manner" along forbidden Indian paths above Augusta. Kent resigned his exhausting duties and returned to England in 1749, but not before recommending a few "worthy" land seekers, like William Bearfutt (or Barefutt) and Anthony Groobs (or Grubbs), to the Trustees.

Bearfutt, "He being recommended as an industrious Man," received his one hundred acres at a place called "the Uchee Old Town" (or Uchee Old Field) near the mouth of Uchee Creek on what is alternately called Uchee, Germany's, or Walton's Island. This small strip of land in the Savannah River can be seen today just above the Fury's Ferry Road Bridge over the Savannah River, or at the end of a narrow road leading from the Greenbrier school complex to the river.

Other than the label "industrious," we're not told why the man with the phonetic name wanted his one hundred acres of land. Anthony Groobs, however, knew exactly why he wanted his one hundred acres, and where. He had been living on that choice site near a stream for at least a year, and "built a corn mill [gristmill] thereon which might be of great benefit to the inhabitants there." The Trustees quickly forgave the miller his trespasses and granted him the extra acreage he wanted down by the old Mill Creek stream.[4]

When Groobs sold his property a few years later to Thomas Reed (also spelled Red or Rede), area settlers began calling the stream "Reed's Creek," the name by which it is called today. In 1785 the mill and surrounding tracts were purchased by prominent landholder, James Stallings, for whom nearby Stallings Island is named (see Chapter 2). Remnants of the dam that helped fuel the old mill are still visible in Bowen's Pond off Steven's Creek Road in Martinez, near a gated community now called "West Lake."[5]

Edmund Gray

Now comes that "pestilent fellow" from Virginia, Edmund Gray.[6] Not all historians agree about his purpose or the number of people this apparent opportunist wished to bring into the Backcountry, but all agree that their opinion of Gray differed widely from his own.

In early 1751 Gray requested a tract of twenty-thousand acres of land on the Savannah River, thirty to forty miles above Augusta, which "he and 30 other Quaker families of substance and force promised to improve to the best of their abilities."[7] Without waiting for the Board's decision, Gray went back to Virginia, collected his own family and six more, and returned to Georgia, where he set up camp along Little River, thirty miles above Augusta.

James Fraser, who had succeeded Captain Kent, was quite taken with the plucky Virginian, and recommended his wish be granted. The Board, however, was not so sure. They did grant him land—five hundred acres on Little River, the eventual northern boundary of Columbia

County—but they withheld any bequest for his entourage until Mr. Fraser had enquired more particularly about them.

The Board might have been wiser to be more generous with the other six families than with Gray, for it was not long before they determined this newcomer was an unscrupulous name-dropper and pretending Quaker, whose real reason for moving to Georgia was to escape debts and other legal troubles he had amassed in Virginia.

Within a few years Gray would move again, this time to escape the wrath of Royal Governor John Reynolds, who accused him of sedition. The Governor may have overreacted because Gray's outspoken political views did not agree with his. Nevertheless, Gray removed himself to neutral lands south of Georgia on the Satilla River, where "thither flocked criminals and debtors anxious to escape the just demands of creditors."[8]

But for all his flaws, Gray earns a prominent place in the annals of Columbia County history. His little settlement on Little River, which he called Brandon, became the first known community in what would become the county. Although the Brandon name disappeared as soon as the pretending Quakers made their exit, the area would be revived twelve to fifteen years later when a group of genuine Quakers received a large parcel of land nearby, which they renamed Wrightsborough (later shortened to Wrightsboro). Some two hundred years later all trace of the little community that Gray built would be obliterated by a lake called Clarks Hill (or Thurmond Lake).

Throughout the 1750's and the rest of the colonial period, other Columbia County names, including Clark, Crawford, Dozier, Germany, Hardin, Holloway, Jackson, McElmurray, and Morris, filtered through the list of landowners above Augusta with increasing frequency. In time the word "trespasser" would fade, as residents became rightful owners of the land that bore their names. These pioneers would put down roots and bequeath their holdings to new generations who carried on the family name and cared for the land they left behind.

But first, Georgia's third royal governor, Sir James Wright, had to make things right with the Indians.

11

As Long as the Rivers Run

Like Europe a century before, Georgia was running out of room. That small strip of land between the Savannah and Altamaha rivers, which James Oglethorpe "shared" with the Indians in 1733, even with the extensions for Forts Frederica and Augusta, was far from adequate. England's southernmost colony was filling up, and hundreds more settlers were on the way.

What a dilemma for Governor Wright. Ever since his arrival in 1760 he had recognized the need to increase the size of Georgia. But he also knew any decision to expand the colony had to balance the wishes of three groups of people: the old settlers (mainly traders), the newcomers (mainly farmers), and the Indians who still occupied the land.

Widespread tales of "savages" lurking in the Georgia woods frightened the newcomers before they arrived. For safety reasons, they said, the Governor should bargain for more Indian land, some for settlement and some for a buffer between the Indians and themselves.

But the traders didn't want the Indians moved. If the Governor pushed the Indians into the interior, then their supply of pelts and skins would be too far away to be profitable. And all the Indians wanted was enough room to hunt and live undisturbed by these newcomers, whose land-grabbing ways were scaring them, too.

What's a Governor to do? Call an Indian conference? Invite neighboring Governors in for support, and order presents for the Indians to strengthen his hand before requesting more of their land? Wright, Georgia's most effective leader between the Trustee period and the Revolution, would do just that—soon.

1763 was an eventful year. For seven years perennial rivals England and France had fought to control the territory between the American colonies and the Mississippi River. Because many of the Indians in that area had allied themselves with the French, the conflict was known as "The French and Indian War." Finally, by early 1763, the English were victorious.

Following the war, key decisions made during peace negotiations in Paris determined the immediate future of the colonies, and paved the way for Governor Wright to secure his extra Georgia land. According to the terms of the treaty, France ceded all her territory east of the Mississippi River to England and gave New Orleans to Spain. At the same time, Spain relinquished Florida to England. Thus, after more than a century of war and diplomatic dispute between the three major European nations, England now controlled most of the territory in the New World between the Atlantic Ocean and the Mississippi River. Only one problem remained—no one had passed the peace pipe to the Indians.

But with France and Spain gone from the scene, England believed she had gained the upper hand with the Indians, too. The red man now had no white father but England, they said, and the English had no competition for the much needed Indian land. Surely the Indians would understand.

They may have understood, but they were not happy. The war between the Europeans might have been over, but the Indians continued to wage surprise, sporadic warfare and feed the fire of "savage tales" whenever the white man advanced too close to their still treasured land.

Acknowledging that severe tensions with the Indians continued to exist, in yet another major decision of 1763 the Crown issued a proclamation forbidding English settlement west of the eastern edge of the Appalachian Mountains. With this act, the Crown hoped to convey to the Indians that there was a limit to what the powerful white father would do or allow. Further encroachment on Indian land was not one of them.

The proclamation was a good move that produced two significant results: (1) tensions with the Indians improved, and (2) all those Northern colonists who were joining caravans going west turned south toward Georgia and the Carolinas. Now, not only was Governor Wright running out of room, but he was running out of time.

The skillful Governor then set the wheels in motion for the last significant event of 1763 for Georgia. With the Governors of Virginia and the Carolinas, Superintendent of Indian Affairs John Stuart, fifteen Indian chiefs, and seven hundred to eight hundred members of the five neighboring tribes all assembled in Augusta, Governor Wright presided over the first major land treaty in the Colony between the Indians and the Crown.

In his welcome speech Governor Wright noted that the weather was fair, and he hoped the talks would be pleasant, too. An eloquent Superintendent Stuart then assured the Indians, "We are all friends and brothers under the command of great King George, the father and protector of the red man and white man alike, who wishes both groups to live together in peace and brotherly friendship."[9]

Finally, on the fourth day of the conference, everyone present adopted the "Treaty for the Preservation and Continuance of a Firm and Perfect Peace and Friendship," which doubled the size of Georgia. In words as flowery as the treaty's name, an Indian spokesman sealed the agreement with a phrase long used by his people when bargains were made, promising to honor this treaty, "as long as the sun shines and the rivers run."

Today, as the twentieth century gives way to the twenty-first, the sun still shines on the Georgia Backcountry, and the Savannah River still runs past the land Native Americans willed to their new friends incrementally, beginning with the Treaty of 1763. But soon after the eighteenth century gave way to the nineteenth, those who first shared their space with the white man and then moved inland so he could have more of their land, have moved on—not by choice, but because a day would come when there was no longer room enough to go around. In the words of the late Dixon Hollingsworth, "If the rivers had run no longer than the white men honored these treaties, all America would be a desert."[10]

12

GEORGIA DIDN'T WANT A CRACKER

If Governor Wright had had his way, there would have been no population explosion in the Georgia Backcountry under his watch. Even
before the land cession of 1763, Wright had planned to follow the same
formula used by the other colonies—settle the coastal area first, then
gradually work his way toward the interior.

The settlers, however, had other ideas, including first pick of that
fertile piedmont land away from the coast. Besides, they did not want
to raise rice or establish large plantations, nor could they afford even the
small price the Governor had set for Georgia's coastal land. Possibly, they
also wanted a buffer zone between themselves and the more aristocratic
culture in Savannah. These largely illiterate pioneers might not have been
welcomed by the Savannah crowd anyway, and they surely would have
felt out of place. This cultural divide among the early settlers of Georgia
would be a continuing factor in the years leading up to the Revolutionary
War and likely beyond.

Governor Wright—lawyer, landowner, and a bit of an aristocrat himself—had another reason for settling the coastal area first. If he could
restrict settlement to those who could afford to pay for the land, then
only those he considered "the better sort" were likely to come. In his eyes

that would be good for Georgia. Money received from land sales would be good for Georgia too.

So it was disappointing to the Governor and his fellow "worthy" land-owners when a different sort of people swarmed into the Backcountry as soon as it was announced that two million acres of choice land was now available in Georgia. And, oh, what names these folks were called: "Banditi, refuse of mankind, idle people from the North, meaner than slaves and worse than Indians, Presbyterians—'ignorant, itinerant preachers who poison the minds of people'—and everyone's favorite catch-all, 'Crackers.'"[11]

It's important to note here that many historians from the American Colonial Period to the nineteenth century wrote from the aristocratic, establishment point of view. The "better sort" themselves, perhaps, or more interested in fostering regional pride than in writing objectively, they filled their books with the attitudes and descriptions listed above. Professor Delma E. Presley of Georgia Southern University, and Professor Grady McWhiney of Texas Christian University are among later writers who balance this uncivilized image of the early Backcountry settlers with background information, and give credit for the positive influence they too brought to Georgia.

The history of the American Southeast did not begin with the voyage of Columbus, the settling of Jamestown, Virginia, or the arrival of James Oglethorpe on the Georgia coast. As noted earlier, events occurring in Europe before this exploration took place profoundly affected the demographics of the New World. It's also true that the people who came to America rarely left their ethnicity behind.

All early Americans could have used the modern custom of hyphenating their nationalities to define who they were: Anglo-Americans from England, predominant settlers of coastal Georgia and the northeastern states; German-Americans, or Salzburgers, in Georgia and other colonies; and the Scotch-Irish, or Celtic-Americans, from the upper regions of the British Isles, who poured into the Georgia backcountry as soon as the land-locked floodgates swung open.

Like the English, the Celtic people were British too, but the two groups were never considered equals. Those who called themselves true

Brits in America came from the English lowlands, while the Celts emigrated from the uplands of England, the Scottish Highlands, or Northern Ireland and Wales.

The difference between these two groups was enormous. Neither approved of the other, and neither wanted to live with or under the rules of the other. The English were educated, organized, and hard working; the Scotch-Irish tended to be restless, illiterate, and given to fun and strong drink, but not to work. The former were planters; the latter raised livestock because it didn't take as long to milk cows or butcher hogs as it did to plant, tend, and harvest crops. In early Backcountry Georgia, the former bought and registered their land, while the latter drove their herds to the first clearing they found, built crude homes but few fences, and made little attempt to establish legal ownership of their land. They loved life, but they loved it simple. They didn't see any need to complicate it with rules.

These Celtic highlanders settled first in Maryland, Virginia, North Carolina, and as far north as Pennsylvania, but the promise of all that land in Georgia drew them south in droves. By the time of the American Revolution, the Celtic people outnumbered all other immigrants across the South, with the greatest number living in the Backcountry of Georgia.

There is much speculation about the origin of the term "Cracker." Some say it came from the cracking sound of whips lashing across the backs of the migrants' mules. The word often falls into the same category as North Carolina "Tar heels," Tennessee "Hillbillies," Indiana "Hoosiers," or any group of poor whites once considered lower class.

During Georgia's beginnings, Cracker usually meant a non-slaveholding white—not necessarily out of principle, but because of price. In fact, Crackers were said to favor slavery because of their own aversion to work, a point that would have supported Oglethorpe's reason to forbid slaves in Georgia several decades before.

Professor Presley, however, has another idea of the origin of this colorful word. In the language of the Scots, the verb "crack" means "to talk boastingly," and Crackers were considered "noisy, boasting fellows." Quoting from *The Chronicle* to Henry VIII, "For the Scottes will aye be bostyng and crakyng, ever sekyng causes of rebellion," Presley concludes: "The 'crakyng' Scots, anti-establishment to the core, were a nuisance to not a few English kings, or southern loyalists."[12]

More than any other group of people, however, the Crackers became Georgia. They did not become educated leaders and landowners overnight, but given time and opportunity they built homes, schools, and towns; abandoned their primitive ways; and ascended the ladder of civilization along with their once antagonistic peers. The same cantankerous people who were against other people's rules were also against high taxes, illegal fees, and religious intolerance. In short, they were perfect candidates to fight for American independence.

Names like Campbell, Clarke, Crawford, Dooley, Heard, Jackson, Johnson, Marshall, and Walton were among the great unwashed democracy that entered the Georgia Backcountry as Crackers. The Clarkes would become military heroes and turn the tide of the American Revolution in the South. The Crawfords and the Waltons were among those who would establish governments at the local, state, and federal levels. And Daniel Marshall, who failed to register a claim for his property on the banks of the Kiokee, would ignite the spark that created the largest Protestant religious denomination in America today, the Southern Baptist Convention.

As Professor Presley concludes, "It was Georgia's cracking pioneers who independently settled and developed the state as it is known today [and] there is no good reason for residents of the Cracker State to refrain from saying, 'I'm a Georgia Cracker and proud of it.'"[13] Although Georgia is now called "The Peach State," Cracker State is one of the state's former nicknames, along with: The Goober State, The Empire State of the South, and The Yankee-land of the South.

Between the land cessions of 1763 and 1773, another group of settlers also placed indelible footprints in the Backcountry. More educated than the Crackers, and more anxious to live by a higher set of rules than even the Royal Government required, the Quakers of Wrightsborough would play a major role in the creation of Columbia County.

13

Quaker Meeting Has Begun

For some of the Europeans migrating to the New World, land and prosperity were not the only reasons to exchange one homeland for another. From the New England Puritans who fled persecution by the Church of England, to the German Lutherans and French Huguenots who feared Catholic reprisals following the Protestant Reformation, religious freedom was more important to them than national tie or personal gain.

For the Quakers of Wrightsborough, Georgia, religious freedom also meant the right to live by a different set of standards than that of their neighbors. This difference would earn them much admiration and the largest land grant to date in the Backcountry. Sadly, about thirty-five years after they settled along Little River near the former home of Edmund Gray, it would also be their demise.

Sometimes called "The Society of Friends," the Quakers originated in seventeenth-century England during a time of political and religious unrest. Politically, they considered it their duty to speak out against restrictive legislation whenever it was imposed, and religiously—because they believed God inhabited a part of every man—they saw no need for a formal church structure or an ordained ministry. So with a powerful, organized church in England and a ruling monarch on the throne, the

Quakers felt they could practice their faith and lifestyle more easily in the New World.

Among the first Quakers to arrive in America were the Maddock family from Cheshire, England, who settled in Pennsylvania in 1682 near their friend and fellow Quaker, William Penn.[14] But soon after descendant Joseph Maddock moved his family to North Carolina in 1755, the Quakers found themselves under oppressive rule again. When their new state set exorbitant taxes on everything from wedding licenses to imported goods, they refused to pay them. Then, when Royal Governor William Tryon retaliated by confiscating their livestock to pay for the uncollected fees, the Quakers prepared to move again.

Joseph Maddock's timing was perfect. In 1767 he and fellow Quaker Jonathan Sell petitioned Governor James Wright of Georgia for enough newly ceded Indian land for forty families to live on, raise livestock, and plant their crops. Judging the Quakers to be an industrious people with good reputations, the Governor granted them twelve thousand acres between Little River, Briar Creek, and the Indian Treaty line. Governor Wright also guaranteed his new tenants civil justice and religious freedom. In return for the Governor's favors, the Quakers named their community Wrightsborough after him.

Instead of forty families traveling from North Carolina to Georgia, however, seventy-five families arrived almost as soon as their land was granted. Not all these families were Quakers; perhaps not even half belonged to the strict religious sect. But everyone who helped establish this new frontier town had to be approved by the Quaker leadership, and make an effort to live by the same work and behavior standards as they did.

Quaker or not, Governor Wright was pleased with the newcomers and quickly granted them more land. By 1775 the little community of Wrightsborough included six hundred people, 124 landowners, and approximately two thousand head of livestock spread across thirty-thousand acres of land.[15]

Unlike the casual Crackers, the Quakers and the Quaker-inspired were a well-organized, hardworking group of people. They built log cabins to live in until lumber could be seasoned for larger, permanent homes, and then turned the cabins into outbuildings. They put up fences, creating cow pens for their livestock, and turned existing Indian paths into wagon roads for travel to Augusta and the Colonial Capital of Savannah. The old Quaker Road, which ran south through Wrens and Waynesboro to an existing road to Savannah, has been replaced, but the slightly altered "Wrightsboro Road" remains a prominent thoroughfare to Augusta to this day. The remaining portion of a third wagon road that links Appling with Martinez today is called Columbia Road.

The Quakers demonstrated their unique lifestyle in a number of ways, including education. Unlike so many early settlers, most Quakers could at least read and write. It was said that a Quaker rarely signed a deed with an "X," and schools were set up in several of their homes to pass these skills along to their children. They also were a structured people who chose committees to police the town and conduct periodic meetings to determine who should be reprimanded for breaking what rule. Quoting from an old list of "queries and advisings," historian Robert Scott Davis relates the following guidelines for proper Quaker behavior:

—Are meetings for worship and discipline duly attended, and do Friends avoid all unbecoming behaviour therein?

—Is love and unity present amongst you, and do you discourage all tale bearing . . . and where differences arise, are endeavours timely used to end them?

—Are Friends careful to avoid the excessive use of spirituous liquors, the unnecessary frequenting of taverns and places of diversion, or being concerned in gaming or lotteries?

—Are Friends careful to live within the bounds of their circumstances. . . . Are they careful not to defraud the State of its dues?

—Advis'd that early care be taken to deal with such as appear inclinable to marry contrary to discipline or with too near kindred, and that those who attend such marriages be dealt with accordingly.[16]

There were, however, other Quaker traditions that overshadowed the meetings, the reprimands, and who could marry whom. To be a Quaker was to be a pacifist. In writing about the Wrightsborough Quakers, the tactful historian Lucien Lamar Knight explained, "They were inclined to the arts of peace rather than to the pursuit of war."[17]

When rumblings of war spread across the Backcountry five to seven years after they arrived in Georgia, the Quakers made no plans to change their antiwar stance and join the march toward independence. At the same time, those in the Backcountry who favored revolution discounted the religious argument and interpreted the Quakers' refusal to bear arms as loyalty to the Crown. Thus, when the war began, the Quakers were thought to be on the side of the enemy. Their homes were burned, crops plundered, and perhaps saddest of all for a community where strong families were an important element of their religion, some of their sons were enticed to join the war effort over the agonizing objections of their parents. Quaker pacifism also placed the community at the mercy of the occasional Indian uprising, at least once driving them to the shelter of Fort Augusta until hostilities died down.

When the war ended, and Eli Whitney's newly invented cotton gin transformed Southern battlegrounds into cotton fields, the Quakers found themselves out of step with their neighbors again. Besides their aversion to war they were also opposed to slavery, and it was not long before their small family farms could not compete with those who used slave labor. They had survived the war, but they would not be able to survive the loss of income once provided by their crops and livestock.

They persevered for a few more years, but just after the turn of the nineteenth century the Quakers left Georgia and joined a similar settlement in Ohio. Some of their non-Quaker neighbors and descendants stayed behind and kept the community of Wrightsborough going for nearly another hundred years. But gradually, following disputes over the coming of the railroad and events surrounding the Civil War, the remaining residents of the town left too.

Little remains of the once thriving settlement of Wrightsborough (now called Wrightsboro). The colonial-style Methodist Church, built in 1810 and a short distance from the old Quaker meetinghouse, is still there and surrounded by the graves of those who once worshiped inside. The Wrightsboro Foundation maintains the church and a few restored buildings across the road. Visitors are welcome to attend the annual home-coming service at the church on the first Sunday in May of each year, and to explore the well-marked remnants of the historic community anytime.

Wrightsboro has not been part of Columbia County since 1870, when McDuffie County emerged from sections of Warren, Lincoln, and Columbia counties. But at the time Columbia County began, this community was the largest and first enduring settlement in the new county.

Had it not been for the settlement at Wrightsborough, the history of Columbia County would have been drastically changed. Descendant Tom Watson might never have become this area's leading nineteenth-century political activist and, currently, McDuffie County's favorite son; William Candler's daughter might not have married the son of Quaker-turned-Methodist Ignatius Few or borne a son who would become the founder of Emory University; and more than a century later, President Herbert Hoover could not have claimed Wrightsborough as the home of his ancestor, Abiathar Davis.

Also, two more Few brothers, Benjamin and William, might not have been among Georgia's leading Revolutionary War heroes, and William might not have waged a ten-year battle of his own to insure that the county seat for the entire Backcountry did not become Augusta. Instead, the soldier-turned-statesman fought against making his neighbors travel thirty horse-drawn miles to vote, conduct legal business, or pay taxes, until he finally convinced the General Assembly of Georgia to give the western end of Richmond County a new name. William Few is the undis-puted father of Columbia County.

Some historians speculate that another group of Quakers may have lived near today's intersection of Washington and Baston roads in Martinez prior to the settlement at Wrightsborough. Not so, says Davis. This legend may be based on the nearby "Quaker Spring," which served as a rest stop or "watering hole" for travelers and their horses during the long ride between Wrightsborough and Augusta. The story was revived when, for a brief period in the late 1900's, a builder named a nearby apartment complex "Quaker Springs." The exact location of the spring is not known.

There is one more Wrightsborough legend with more than a shred of truth that, on the heels of the Revolutionary War when other Georgia counties were being named for military leaders, the Wrightsborough pacifists chose to name their county "Columbia" after the explorer Christopher Columbus, instead. There is no written record that this story is true, and it is true that by 1790 the Quakers were not the majority in the new county.

There are, however, many reasons, including two hundred years of tradition and the absence of any other explanation for the county name, to believe this story is more truth than fiction. After all, as many have surmised, every other place or institution in America called "Columbia" today traces its name to the famed explorer and it is logical to include Columbia County, Georgia, in that number, too.

14

RUM, TRINKETS, AND

TWO MILLION ACRES MORE

B y the early 1770's Governor Wright must have thought his clock was running in reverse. Georgia's land allotment, especially in the Backcountry, was filling up again. Ever since the land cession of 1763, Quakers, Crackers, planters, and frontiersmen had flocked to Georgia's warm climate, fertile soil, and what they mistakenly considered unlimited space. Other men might have been proud of such an achievement, but not the very proper Wright. Georgia's mushrooming population were not the sort of folks he had in mind.

This time, as Wright prepared to negotiate for still more Indian land, perhaps he would be successful in attracting his desired "better sort" to Georgia—men like Thomas Brown, the wealthy shipbuilder's son from Yorkshire, England, who was waiting in the wings. If Wright's diplomacy with the Indians worked once more, Brown and others like him might establish future settlements in Georgia, including a town in the Backcountry that one day would be called "Appling" and become the seat of a new county.

Space, however, for his preferred tenants, or anyone else pointing ships and wagons toward Georgia, was not the only reason Governor

Wright began bargaining for more land so soon after the Treaty of 1763. Before his term of office was over, this Governor would increase the size of his colony by another two million acres, but it was a different kind of space he and his mixed multitudes needed now. The balancing act that Wright had worked so hard to stage between the older settler-traders, the eager newcomers, and the landholding Indians a few years before had all but fallen apart.

If anything, all the old animosities between these three groups of people had intensified. The traders still wanted freedom to travel across Indian or settler-owned land to exchange English goods for Indian pelts and skins; the settlers were still terrified of the Indians and wanted "the savages" moved farther away; and the Indians were beginning to realize the days of sharing their land with the white man were over.

Call it politics, the craftiness of man, or living by their wits, but the next scheme for increasing the size of the Georgia Colony was in place long before Wright and representatives from each Indian tribe returned to Augusta. Some say it was the Cherokees' idea, while others credit the traders—and "credit" was the trademark of the new plan no matter who thought of it first.

In spite of Oglethorpe's well-intentioned regulations for trading with the Indians, and the Trustees' initial ban on rum, the traders had always found a way to bend those rules and squeeze a little more profit from the Indian trade. Sometimes it was a single trader who did not wait for the skins to arrive in Augusta, but met the Indians on the road between the hunting grounds and the trading post so he could tailor the transaction to his own advantage.

Typically the trader would bring the latest goods from England, plus plenty of rum to sweeten the deal. Just as typically the Indian would purchase more rum and trinkets than his pelts and skins were worth, and incur more debt than he could repay with the next load of skins. With an estimated Creek and Cherokee population of five thousand bartering with hundreds of traders, it's easy to imagine how quickly their combined debt to the traders reached forty-thousand to fifty-thousand pounds.

But everyone, it seemed, was indebted to someone. The Indians owed the traders for rum and supplies; the traders owed the Augusta merchants for the wares they sold to the Indians, but could not pay for until the Indians paid them; and the merchants owed suppliers in England for the goods they furnished the traders. That is why the new plan between the Cherokees and the traders seemed ideal. The Cherokees would give up land to the Governor, who would sell it to prospective settlers and use the money to pay off the Indian debts to the traders. Then the domino effect would take over as the traders paid the merchants and the merchants honored their obligations to England.

Everyone should have been happy, but they were not. The Cherokees' generosity was not entirely theirs to give. Most of the debts belonged to them, but most of the land they agreed to give up belonged jointly to the Creeks.

Talk about a warpath. The Creeks were still unhappy about the 1763 cession, and they were in no mood to relinquish still more of their cherished hunting grounds to the white man, especially if such a transaction would also benefit their not-so-bosom land partners, the Cherokees.

Governor Wright, however, was a shrewd trader himself. Following a trip to England for the Crown's permission to pursue another land cession with the Indians, he once again summoned Indian Affairs Superintendent John Stuart and tribal representatives to Augusta. With Stuart and the Cherokees already on his side, he needed only the approval of the unhappy Creeks for his plan to work.

It was not easy, and it may not have been a permanent healing, but his plan worked. First, there were the customary gifts—except that they were more plentiful than in the past. Then Wright asked for an astonishing five million acres stretching sixty square miles from above Little River to the Ocmulgee River, or between the present-day cities of Athens and Macon. The gifts helped, but five million acres was just too much to ask. Instead, though with great reluctance, the Creeks agreed to cede two million acres north and west of the cession of 1763. But perhaps the smaller amount of land was all that clever "trader Wright" wanted in the first place.

To say the Treaty of 1773 softened the animosity between the various groups, however, is not quite true. Wright and the now debt-free Cherokees might have been pleased, but the Creeks continued to nurse their anger against the settlers who were now staking claims to their land, and the "savage Indian tales" increased. Also, although the price of the new land was pitifully small by our standards—as low as ten acres to the pound—the mostly Cracker settlers could not afford to pay even that amount. Thus they too were angry with the Governor who had also discontinued the grant system. Then, when the Indian uprisings and settler complaints became so severe the Governor halted the Indian trade, the traders also turned against him.

All the Governor's intentions seemed to backfire at the same time. What Wright did not realize was that this treaty he had been so proud to enact would be the catalyst that propelled the Colony of Georgia to join the march toward independence. Wright was Georgia's most effective Royal Governor, but his eyes were so focused on increasing his own territory that he may not have seen the Revolution coming.

Six months after the land cession of 1773, a group of northern colonists, angry at high, new taxes on imported English goods, poured forty-five tons of tea into Boston Harbor. Southerners in the Georgia Backcountry, who were already upset at their Governor and the mother country he represented, would soon merge their hostility with that of their northern neighbors and join a costly, savage war. But first, for a few intervening months, Governor James Wright welcomed his "better sort" to Georgia's newly ceded lands. Some of those newcomers would settle in the Backcountry and add a defining chapter to Columbia County history.

15

God, Rebellion, and Loyalty to the Crown: The Three Pillars of Columbia County

Daniel Marshall was already in Georgia, preaching a new kind of Gospel on the banks of the Kiokee, when rumors of separation between the colonies and the Crown swept through the Backcountry.

William Few was on the way, joining his family who had settled on Quaker land a few miles to the west. Intelligent, principled, and destined to make history rather than watch it happen, William and his brothers, Benjamin and Ignatius, would not only overcome their Quaker resistance and support the Revolution, but take up the reins of responsibility in their adopted state when the conflict was over.

Neither a preacher nor revolutionary, new arrival Thomas Brown had something else on his mind—building a lavish manor on a portion of recently ceded Indian land a few miles northwest of the Marshall home. War and loyalty to the land of his fathers would intervene, but without this country gentleman's brief sojourn here, Columbia County's beginnings would bear little resemblance to the chain of events that happened next.

Daniel Marshall: God's Man in Georgia

To understand why Connecticut-born Congregationalist Daniel Marshall became a Baptist and moved a thousand miles away, we need to pick up the Protestant Reformation story back in England.

Although the Church of England had joined the other sixteenth-century Protestant reformers in separating from the authority of the Roman Catholic Pope, considerable church hierarchy remained. The more extreme Protestants, or those for whom a personal faith in God was more important than allegiance to an established church, found such a condition unacceptable. Believing the Reformation hadn't gone far enough, they left the Anglican Church and called themselves "Puritans."

By 1620 a group of Puritans every American child knows as "The Pilgrims" emigrated to America to establish a holy commonwealth, where they could live in both civil and religious freedom, and where neither the state nor the church dominated the other. Once they were settled in Massachusetts, the Puritans renamed their church "Congregational." Unlike the system they had left behind, only the members and a small, overseeing body would determine how the new church was run.

It was scarcely a dozen years, however, before some members of the new church began to sense the old, familiar restraints. When ordained clergyman Roger Williams expressed his misgivings to the church leaders, he was rebuffed and denied permission to preach in any Congregational pulpit from then on. In response, Williams and his small following started a new settlement they named "Providence" and a new church they called "Baptist." The settlement would become the Colony of Rhode Island, and Baptist churches would soon dot the colonies.

Williams, however, did not start a new religious denomination. Baptists had existed in Europe for some time. Stressing personal faith and baptism by belief rather than at birth, these Christians were originally called "Anabaptists," meaning "rebaptizers," since most had already been baptized as infants. A few generations later, after those who were baptized both as infants and as adults had died out, the Anabaptists dropped their prefix and adopted the denominational name we use today.

Nearly a hundred years separated the missionary efforts of Roger Williams and a movement called "The Great Awakening," which in 1735 swept across New England and into Daniel Marshall's heart. By this time the Congregational Church had become the very state church their ancestors had rebelled against, and the now powerful, overseeing body was far from receptive to the evangelistic "fire in the bosom" that some of their people were experiencing now.

Most of the "awakened," including the Marshall family, left their Congregational churches and joined Baptist churches nearby. But by that time much of the "fire" in the Baptist churches had also gone out. The Marshalls and other dissatisfied members soon left what had become known as the "Regular Baptists" to begin a new denominational branch called "Separate Baptists."[18]

Still, the fire in Daniel Marshall's heart burned brighter than most, so much so that he left Connecticut and moved to Pennsylvania to begin missionary work among the Indians. Pennsylvania, however, would be only the first stop in what was to become a lifelong quest to deepen his own spiritual understanding and share that knowledge with others. Soon Marshall's journey continued southward to Virginia and the Carolinas, and eventually to the banks of the Kiokee in Georgia.

Hardly a Columbia County resident exists who has not heard of Daniel Marshall or the Kiokee Baptist Church he established in 1772, served until just before his death in 1784, and which still reveres his name. The large, modern building on Ray Owens Road in Appling, however, is but the latest in a series of structures housing the oldest, continuing Baptist congregation in Georgia. From 1937 to 1995 the congregation worshipped in the smaller building next door, now used as an office and activity complex. The only other Kiokee Church building still standing is the much-visited 1808 colonial brick church on Tubman Road in Appling, where Daniel Marshall's son, Abraham Marshall, and grandson, Jabez Marshall, followed in his hallowed footsteps. Weddings, baptisms, and other special occasions are held in this well-maintained building to this day.

There were, however, no church buildings on the Kiokee when Daniel Marshall began his ministry there. Legend says he and his followers worshipped under trees, in crude lean-tos, and eventually in a primitive, log-hewn shelter long since destroyed. But as was said of the great London architect Christopher Wren, "If you seek a monument to this man, look around you."

The obelisk bearing Daniel Marshall's name in the center of Appling today is but a small monument to the man who, without formal training, began his ministry at the age of forty-eight, followed his heart and his God to a distant land, and planted a seed that by the turn of the twenty-first century had harvested some forty-thousand churches, sixteen million members, and the largest Protestant denomination in America—The Southern Baptist Convention. The Marshall legacy increases when we learn that in 1817 Daniel's son Abraham became a founder and early trustee of the First Baptist Church of Augusta, Georgia, where the Southern Baptist Convention was formed in 1845.[19]

For further information on Daniel Marshall or the Kiokee Baptist Church, consult *Georgia's First Continuing Baptist Church* (1995), by Waldo P. Harris, or visit the Marshall historic site on Tubman Road, which was developed by the Georgia Baptist Convention on land donated by the family of the late Robert Pollard.

William Few: Civil Servant Extraordinaire

Today, for most residents of Columbia County, this former resident, war hero, and politician is little more than a name on a road sign between Windmill Plantation and Patriots Park. The road naming may be a sign of honor, but it is only a token of the county's debt to this extraordinary man. Without the efforts of William Few, Columbia County might not exist.

The small Maryland and North Carolina communities where Few was born and reared offered little more than a meager subsistence to support a family, and almost no opportunity at all for an education. So in 1773, when two million acres of Indian land became available in Georgia, the Fews were among a host of colonial pioneers to migrate south.

For the young man with multiple skills and an eager mind, however, his education still would not come from formal training, but from family example and his own desire to learn. Although he was only in his mid-twenties when his parents and younger siblings left North Carolina, William remained behind to settle his family's affairs. From this experience, plus some fruitful mentoring by local attorneys, he gained enough knowledge of the legal system to practice law soon after he joined his family on the Wrightsborough tract in Georgia. But when it became apparent that American independence could not be won apart from war, William and his brothers Benjamin and Ignatius set aside their pacifistic Quaker leanings and joined the Revolution. All three became officers in the local militia and figured strongly in liberating the Colony of Georgia from the British.

By war's end the Fews were living in Brownsborough on land confiscated from British loyalist Thomas Brown just north of present-day Appling. William repaid his "spoils-of-war" reward with nearly superhuman service to his adopted state and community. Before leaving Georgia in 1799, he would become her delegate to the Continental Congress, state surveyor-general, member of the Georgia Legislature, signer of the U.S. Constitution, U.S. Senator, and judge of the state's Second Judicial Circuit. He also would begin a ten-year legislative journey that led to the forming of Columbia County.

Few remained in Georgia throughout the Revolution, past the birth of the county and well into the formative years of both his state and the new, independent nation. But after years of military and political achievement, when he asked the Georgia Legislature in 1795 to appoint him to a second term in the U.S. Senate, (U.S. Senators were not elected by popular vote until passage of the seventeenth Amendment in 1913), his request was turned down. Quite likely the tireless activist, who was well known for his strong stand on controversial issues, had acquired a political enemy or two along with his astonishing success.

For whatever reason Few lost his Senate bid, when his term on the judicial circuit ended in 1799, he moved to Fishkill Landing, New York, where he remained for the rest of his life. Georgia's loss, however, was New York's gain. In the thirty years William Few lived in the small town on the Hudson River, he served as Alderman of the town, member of the

State Assembly, president of the Manhattan Bank, State Prison Inspector, and U.S. Commissioner of Loans.

When the Brownsborough name was dropped and the land parceled out and renamed, William Few's property became part of the Winfield community. Today a historic marker identifies the site of his clapboard house and surrounding farmland which later residents called "Pecan Grove." The original house burned in 1930, but in an effort to preserve the historic value of their home, then owners A. D. (Ralph) and Lula Dozier rebuilt the house as nearly as possible to the specifications of the old.[20]

For 150 years following his death in 1828, Few's remains lay in a neglected church cemetery near his final, New York home. Prior to the nation's 1976 bicentennial celebration, however, with the aid of Governors Jimmy Carter of Georgia and Nelson Rockefeller of New York, the Georgia Bicentennial Commission returned Few's remains to Georgia. Sympathetic to the bureaucratic red tape encountered by the committee, Governor Rockefeller was heard to say, "I'll get him back there if I have to dig him up myself."[21]

After some discussion about where his final resting-place should be, in the Fall of 1973 William Few's remains were reinterred beneath an appropriate monument in St. Paul's churchyard in Augusta. The Bicentennial Commission based their decision on St. Paul's accessible and well-maintained location, the tombs of other war heroes at the same site, and the fact that, during the American Revolution, William Few was a resident of Richmond County. Columbia County did not yet exist.

Thomas Brown: Villain or Victim?

To area natives the name Thomas Brown is synonymous with thirteen legendary ghosts that still haunt the hills near the Ezekiel Harris House on outer Broad Street in Augusta. Visitors shudder as they hear of the barbarian who brutalized American Patriots because they dared to fight against King George, that great grantor of lands and protector of his subjects in the New World. School children shudder, too, as they learn about the man who tried to douse the very flames of liberty their ancestors gave their lives to gain. But the British Loyalist, who once owned large parcels of land in what would become Columbia County, had other entries on his resume besides "hangman of 13 American Patriots" during the Revolutionary War.

Thomas Brown was exactly the "better sort" Governor Wright had hoped to attract to Georgia's newly acquired Indian land. Wealthy, energetic, and full of gentleman-planter ideas, Brown and his entourage landed in Savannah in November, 1774. He was twenty-four years old.

More than half the 5,600 acres Brown received for his intended plantations lay above Little River, the eventual northern boundary of Columbia County. But with the Creek Indians still upset over the amount of land their leaders had bargained away, Brown restricted his initial settlement to an area between the forks of the Kiokee, where other settlers could come to his aid in case of an Indian attack.

Brown's carpenters began work immediately on a plantation house, servants' quarters, and stables for the transplanted English manor he would call "Brownsborough," and where he would never live. Long before his manor house was complete, Brown and most of the Georgia Backcountry would be on opposite sides of the war for American independence.

Rumors about the young man from Yorkshire, England, arrived in Georgia before he did. Not only were a growing number of Georgians already angry at the Crown for enacting their laws without their consent, but they believed the King was sending a spy to Georgia to fan Indian resentment into a war against them. Someone pieced the rumors together and concluded Brown was that man.

He may have been wealthy and industrious, but Brown was far from wise about conditions in his new land. No one told him about the extent of anger in the Colonies, or the impending revolution against the Crown. Therefore, when he refused to speak out in favor of revolution, the spy theory and his own frustration grew. Brown's motive for coming to Georgia in the first place was based on Governor Wright's "enthusiastic proclamations" about the colony in 1774.[22]

"I don't want to take up arms against the land of my birth," he said, "nor do I want to fight against those with whom I plan to spend the rest of my life."[23] Being left alone would have been fine with Brown, but in those volatile, prerevolution days, neutrality was not an option.

While his own house was under construction, Brown often lived with his friend James Gordon at New Richmond (North Augusta today), across the Savannah River from Augusta. On August 2, 1775, more than a hundred Liberty Boys paid a visit to Brown and demanded that he join the Continental Association, whose members favored revolution. When he refused, the revolutionaries threatened to destroy his friend's property. An equally determined Brown went inside for his pistols before facing the angry crowd.

"Leave," he ordered, "or prepare to face the consequences!"

The Liberty Boys stood their ground, and Brown soon proved he was no match for the well-armed mob. With drawn swords they rushed at the presumed traitor-spy, grabbed his guns, fractured his skull with a rifle butt, and carried the semiconscious Loyalist back to Augusta for public display. After the viewing they tied him to a tree, shaved his head with knives, tarred and feathered his legs, and burned his feet so badly that he lost two toes. When he was nearly unconscious, Brown gave in to their demands and signed the revolutionary pledge. His captors then let him go.[24]

Brown's friends took him back to South Carolina where, after months of recuperation, he recanted his Continental Association pledge, joined the British Army, and fought against the revolution.

Thomas Brown became a skillful warrior, rising to the rank of colonel and achieving acclaim as the leader of a special fighting force known as "The East Florida Rangers." Though his side would eventually lose the war, following a British victory in Augusta during the Revolution Brown did indeed conduct a "hanging" in the Robert Mackay "White House," not far from the Ezekiel Harris House on display in Augusta today, and earn his barbaric reputation. Whether his reported cruelty was motivated by revenge for the cruelty that had once been committed against him or carried out by order of his military superiors, will always be a matter of opinion. In any event, the story of Thomas Brown remains one of the Georgia Backcountry's tallest Revolutionary War tales.

After the war, Brown's property, like that of all British Loyalists in the Colonies, was confiscated by the victors and given to those who had fought for independence. As Brownsborough beneficiary William Few was moving into his new home, former owner Thomas Brown was finally becoming a gentleman planter—not in Georgia as he had planned, but in the British-owned Bahamas, where he was again granted land by a grateful King.

Today Brownsborough is called Appling, Winfield, Leah, and Columbia County. Remnants of the plantation, and memories of a young man who exchanged his manor dreams for an unwanted suit of arms, may be seen off Crawford Road behind North Columbia Elementary School in Appling.

Though Daniel Marshall supported civil independence from the Crown as much as he had favored religious freedom from her church, the now elderly preacher left the fighting to younger men, including his own sons. But like a three-legged stool, Marshall's influence and quite likely his prayers, along with William Few's diplomacy and Thomas Brown's land, represented three pillars upon which Columbia County would emerge—after Georgia and all the colonies recovered from a terrible but victorious war.

16

Breaking the Ties That Bind

Listen my children and you shall hear
Of the midnight ride of Paul Revere,
On the eighteenth of April in seventy-five;
Hardly a man is now alive
Who remembers that famous day and year.

—Henry Wadsworth Longfellow

Thomas Brown was not the only one who opposed the war against the Crown. Historians believe as many as one in four colonists remained loyal to Great Britain throughout the Revolution. In Georgia that ratio was one in three. At the time of Paul Revere's famous ride, few Backcountry souls were signing the "Liberty-Boy" pledge.

For a number of reasons Georgia's ties to the Mother Country were stronger than those of her neighbors to the north. As the youngest colony, barely forty years old in 1775, more of her citizens were recent arrivals from England and fewer had put down firm roots in the New World. But whether they were still fond of the land they left behind, more intent on establishing new homes than in founding a new nation, or opposed to war on religious (Quaker) grounds, there was one overriding reason why Backcountry Georgians did not want to break away from the Crown— the Indian threat was still very real here, and they believed they needed the British to protect them from harm.

As one colony after another strengthened its militia and took up arms during the spring and summer of 1775, the Georgia Lowcountry also began favoring war. But the Indians were not as much of a danger to Savannah anymore, and even that part of Georgia did not understand the Backcountry's reluctance to join the fight. By August, when liberty-minded citizens, including a few from the Backcountry, met in Savannah to declare themselves on the side of independence, at least sixty men from the "Kyokee and Broad River settlements" wrote a strong dissent to the resolution.[25] Many of these same men, including William and Benjamin Few, would eventually change their minds and become revolutionaries. But with strong feelings both for and against the war in the same community and sometimes in the same family, the Revolution in Georgia, and to some degree in South Carolina, has been called America's first Civil War.[26]

Like most conflicts, the war between England and the colonies was a contest between two rights. As late as 1760, when George III ascended the throne, Americans were proud of their connection to the British Empire, and the British were quick to aid the colonies. That the new King receives the lion's share of blame for destroying that bond may have more to do with the circumstances of his reign than with the decisions he made that turned the colonists against the Crown.

Ordinarily Prince Frederick, eldest son of King George II, would have succeeded his father to the throne. But by 1760 Frederick also had died, which left responsibility for the empire to his twenty-two-year-old son, George III.[27] Even a seasoned leader would have had difficulty managing the critical events to come. But for the youthful and, at times, mentally unstable King to immediately encounter growing unrest in the American colonies, deciding between options posed by his advisors was likely the extent of his ability to rule.

Seeds of American rebellion began sprouting soon after the French and Indian War ended in 1763. Waged between Britain and a coalition of French and Indian troops for control of the Ohio Valley and, thus, for expansion of the colonies, this conflict had lasted seven years and consumed much of the Crown's military treasury. To continue sending British troops to America while defending themselves against their enemies at home, Parliament had to replenish those funds. When the lawmakers voted to pass along some of this cost to the colonies, the British considered their decision justified. Angry colonists called it "taxation without representation."

When neither side seemed able to understand the other's point of view, the gulf between them grew. No matter how many revenue-producing "acts" the lawmakers passed, the colonists denounced each one. The Stamp Act, which required adding small, embossed stamps to every sheet of paper used for documents or publication, was the first to ignite colonial ire, and for good reason. No contract, deed, or license would be legal, and no publication could be sold, if it were not printed on stamped paper.

Anti-stamp protests surged throughout the colonies. A specially formed "Stamp Act Congress" sent petitions of complaint to Parliament, and the "Stamp Men" who distributed the stamps feared for their lives. Also, because of the added expense of the stamps, printed matter like the *Georgia Gazette* (forerunner of the *Augusta Chronicle*) temporarily ceased publication. Scarcely a month after the stamps arrived in Georgia, a wise Governor Wright acquiesced to his citizens' demands, gathered up all unsold stamps, and sent them back to England. After six months of debate, Parliament repealed the offensive Act.

With British tempers rising, Parliament looked for other ways to convince their American citizens they would have to absorb some of the cost of their own protection. But in 1767, when the Crown enacted import duties on glass, lead, paint, paper, and tea, the colonists refused to pay the first cent of these additional duties. Parliament's belief that "they will not grudge us their mite to help the heavy burden we bear"[28] reveals how little the Crown understood the mood of the colonists.

With colonial tempers continuing to rise, following this new round of taxation merchants in every state except New Hampshire refused to import any more British goods, whether they were taxed or not.

Finally, after three years of declining sales to the colonies, the British economy began to suffer, and these later duties also were repealed on all goods except tea. Although the colonists were not happy with the compromise, they could not sustain their painful boycott any longer and in 1770 began importing British goods again—with the exception of tea.

What might have been a workable solution began to fail when warehouses in Britain started overflowing with unsold tea, and the tea merchants begged Parliament for help. Thus, in 1773, came the Tea Act, which reduced the price of tea and exempted merchants from paying import duties when it reached them in England. This tax, however, would continue to be levied when the tea arrived in the colonies.

The colonists considered their new, bargain-priced tea a bribe, and when shiploads of the beverage began arriving at American ports, they were halted and returned to sender—except for Boston. Consequently, in mid-December 1773, after the Royal Governor of Massachusetts resolved to land the tea there anyway, angry townspeople poured 342 chests of tea into Boston Harbor.

The Boston Tea Party was the beginning of the end for the mother country and her colonies. All England was outraged at the wanton waste of the valued tea and demanded the colonies be punished. In March 1774 Parliament responded by revoking the Massachusetts charter and closing the port of Boston to all trade. Concerned Georgians joined fellow colonists in sending food and supplies to their stricken countrymen, and wondering when the fate of Massachusetts would become their own.

Six months later, minus the delegation from still undecided Georgia, the First Continental Congress met in Philadelphia. The agenda was obvious: protest British actions against Massachusetts, declare colonial rights and, fearing reprisals, make themselves ready for war. In April 1775, when the Massachusetts Governor learned a cache of arms had been stored in Concord, twenty-one miles west of Boston, he sent troops to destroy it. When his troops encountered a small band of militia in the nearby town of Lexington, shots were fired, neighboring militiamen raced to their countrymen's aid, and the outnumbered British were forced to retreat. The long anticipated Revolution had begun.

17

WAR IN THE BACKCOUNTRY

To read the story of the Georgia Backcountry for much of the next decade is to wonder if the American Revolution took place there at all. It's rare, in fact, to find a history book with more than a brief reference to Georgia during that monumental period in our nation's past. Even when Georgia is mentioned, it's rarer still to read of any wartime action in the state outside of Savannah.

But war did come to the Backcountry. Local historians Edward Cashin, Heard Robertson, Charles Jones, and Berry Fleming especially have combed the record to document what took place on Richmond, Wilkes, and future Columbia County soil during that terrible time. Dead and wounded soldiers, burned homes and displaced families, and land so painstakingly transformed from forest to farmland only a few years before lying plundered or confiscated from one party and given to another, all prove that war did, indeed, occur in the upper part of the reluctant thirteenth Colony, too.

Except for occasional skirmishes between supporters of liberty and the Crown, however, fighting which spanned nearly eight years in the northern colonies consumed less than half that time in the South. The British knew they had stronger opposition in the North and must have planned to put out the larger fires first. Perhaps, too, a still popular

Governor Wright, among liberty seekers as well as loyal subjects of the Crown, had persuaded his superiors that Georgia was not part of the enemy anyway.

But the idealistic governor's hopes were short-lived. Once patriotic fever caught on in Georgia, those who favored revolution in the southernmost colony—alternately called Patriots, Liberty Boys, Sons of Liberty, or Whigs—became as pro-American as their countrymen in the other twelve. In July 1775 leaders throughout the Colony met in Savannah to establish Georgia's Provincial Congress. Belatedly, the men from Georgia then adopted the provisions of the First Continental Congress, and sent delegates to the Second Continental Congress already in session in Philadelphia. Almost immediately the newer Colonial Government grew stronger as Governor Wright's royal government weakened.

Early in 1776, in an effort to restrict Governor Wright's ability to monitor British military movement along the Georgia coast, the Council of Safety (the Colony's governing body when the Provincial Congress was not in session) placed him under house arrest. Loosely guarded, Wright soon escaped to a waiting ship off Tybee Island near Savannah and returned to England. Archibald Bulloch, President of the Provincial Congress, then became the Colony's first American governor, and for the first time in a year Georgia had one government instead of two.

On August 10, 1776, when news reached Savannah that Georgia's delegates to the Continental Congress—Lyman Hall, George Walton, and Button Gwinnett—had joined their counterparts in signing America's Declaration of Independence five weeks before, Governor Bulloch summoned townspeople to the public square to announce the news. Ecstatic citizens cheered, fired ceremonial cannons, and celebrated for days.

But any hopes Georgia had of avoiding a war to seal that independence also were short-lived. Although Georgians furnished food, timber, and other supplies to support the war effort from the start, perhaps they thought victory would be declared before they were asked to send their sons. Whatever their thoughts, by the time their sons, fathers, and patriotic neighbors were summoned, there would not be nearly enough manpower to defend their cause.

Almost from the beginning of the hostilities, about two thousand of those one in three Georgians who opposed the war fled the Colony. Some sailed for England, the West Indies, or Nova Scotia, while others moved to Florida or to remote sections of the colonies still untouched by the war. Few of the departing Loyalists would ever return to Georgia, even when ordered back under threat of confiscation of their property. Eventually men from North and South Carolina would come to Georgia's aid. Some, like popular Backcountry hero Elijah Clarke, would never leave.

By late 1778, with the war tipping toward General George Washington's American forces, British General Archibald Campbell revised his war strategy and headed south. Georgia and South Carolina would be easy targets, his advisors said, and victory in the South would be good for his army's sagging morale. Freshly energized, they would then move up the Atlantic coast and, like a game of dominoes, reclaim the other colonies for the British, too.

The first phase of Campbell's scheme went exactly as planned. Just after Christmas his seasoned troops took unfortified Savannah with so little effort the city suffered no damage at all. Scarcely a month later, in February 1779, the confident general moved upriver toward equally unprotected Augusta and captured the stronghold of the Backcountry without the loss of a single man. All of Georgia, he boasted, would soon be in British hands.

Campbell was undisputedly the better soldier, and his army larger and better trained than the Patriots. Besides, following his initial successes, enough formerly undecided Georgians to make up fifteen to twenty additional militia companies took the oath of allegiance to the Crown. This new band of Loyalists would have an enthusiastic role model to follow—Campbell's aide-de-camp, Thomas Brown.

Like all mortals, however, Archibald Campbell had no crystal ball. He also lacked intelligence information on the fire in the bellies of the liberty seekers across the towns and villages of the Backcountry, including a small, unofficial Whig militia lurking in the forests above Augusta. Their commander had no commission, and he couldn't write his name. Yet before this war was over, Elijah Clarke and the devoted band of frontiersmen he trained and led into battle would have a greater impact on the outcome of the revolution in Georgia than Campbell, Brown, and their bloated militias combined.

It did not take long for Campbell to discover that his Augusta victory was razor thin or to rethink his timetable for becoming "the first officer to take a stripe and star from the rebel flag of Congress."[29] He was further disappointed when his promised Creek and Cherokee reinforcements did not materialize once he reached Augusta, or when those recent converts to the Crown proved to be as undecided about the war after taking their loyalty oaths as they were before.

Realizing he did not have sufficient manpower to defeat the Backcountry militia and, at the same time, defend himself against the growing number of Whigs camped across the river from Augusta, Campbell ordered about 750 troops to face the frontiersmen, while he withdrew downriver to regroup.

With Colonel James Boyd in command, the smaller British contingent rode as far north as Kettle Creek near present-day Washington, Georgia, where they stopped for a much-needed rest. For a few hours, while their horses grazed and some of the men slaughtered nearby cattle for food, their attention was not on the war.

Boyd, however, was unaware that the militia units he was planning to fight were also on their way to Kettle Creek, and they were not coming there to rest. Catching Boyd and his men off guard, the combined forces under Clarke, John Dooly, John Twiggs, and South Carolina Colonel Andrew Pickens surrounded the inattentive British, killed a hundred of their men, and fatally wounded Boyd. The surviving British quickly withdrew.

The Battle of Kettle Creek would not be the last encounter between the Southern revolutionaries and the Crown, nor the last the British would lose. But Georgia's first success of the war was the last time the British would doubt the power an ordinary, well-led militia could wield against them. And it would not be the last the British would hear from Elijah Clarke.

18

The War within a War

Two stories intertwined in Georgia throughout the Revolution: the war itself, and the struggle to maintain her fledgling government once Governor Wright and his Royal Government were displaced. Often, for those who were more adept at tending farms than forming governments, the political battles among the Patriots themselves would be as troublesome as their military clashes with the British, and each conflict would profoundly affect the other.

Conscious of the need for legal authority following the Declaration of Independence, the Second Continental Congress asked each state to set up a formal government of its own, including a workable constitution. Georgia's already functioning Provincial Congress worked through the winter of 1776–1777 to create the document, "Rules and Regulations," which would serve as the state constitution for the next twelve years. At the same time, her existing twelve parishes were divided into eight counties, with the former St. Paul's Parish becoming Richmond County, and the recently acquired Indian land above Little River renamed Wilkes.

Acting Governor Bulloch set an early May date for the initial meeting of the new legislature, at which time the delegates would choose Georgia's first constitutional governor. Bulloch was considered the favorite to succeed himself, but within a month he contracted a serious illness and died.

Button Gwinnett, one of the signers of the Declaration of Independence, became Georgia's second acting governor, a position he hoped to make permanent in May. But a lot would happen before then.

Perhaps they should have worked longer on those "Rules and Regulations," or spent more time discussing how to put them into practice. Like the once-abused boundaries between the land still held by the Indians and the territory they ceded to the Crown, Georgia's early government either had no established boundary between military and political responsibility, or none that was recognized by both sides. So when the Continental Commander of Georgia's revolutionary forces, General Lachlan McIntosh, assumed he had authority to make military decisions himself, and the acting governor believed the role of Commander-in-Chief was his alone, not all battles occurred between the Patriots and the British. The resulting clash between McIntosh and Gwinnett would be catastrophic for both Georgia and the would-be governor.

In Gwinnett's mind, defeating the sizable British force camped in nearby Florida was Georgia's best line of defense. Although similar forays into Florida already had failed, Gwinnett organized a new assault without consulting McIntosh. This offensive also failed, but it succeeded in sharpening the hostility between McIntosh and Gwinnett. By the time the general called the governor a "scoundrel and lying rascal,"[30] even normal Gwinnett supporter George Walton agreed with McIntosh, comparing the "scoundrel" to Alexander the Great who thought himself "the lord of the earth."[31]

On May 8 Gwinnett's failed Florida coup plus his public feud with McIntosh cost him the election. John Adam Treutlen became Georgia's first elected governor, an honor Gwinnett bitterly wanted for himself. No one was happier with this turn of events than General McIntosh.

A few days after the election, a still angry Gwinnett challenged McIntosh to a duel, an acceptable way in those days to preserve a gentleman's honor. On the appointed day the former governor and the current general met at dawn on the outskirts of Savannah, paced the customary twelve steps apart, turned, and fired. The spectacle was over in seconds. Each man found his target; both fell wounded to the earth.

McIntosh recovered quickly, but when Gwinnett died of gangrene four days later McIntosh was accused of murder. The preposterous charge brought by Gwinnett's supporters didn't hold and McIntosh was acquitted, but sentiment continued to run so high against the general that he asked to be reassigned. In the fall of 1777 the Continental Congress honored his request, essentially depriving Georgia of her finest military leader, and sent General Robert Howe to Georgia to take his place. A little more than a year later the weaker, less effective Howe was in command when all of Georgia fell to the British.

In July 1779 a triumphant James Wright returned to Savannah, where he would remain to govern the recovered British colony for another three years. Georgia's Provincial Government, however, which had moved to Augusta for safe keeping, continued to function in spite of internal upheaval and external threat, including a period when the Georgia leaders split into two factions and another governor was killed in a duel.[32]

Somehow the resilient Backcountry managed to maintain a semblance of order and keep their patriotic hopes alive, until all of Georgia was back in American hands.

19

Blood, Sweat, and Terror
in the Backcountry

Following repeated American losses in Georgia and South Carolina throughout 1779 and into the next year, there developed a growing fear that the revolutionary cause, at least in the South, was lost. Some even suggested relinquishing the southernmost colonies to the British and focusing on the other eleven as the first United States of America.

This plan, however, did not survive the proposal stage. After reading a passionate letter from Backcountry Georgians, including George Walton and William Few, delegates to the Second Continental Congress agreed that "No part of America should expect to be free while England retains both ends of the Continent."[33] Canada to the north might be acceptable, but a second "Canada" to the south was unthinkable. However, despite earlier successes by Elijah Clarke and his fighting pioneers, before passion could lead to victory in all thirteen colonies, Georgia would experience at least two more major defeats, one in Savannah and one in Augusta.

On the heels of the American victory at Kettle Creek, the new Continental Commander of the South, General Benjamin Lincoln, now believed his troops could retake Savannah. Scarcely a month later, the general's elation was tempered by the loss of as many Americans at the battle of Briar Creek near Savannah as the British lost at Kettle Creek above Augusta. The Patriots were still outmanned and, for the most part, outsmarted by the British.

But by September 1779 help appeared to be on the way. Because of long-standing rivalries still taking place in Europe, one of England's enemies became America's friend. Suddenly, and without conferring with General Lincoln, Charles Hector, comte d'Estaing, of France and his naval fleet appeared off the coast of Savannah. Immediately the confident count planned an attack on the city and volunteered to lead the charge, which he predicted would take about a week to win.

Had d'Estaing and his experienced troops begun their assault immediately he might have achieved his goal. Instead, his first move was to take on the role of a gentleman, essentially offering British commander, General Augustine Prevost, time to decide if he wanted to surrender then, or after his French troops had sacked the city. The general accepted the delay, sent for reinforcements, and turned the Frenchman down.

The great Siege of Savannah began on September 23 and lasted nearly a month. Rather than rout the city as he had planned, d'Estaing lost nearly a third of his four thousand men, including the dashing Polish nobleman, Count Casimir Pulaski, who led the final battle and was mortally wounded in the process. The British were superb in their defense of the city, Count d'Estaing sailed quietly back to France, and the disheartened Americans would have to wait another three years for control of Georgia's first city to return to them.

The battle for Savannah was one of the worst setbacks of the war for Georgia, and another example of how different the outcome might have been if all the would-be heroes had fought under one plan. The Frenchman's efforts were admirable, but General Lincoln should have been the one to dictate how and when the battle was waged, not d'Estaing.

In a postscript to the Savannah story: more than two hundred years later, when the first exchange students from Columbia County's sister city, Nowy Sącz, Poland, arrived in Georgia, they asked to be taken to Savannah to see the Pulaski Monument. This tribute to a fallen soldier from their country, who died heroically for a cause he did not have to undertake, still stands in Monterey Square in the city he tried valiantly to save.

In contrast to Patriot gloom following the failed Savannah siege, and not long afterward the loss of Charleston, the British were counting the days to victory. And who better to send to the Backcountry to quell any remaining rebel disturbance than the supreme Loyalist himself, Colonel Thomas Brown. Whether Brown considered his new assignment vindication for the treatment he once had received in Augusta, he had no trouble carrying out a new British mandate that, "those who have once borne arms with us and afterward joined the enemy, shall be immediately hanged."[34]

Fact is difficult to separate from fiction during Thomas Brown's thirteen-month stay in the Backcountry, but from his arrival in May 1780 to the present day, tales of this "barbaric butcher" and his cruelty to soldier and civilian alike abound. At least two incidents are found in all the record books. Both figure prominently in the outcome of the war in the Backcountry and, therefore, in the potential lost colony of Georgia.

For more than a year Elijah Clarke dreamed of leading an expedition to retake Augusta, but by September 1780 the celebrated hero of Kettle Creek and his fellow militiamen had had enough of Thomas Brown. Not only had they heard the barbaric tales, but they had experienced them firsthand. Their homes had been burned, their crops plundered, and members of their own families murdered before their eyes.

Although he called for one thousand men to join him, Clarke would make do with the 500–600 who shared his resolve. Pinpointing Brown's Augusta location, he divided his men into three companies and prepared for a three-pronged attack. The triple assault caught Brown by surprise, allowing him only time enough to gather men, arms, and a few supplies and dash to safety inside the Mackay Trading Post.[35] For the rest of the day the two sides exchanged fire, while Brown resisted Clarke's repeated demands that he lay down his arms and surrender.

Under cover of darkness both sides spent a busy night. Brown's men dug a trench near the house for an earthen shield, reinforced the walls of the house with clay and sand, and tore up floorboards to nail over the windows. Perhaps they couldn't leave, but their fortified prison would blunt most of the enemy's firepower, and they had plenty of ammunition to fire back. At the same time and about 150 yards away, Clarke's men dug an outer trench completely around the house. With their circular foxhole filled with determined Americans, and two confiscated British cannons pointing directly at the house, they were confident the battle was already won.

By morning both sides were astonished at what the other had accomplished overnight, but neither would bow to the other's pluck. More than anything else, the next four days would be a battle of wills between Clarke and Brown.

Amid cannon shots and musket fire on day two, Clarke continued his calls for Brown to surrender. But Brown ignored the cries of his men and the pain from his own wounds, and refused to give up. A small band of Indians arrived to reinforce the British on day three, the same day Clarke cut off all water supply to the house. Without water and with food so scarce, Brown and company had little more than raw pumpkins to eat; pitiful pleas for water, medicine, and their leader's surrender could be heard throughout the day. An unmoved Brown ordered his men to substitute their urine for water, and for those still standing to fight on.

Knowing that some of Brown's men were dead and others weakened from their ordeal, on day four Clarke's strategy changed. His men would emerge from their foxhole, approach the house, and use every weapon they had left to swamp the enemy out. It was a good plan, but Clarke would not have a chance to see if it worked.

Unknown to Clarke, Brown's last act before entering the trading post on day one was to send a messenger for help. Brown had to wait four days to see if his plan worked, but just as Clarke was preparing to storm the last of the barricaded British, a sickening sound arose from the river behind him. Colonel John Cruger and five hundred reinforcements from the British Outpost at Ninety-six, South Carolina, had arrived in the nick of time to rescue Brown. Ironically, the stubborn Loyalist had just signaled his intent to surrender.

Even if all of Clarke's men were still surrounding the besieged British, they would have been no match for Cruger's fresh, better-armed troops who now surrounded them. With the Americans appearing to have the upper hand from the start of the confrontation, either by desertion or permission many of Clarke's men had gone home to visit their families. Now, with reduced manpower and much of his ammunition gone, Clarke would be the one to admit defeat, not Brown. On day five, with sixty Americans lying dead or wounded, Clarke was forced to flee with those still able to ride or run away.

In the gruesome aftermath of the failed siege, Brown followed his commander's orders—and cemented his barbaric reputation—by hanging some of the wounded Americans from the stairway inside the trading post. Whether Brown hanged the fabled thirteen—one for each of the rebellious, American colonies—or five, or another number as others suggest, and lay on his cot in delirium at the sight of the twisting, dying bodies as legend claims, the battle and its terrible outcome are true.

Nine months later the Loyalist and the freedom fighter would meet again. This time Clarke would join the victory celebration, and Brown would be the one to slink away.

20

NOT A SINGLE SERVANT OF THE KING

ON GEORGIA SOIL

If anything could be certain following the siege at the Mackay House, it was that the outcome of the war for American independence was still uncertain. Euphoria and gloom had traded sides so often since the war began that neither side could afford to rest after an isolated victory, nor lay down arms following a discouraging defeat.

Thomas Brown did not do much resting during the fall of 1780, except to recover from his latest wounds and bask in a sea of praise. Brown may have been a "butcher" to the Patriots, but to an overjoyed Governor Wright he was a courageous hero who stood firm in Augusta against "the most barbarous wretches that ever infected any country."[36] Labels, it seems, depend on the labeler's point of view.

Brown now resumed his activities in the Backcountry by sending Cruger after the retreating Clarke, and dispatching his own troops to continue acts of plunder against those who had fought against him. Cruger was too late for the swiftly moving Clarke, but the plunder was most severe in Wilkes County, where the militia leader and many of his fellow fighters lived.

Clarke's next mission was a humanitarian one. In late September, rather than attempt a rematch against Brown just then, he led a group of frightened women, children, and elderly men to the remote Watauga Valley in North Carolina (now Tennessee) to wait out the war. During their return trip, the Clarke party surprised a company of British troops who had been sent to King's Mountain, South Carolina, to intercept them. In a near repeat of the battle at Kettle Creek, the Patriot militia killed the British commander and soundly defeated his men. Now, with surging Patriot courage and sagging British morale, the swapping of emotions in the Backcountry was about to occur for the last time.

Isolated skirmishes in Georgia continued to turn in favor of the Americans throughout the fall and winter of 1780–81, leading both Governor Wright and Brown to cry loudly for aid. The governor not only begged for more troops, but for food for the destitute citizens of Savannah who had "no beef or pork and no money to buy any."[37] Brown had a different problem: The "barbarous wretches" near Augusta were doing some plundering, too. They pilfered his warehouses, ambushed boats bringing in fresh supplies, and stole the clothes off his men's backs.

By spring of 1781 the war in the South took an escalating turn. Two imposing generals, Lord Charles Cornwallis, commander of the British forces, and Nathanael Greene of the American Army met at Guilford Courthouse, North Carolina, in a defining battle of the war. The British were barely victorious, but at a terrible toll. As Greene reported to General Washington, "We were obliged to give up the ground and we lost our artillery, but the enemy . . . are little short of being ruined." Cornwallis' report to England was equally grim: "Another such victory would destroy the British army."[38] Following the loss of nearly a third of his men, Cornwallis retreated to the North Carolina coast. Soon he would turn north toward Virginia and, for him, the final battle of the war.

Meanwhile, based on reports that small militia units were having success in the Georgia Backcountry, General Greene focused his attention farther south. About the middle of May he sent Colonel Henry "Light Horse Harry" Lee of Virginia to join Colonel Elijah Clarke and his Kettle Creek partner, General Andrew Pickens of South Carolina, to "repair to Augusta and reduce the town."[39] General Greene might not have known Clarke's militia had been in place for some time, but serving under a subordinate commander because Clarke was at home recovering from smallpox. By the time the assault began, healthy or not, Clarke would be there, too. It was no secret that, in addition to his leadership skills, Elijah Clarke was the inspiration behind much of the revolutionary success in the Backcountry.

When Thomas Brown arrived in Augusta the year before, he built two forts along the river: Fort Cornwallis, a reconstruction of the former Fort Augusta near present-day St. Paul's Church; and a short distance upriver, the smaller Fort Grierson, named for its first and only commander, Colonel James Grierson. The final battle for Augusta and the Backcountry would be fought entirely at these two forts.

The Americans planned to attack Fort Grierson first. Since they enjoyed a good supply of manpower, two companies were directed to approach the smaller fort from the sides. At the same time, Colonel Lee stationed his troops near Brown, who waited inside well-fortified Fort Cornwallis. Still another company patrolled the area between the two forts to keep Grierson's men from fleeing to Fort Cornwallis, or Brown from coming to Grierson's aid.

The British knew they were outmanned, but they had greater experience and a good supply of ammunition on their side. Thus, when Thomas Brown heard the familiar call for surrender before the battle had even begun, he confidently issued his stock answer, "No."

But the Americans were also more experienced now, especially in recognizing the military chain of command. Gone were the days when politicians directed the affairs of the military, or military leaders squabbled among themselves for control. Commanding General Greene had instructed Lee, Pickens, and other capable men to lead the charge, and they followed their well-respected leader's plan. The commanders, however, knew their success depended largely on local militia leaders who were more familiar with the area than they were, especially Elijah Clarke who understood the mind of Thomas Brown.

The attack on Fort Grierson ended almost as quickly as it began. In addition to manpower and guns, each American soldier also carried an axe with which he planned, literally, to chop the small, wooden structure down.

It did not take Colonel Grierson long to see the futility of mounting a defense. Before the approaching guns and axes could be turned against them, he quickly led his forces out the side of the fort nearest the river and farthest from the attackers. Though more than half of his men were killed or wounded in the assault, Grierson and a few others managed to escape by racing along the riverbank and, under protective fire from Brown, outmaneuver the Americans and reach the safety of Fort Cornwallis.

Thomas Brown did not intend to lose Fort Cornwallis too. Although the memory of the earlier siege at the MacKay House was still fresh, this time he was better prepared. With more munitions and supplies, and messages already on the way to outlying British commanders including his previous liberator, Colonel John Cruger, Brown was confident he could at least outlast his opponents, if not drive them completely away. But this time Cruger would never receive his message, and no other British force would be able to break through enemy lines in time to save Brown.

Once again the Americans began digging approach trenches from the river to both sides of the fort. However, with their low ground and Brown's repeated assaults directly into the trenches from his higher position inside the fort, some other plan would have to be made if the Americans expected the advantage to shift toward them.

That's when Colonel Lee decided to build a "Maham Tower."[40] The thirty-foot tall structure, framed with notched logs and filled with dirt and stone, would be capped with a platform strong enough to support their largest gun, and high enough for Lee's forces to fire down into the fort.

The tower took nearly a week to complete, time enough for both sides to calculate their defense. An abandoned house between the tower and the fort offered initial protection for those working on the tower, but Brown burned several other buildings to keep the Americans from turning them into shields, too. When Lee noticed Brown had left two houses standing, he suspected a ruse. Without knowing Brown had dug tunnels from the fort to the houses so he could mine them with explosives, Pickens sent in inspectors to see if the buildings could serve as nighttime shelter for his men. No one discovered Brown's plan, but Lee's suspicions caused the men to abandon the idea of making those houses their temporary home.

That decision alone may have determined the outcome of the battle. When Brown heard the commotion of the inspectors inside the buildings, he assumed his attackers had fallen into his trap. Later, when quiet returned and he also assumed the Americans were asleep, he gave the order to detonate the explosives. The blast leveled the buildings, but not a man was harmed. Lee was correct, and Brown's clever plan accomplished nothing.

On May 31, the day before the Patriots' cannon was to be mounted on top of the finished tower, Lee and Pickens gave Brown one last chance to surrender. Stalwart and optimistic to the end, Thomas Brown considered it his responsibility to defend his position "to the last extremity."[41] He, too, built a platform as high as possible in one corner of the fort, mounted his two guns in the direction of the tower, and waited for the barrage to begin.

Brown's best artillery, however, was no match for Lee's sharpshooters, whose elevated position now gave them a sweeping view of the fort. By noon on June 2 the Americans had silenced the British guns. Earthen bulwarks inside the fort saved the lives of most of Brown's men, but the fort itself was all but destroyed.

Brown had one more card to play. He primed one of his sergeants to act as a deserter and sent him out to burn down the tower. Once again Lee's suspicions were aroused and, for precaution, he placed the alleged deserter under guard—and foiled yet another of Brown's plans.

On June 4 the Americans gave Brown an ultimatum—surrender or we will level a final assault on your position and you will suffer great loss of life. But June 4 was also the King's birthday, a day even the Patriots understood to be sacred to a British citizen. Sensing the end of their confrontation at last, Lee and Pickens held off their fire and allowed Brown another day to work out the details of his surrender.

On June 5 Brown and his remaining garrison walked out of what was left of Fort Cornwallis, laid down their arms, and gave themselves up to the mercy of the Americans. Knowing the extent of the hatred between the local militia and Thomas Brown, Lee and Pickens gave stern orders that none of the surrendering men be harmed. Under heavy guard, Brown and most of his surviving officers were sent to Savannah for medical treatment and parole.

But no orders from Commander Lee on down were able to prevent one final round of bloodshed. Before they could be stopped, and with their intended target, Thomas Brown, safely out of the way, a group of angry Patriots killed Colonel Grierson and a handful of his men.

Lee, Pickens, and especially General Greene were furious at this breach of military ethics and launched an investigation to learn which of their soldiers had so grievously killed an enemy after he had surrendered. The investigation was fruitless. If anyone knew who the guilty parties were, they were not talking. To them, the long-standing antagonism between the Patriots and Thomas Brown or anyone associated with him made any ethics breach an entitlement rather than a crime.

Officially the thirteen American colonies would continue to be British subjects until the Treaty of Paris transformed them into independent states in September 1783. Practically, however, with Savannah weakly defended and no major battles left to be fought in the South, the Revolutionary War in Georgia ended with victory in the Backcountry, June 5, 1781. The unlearned frontiersmen, whose passion for their cause burned brighter than all the manpower and guns they struggled against, had won a war no prophet or military strategist would have believed possible when hostilities began six years before.

General Campbell's prediction in 1779 that he would be the first to "take a stripe and star from the rebel flag of Congress" and then move north until all thirteen colonies were back in British hands had not come true. Georgia was neither the first nor the last colony to root out her oppressors, but her victory went a long way toward raising the possibility that all the colonies would soon be free of British control.

Four months later, on October 17, 1781, British General Lord Charles Cornwallis surrendered to General George Washington's army in Yorktown, Virginia, signaling the end of the British effort to put the rebellion down. Although Governor Wright and a small British contingent remained in Savannah, nothing but minor skirmishes occurred there until those still loyal to the British cause were allowed to evacuate the following July. Thus, in the words of historian Charles C. Jones, Jr., "With the departure of the British garrison from the Georgia Capital there lingered not a single servant of the King on Georgia soil."[42]

Not every British sympathizer, however, chose to leave. Those who chose to change their allegiance rather than leave their homes became independent American citizens, too. Throughout Georgia, more than four thousand land grants once given to the departing Loyalists were confiscated and either given as rewards to those who had fought for independence or sold. If that number seems excessive, we should remember that in the devastating aftermath of the war, land was all the wealth most people had left.

After his parole Thomas Brown continued to lead those ineffective skirmishes near Charleston and Savannah until he retired to the Bahamas on new land granted by the Crown. Some records claim he became mired in criminal land dealings in his new homeland, was arrested, and returned to England to die in prison. But later research does not support those allegations.[43] More likely, poor record keeping, misunderstanding of land rules, or the desire of some to keep Brown's "bad-boy" image alive obscured the final chapter of his life.

There is evidence that Brown served a term in prison, but not that he died there. Rather, with a resilience reminiscent of his wartime reputation, he paid his alleged debt to his creditors and society, and returned to the Island of St. Vincent in the Bahamas to farm and raise a family at the long-delayed manor home he had wanted to build in Georgia thirty years before.

Two months after the victory in Augusta, a grateful Georgia Legislature awarded Elijah Clarke the confiscated home of wealthy Wilkes County Loyalist Thomas Waters. Clarke would continue to serve his adopted home state by leading campaigns against marauding Indians and participating in other missions of the state militia. The unschooled soldier, recognized by many as the finest Revolutionary War hero in the Georgia Backcountry, also raised a family, including son John, who would drop the "e" from the family name and in 1819 become governor of Georgia.

Generations later other Georgians would name a state park in Lincoln County after the man who helped secure the area where, in the mid-twentieth-century, the U.S. Army Corps of Engineers refigured the Savannah River to create a mammoth lake and dam called Clarks Hill. Although we have no record of a relationship between the soldier and the much more modern lake, the Clark name serves as a symbolic reminder of our military hero. Visitors to the state park, however, will find a tangible memory of the man. Elijah Clarke—still spelled with his distinctive, final "e"—is buried on the state park grounds.

Colonel "Lighthorse Harry" Lee returned to his Virginia farm, entered the politics of his new nation, and raised a family too. Years later his son, Robert, would follow in his military footsteps, and become the still revered commander of the Army of Northern Virginia during the Civil War.

General Nathanael Greene was awarded the choice, confiscated rice plantation called Mulberry Grove near Savannah, while his grateful friends in Augusta named their finest residential street after the man who commanded the final battle for their town. Sadly General Greene died of sunstroke the following year, but his wife befriended a visiting inventor from Connecticut named Eli Whitney, with whom she discussed the plight of cotton farmers searching for a convenient way to separate the cotton boll from its seeds. However indirectly, Greene's legacy also includes winning one more battle in the postwar South. The cotton gin revolutionized the Southern economy.

Other Backcountry soldiers just wanted to go home, plant their crops, and resume the life they expected to lead when they left Europe or migrated from the Northern colonies before war interrupted their plans. Some, including Lieutenant Colonel William Few of the Upper Regiment of Richmond County, were already dividing their time between ending hostilities and turning their attention toward governing their new, independent municipalities and nation. Firmly established in Brownsborough on a portion of the confiscated property of Thomas Brown, William Few would continue to fight another battle, until a new county called Columbia emerged from the ravages of war.

21

FROM COLONY TO COUNTY

B e it enacted by the Senate and House of Representatives of the State of Georgia in General Assembly, that the county of Richmond shall be divided into two counties. . . . Beginning on the river Savannah, at the mouth of Red's [Reed's] Creek, from thence a line shall be drawn running South 45 degrees West, and all that part of Richmond County lying above the aforesaid line shall be one county known by the name of 'Columbia.' "

—From "An Act to Divide the County of Richmond,"
December 10, 1790
—Edward Telfair, Governor

During the Revolutionary War period it was not unusual for Backcountry Georgians or leaders throughout the colonies to wear many hats, but William Few wore more than most. Planter, lawyer, politician, and advocate for American independence, the man most responsible for the founding of Columbia County reserved his strongest passion for establishing the postwar government, not only of his new, independent nation, but for his state and community as well.

At the same time, neither was it unusual for a politician serving in one level of government to hold office in another. Therefore, when Backcountry statesman William Few served simultaneously as a member of the United States Congress, delegate to the Georgia State Assembly, and justice of the Richmond County Superior Court, he might have had trouble juggling all those responsibilities at once, but he broke no code or law.

Others, like fellow Revolutionary War soldier George Walton, wore multiple hats too. Walton, Georgia's youngest signer of the Declaration of Independence, would serve as a U.S. senator, Georgia governor, and chief justice of the Richmond County Superior Court—and champion as hard for the organization of Richmond County as did William Few. But since each of these men had different ideas about how their county government should be formed, they were seldom on the same side of any vote to see that organization through. Of one thing following the American Revolution, however, both men were united. You cannot tear one structure down without building something else in its place. With the Royal Government gone, responsibility for managing the affairs of their newly independent towns and state now fell to them.

According to the new Georgia Constitution, which both Few and Walton helped write, each county was required to choose a county seat where residents could vote, record documents, and hold court. But with a thirty-mile shoreline along the Savannah River, and forty miles to the far edge of the Wrightsborough settlement, Richmond County covered 1,200 square miles. A territory this large meant a long, time-consuming distance for residents to travel in those pre-horseless-carriage days, unless that county seat was centrally located. Or so thought Brownsborough resident William Few.

George Walton disagreed. A central location might have been fine with him if Brownsborough had been a little more civilized, like his already established hometown of Augusta. With Walton's power, or perhaps because more members of the Richmond County delegation to the Georgia General Assembly agreed with him than with Few, the 1780 session of the State Legislature enacted the following: "The remote situation of Brownsborough rendering it a very unsafe place for a Gaol [jail] and Court-House, it is enacted that [these buildings] for the County of Richmond be built in the Town of Augusta."[44]

Initially, as indicated by the mandate of 1780, the Assembly agreed that Augusta was the better location for a county seat, and they commissioned William Candler and William Few's brother, Benjamin, to begin constructing a gaol and courthouse there. But as Few's Brownsborough idea gained strength among citizens and legislators alike, that construction project was put on hold—for ten years.

Resolutions, indecisive votes, and further delays on the Richmond County situation consumed every session of the Georgia Legislature until 1789, when some obvious factors broke the deadlock. Despite this very public controversy, people still were flocking to the Backcountry. Suddenly, their leaders discovered, whenever population increases, the need for new services and infrastructure increases, too. Richmond County was now simply too large to handle that much business from that many people and, some feared, that much crime.

It would take another year, but by December 1790, ten years after the initial act to create the Richmond County seat in Augusta, the Assembly voted to split the county in two, and Columbia County was born. George Walton finally had his way and, in the words of historian George Lamplugh, "that tenacious champion of Brownsborough, William Few, had his county, too."[45]

Today, a little more than two hundred years later, more than 100,000 people also "have" their county. Some of that enduring, ballooning population have ancestors who joined William Few in celebrating Columbia County's birth. It was they who harnessed her rivers, planted her fields, birthed her villages, and welcomed newcomers to her no longer uncivilized lands. Together, newcomers and new generations of the families who came before would enter a new century with fresh determination to continue developing all their trades and towns.

1856 Columbia County Courthouse, Appling, Georgia. Courtesy Lynell Widener.

22

ON THEIR OWN

Just as our giant clump of clay evolved through a succession of earth movements before it became the land where Columbia County was born, so now a small group of newly independent people, free from the rule of other nations or the constraints of a larger community nearby, would accept the task of governing themselves.

But where to begin? Despite their sometimes quarrelsome alliance with Richmond County, a local government had already been established there. Now William Few and company would be on their own. How would planters and frontiersmen pick up the delicate reins of leadership and manage a county when most had held little but plow handles and implements of war in their calloused hands? Perhaps they were not as inexperienced as it seems.

From colonial days to the Declaration of Independence, Savannah was the capital of Georgia. But when the war to secure that independence became more intense in Savannah than in the Backcountry, the Georgia Legislature moved the seat of government to Augusta for safekeeping. As planned, when the war ended the capital officially returned to Savannah. But since the bulk of Georgia's population and many of her lawmakers lived in the Backcountry, at least half the legislative sessions continued to be held in Augusta. Finally, in 1786, and for the sake of convenience,

Augusta became the official capital of the state until a new site could be established in Louisville ten years later.

Thus, with the war over in the Backcountry in 1781, those who would emerge as leaders in Columbia and Richmond counties had nearly ten years of government experience by the time the counties were separated near the end of 1790. As mentioned before, men like George Walton and William Few gained valuable experience by serving simultaneously at county, state, and federal levels. Those who served as military leaders during the war also were schooled in leadership. Perhaps we should add that those who had staked out new lives and livelihoods on a sparse frontier received a kind of management training, too.

Besides establishing a new county government, like all Americans, Backcountry Georgians were still recovering from war. Not only were those who had left home and land behind to fight for independence returning to plundered property, but most farmer-soldiers received little or no income during those turbulent years. Neither were they paid for the weapons and equipment they supplied, nor for the valuable farm horses they rode—and often lost—in battle. It's doubtful we will ever know the personal cost of the Revolutionary War, but it is certain our forefathers paid a price we cannot repay except in gratitude for the freedom they won for themselves and bequeathed to us.

As quickly as possible, however, a grateful state hastened to compensate her fighting men when they returned from war. But with postwar currency either worthless or in short supply, Georgia used the confiscated property of departing Loyalists to repay her veterans or provide for their widows and orphaned children. Called "bounty grants" and distributed in proportion to military rank, some two thousand veterans or their survivors were given approximately 750,000 acres of land in "back pay."

Once again, similar to the years following the land cessions of 1763 and 1773, new settlers streamed into Georgia. Also as before, new immigrants from Europe were likely to settle along the coast, while Northerners moving south in search of richer farmland or warmer temperatures stopped their wagons in the fertile piedmont of the Backcountry just west of the Savannah River. By early 1790, before the division of Richmond

County, the population of the Backcountry equaled that of the rest of Georgia, with more than eleven thousand people living in Richmond County alone. A decade later, the population of Columbia County outpaced Richmond County 8,300 to 5,500. Between the Revolution and the Civil War Georgia's population would double eight times, and her heavily populated counties along the upper Savannah River would lead the world in the production of cotton.

Georgia, the last of the thirteen original colonies, became the largest state in the Union following the Revolution. Land grants were still available to individual landowners who agreed to develop the property for their own use, and Georgia's claim to stretch from the Atlantic Ocean to the Mississippi River was a powerful lure to the new wave of settlers eager for a share of that limitless space. With visions of lucrative tobacco fields or cotton bales in their eyes, these newcomers saw no obstacle to acquiring great quantities of land and ultimate wealth, except for the small fees—about $4 per 100 acres—they paid to register their otherwise free land.

As expected, enterprising newcomers soon bolstered Georgia's postwar economy. But along prosperity's way a new creature called "land speculator" would make a scandalous appearance, and the remaining "custodians"—those Native Americans who once shared the land they occupied before the white man arrived—would relinquish the last of their hunting grounds and move on to a new frontier of their own.

But first the citizens of Columbia County had to build that courthouse they fought so hard to locate way out in their uncivilized woods.

23

Columbia Courthouse: The Town and Buildings One and Two

The County Courthouse is the legal center of the community, the personification of its citizens, the silent witness to its birth and growth, and a symbol of the sovereignty of its people.[1]

The citizens of Columbia County did not have to wait for a new courthouse before they could exercise their rights as United States citizens to hold court and vote. All during the long controversy over the location of the Richmond County seat, temporary polling places with added space for a justice of the peace were alternately established in Brownsborough, Augusta, and "where the road crosses Little Kioka [Kiokee] Creek leading to the 'Meeting House.'"[2] The Meeting House was likely the original Kiokee Baptist Church located near the existing Appling Courthouse. However, since Brownsborough covered a larger area than Appling does today, the polling places outside Augusta may not have been near each other at all.

But now that the location decision was up to them, these citizens of a new county were required by law and at their own expense to build a courthouse and jail. Perhaps it is fortunate that they also were not required to agree where that location should be. In a debate that would recur each time a new Columbia County Courthouse was built for the next two hundred years, not everyone wanted the county's first courthouse in the same place. And what was the major point of disagreement? Reminiscent of William Few's ten-year feud with George Walton about the Richmond County Seat, in all but one instance, someone complained that the new site was not centrally located.

Details of the first Columbia County Courthouse are sketchy, but most records place the small, circa 1792 wooden building on five acres of land donated by William Few, Sr., in Cobbham, a small community near the current Columbia-McDuffie County line. Builder William Stevens was paid 255 pounds (about $500) for his work, with a threatened deduction of forty shillings (two pounds) if he did not supply a promised clerk's table and fix the upper windows so they would open. A few years later the commissioners called Mr. Stevens back to replace the locks and hinges on his troublesome windows, for which he was paid $3 more.

There also is a record of another "first courthouse" in the county. According to historian Pearl Baker, in a letter to Superior Court Judge George Walton, whose court continued to handle Columbia County business until their court facilities were open, the commissioners wrote: "The Courthouse at Cobb's Place is sufficiently finished for business, and the Jail will be before the sitting of Court."[3]

Is there a discrepancy here? Probably not. Mrs. Baker also writes that one of the temporary polling places in use before Columbia County was formed was located in Cobbham, a small village that grew up around the plantation of the community's largest landholder and namesake, Thomas Cobb. By the same token, even after Cobbham became the recognized name of the community, it would not have been unusual for some to continue the common practice of adding the word "Place" to the name of a prominent citizen. Hence, Cobb's Place was quite possibly the forerunner of Cobbham. It is doubtful that even the celebrated Mr. Cobb would have had two villages named for him, and a former polling place would be a fine site for a courthouse.

We do know there was some delay in completing the 1792 building because of a disagreement over whose land would be chosen for its location. Both Mr. Few and his neighbor, William Appling, had offered the county similar five-acre lots. But the commissioners chose the Few location even though most people agreed Mr. Appling's site was more centrally located. It is also doubtful the jail was completed before the first sitting of the court as promised, and perhaps it was not at the same site as the courthouse at all. Jail may be a misnomer anyway, since we know an outdoor "Stocks, Pillory, and Whipping Post," were erected, surprisingly, on Mr. Appling's land in 1796. Perhaps the split location was a compromise to honor the wishes of both men.

We have no description of the little courthouse, except for its flaws, but according to Mrs. Baker there is a colorful reference to what might have passed for the first "jail": "The stocks were to be sufficiently large to accommodate two persons, with a hatch through which their heads could protrude for pelting . . . [and] the whipping post was to be built on a substantial floor, eight feet square and 10 feet high."[4] The pillory was similar to the stocks, except that the holes for the heads were closer to the floor, presumably so the offender could sit down during the pelting.

In a late twentieth-century assessment of the county's early "judicial system," longtime Appling resident, Clerk of Court and State Senator G. B. "Jake" Pollard, Jr., surmised that this apparatus was probably used only for misdemeanor offenses, while more serious crimes were handled at "the hanging tree." Although no official record exists of such an execution site, according to local legend there was a large oak by that very name behind First Mount Moriah Baptist Church in the center of Appling, until it was cut down sometime in the late 1990's.

But we hardly have time to continue our debate over the first courthouse, because talk of its replacement began surfacing as early as 1799. Whether there were more problems with the first building than the windows, or the commissioners were bowing to continued pressure to move to a "central location," is not certain. From Mrs. Baker's account we learn of Judge Walton's criticism of the Columbia County commissioners for their continued squabbling over the location of the courthouse. In his final words of a lengthy tirade, Walton advised the commissioners to "give way to a more happy understanding."

The commissioners did not follow Walton's advice right away, and it would take longer to plan the new building than to build it. But whether by argument or finally by gentlemen's agreement, they accepted William Appling's offer of five acres of land for a new courthouse at the cost of one shilling per acre. With twenty shillings or two dollars to the pound at the time, that would make the cost of this property about 50 cents.

The new building would be larger than the old one, and conveniently located in the center of a community they simply called Columbia Courthouse. By 1816, a few years after the second courthouse was finished, this community would change its name to Appling, in honor of the family who once owned the courthouse land. Appling then became the county seat, which—although a courthouse "annex" was built in Evans in 2002—it remains to this day

Plans for the second courthouse were finished by 1808 and recorded in the "Journal of the Minutes of the Court." The outer dimensions of the new, brick building were to be fifty-by-thirty feet, and it was to be placed on a stone foundation three feet thick. Other specifications, from the number of doors and windows to the size of the clerk's table in front of the judge's seat, also were given in minute detail. Perhaps the commissioners did not want to repeat the unguided mistakes of the first courthouse.

David Stanford, whose $6,869 bid was the lowest offered for the courthouse project, was a builder of some renown. Stanford even made his own brick, which may explain why the building, complete with an eagle over the front door, was begun in 1808, but not finished until 1812. Nevertheless, the happy commissioners paid Stanford in full plus another $125 for extras, including $20 for the eagle he apparently could not make himself.

Business was brisk at the county's new courthouse. Taxes were levied and collected, candidates for all levels of government chosen there on Election Day, and court proceedings carried out in the new courtroom just past the clerk's office on the main floor. But it was the County Commission who made the most use of their proud, new facility, and of all the business they transacted there, no item appeared more often on the agenda than something to do with roads. Since tax revenues could not begin to cover the cost of these projects, and assistance from the state government was sparse to none, our ancestors had to devise a plan to fund, build, and maintain those miles of rural roads themselves.

Once a decision was made to construct a road, three road commissioners were chosen to oversee the building and upkeep of each minor road or portion of a major route. The county would then pay for the materials, but the labor was the responsibility of those whose property the road passed by. For example, if you owned a half-mile of property, you were responsible to build and care for that much of the road. For roads that were not bordered by private property, all able-bodied male citizens in the county were required to give twelve days of labor a year to keep the roadways open.

Lest we become romantics and begin a campaign to return to those good, old, public-servant days, it is necessary to point out that this plan was not as effective as it sounds. Those road-dominated commission meetings often became high-spirited discussions on how to complete this work without depending on the undependable to get it done. According to Mrs. Baker, besides appropriating more money to hire contractors to do the work, the method the commissioners chose has a familiar ring: "County roads were built and maintained according to the 'loudest wheel' system." In other words, the more "high-spirited" the request, the quicker you were likely to get your road.

Records of the county's earliest court proceedings can be found today in piles of leather-bound volumes stored in the Columbia County Historical Society building in Appling. Gleaning from early grand jury presentments within those now musty tomes offers a colorful glimpse into some additional concerns voiced by the residents of early, nineteenth-century Columbia County.

Following the March 1832 session, we read: "The Grand Jury of Columbia County feel highly gratified that they have nothing of a criminal nature to complain of." But, as noted in another entry, by the September term the moral climate of the county appears to have changed. They report: "It is with painful feelings that we have witnessed the deleterious effects proceeding from the use of spirituous liquors."

By the following March the grand jurors' indignation had increased: "It must be obvious to every observant mind that the numerous tippling-houses and dram shops in our county are evils of awful magnitude. . . . These houses are the usual haunts of the idler, the profaner, the drunkard, and the unprincipled gambler." The jurors then proceeded to scold tavern-owners and other purveyors of evil, while complimenting the clerks of the Superior Court and Court of Ordinary (Probate Court today) for "keeping their books neatly and correctly."

From jury pools to road builders and those who planned or assigned their tasks, the people of Columbia County learned to manage their county well. While some of her leaders continued to serve and mature in the duties that fell to them, others felt the call to wider service and extended their influence to the state and nation. At the same time, historic events in and beyond county borders would just as greatly influence those who remained behind.

24

THE TRANS-OCONEE REPUBLIC
AND THE YAZOO LAND FRAUD

Building a courthouse and establishing a new government took priority during Columbia County's first decade, although for some of her citizens local matters were not their only concern. What was happening in Georgia's unsettled, western lands soon became a priority too, not only for Columbia County, but also for Georgia and the nation.

Land has always lured the pioneer. More land, better land, more land than his neighbor or, as in vast, western Georgia, bargain-priced land a person could buy for a low price and sell at great profit was a temptation some could not resist.

Who could blame the men of Georgia and their counterparts in neighboring states for wanting their share or, because there was so much land available, more than their share? More wars have been fought over land, we are told, than for any other reason since the world began. During the final decade of the eighteenth-century and into the nineteenth, Georgia's western lands would spark at least a war of words between a group of speculators and those who condemned their selfish acts. But before the profiteering began in earnest, one man with local connections and a familiar name would make an outlandish claim for a large portion of that land.

Elijah Clarke, Southern hero of the Revolution and victor over Thomas Brown, may have laid down his arms when the war ended, but given another chance to flex his military muscle he was ready to fight again. Thus, in 1794, when Edmond Charles Genet of France needed help to drive the Spanish out of Louisiana so he could set up a French Republic there, Clarke reassembled his former band of revolutionaries and led the Louisiana charge.

But Clarke and Genet had neither sought nor received the blessing of the American government for what they planned to do. President George Washington was highly displeased with Genet's intentions and appealed to France to recall their man. France obliged, leaving Clarke and his men without a battle to fight—at least in Louisiana.

While traveling from the Georgia Backcountry to Louisiana, the Clarke party had passed through Georgia's highly publicized western lands—or, to be more accurate, Georgia's highly publicized but not clearly titled western lands. Spain still claimed part of that territory, and scattered bands of Creeks and other Indian tribes continued to live there. No treaty or land cession had yet declared that the remaining Indian land belonged to Georgia.

War hero or no war hero, Elijah Clarke was as land-hungry as any newly independent American. He also had little love for the Creeks who had fought with the British in the Revolution, or the Spanish who had fought against the British and the Americans ever since the rivaling Europeans came to the New World. Therefore, on his return trip to Georgia, Clarke marched boldly to the western bank of the Oconee River, took possession of an area ten miles wide and 120 miles long, which he called "The Trans-Oconee Republic," and put himself in charge. Clarke then allotted 640 acres plus a promise of more land in the future for each of his men, and began building settlements for their families and forts to protect them all from the Indians.

The new land baron may have been a military genius, but he was greatly lacking in protocol. When anyone questioned his right to usurp such a large quantity of land, Clarke merely announced that the land had been part of Georgia since the Indian land cession of 1773, and since he and his men were part of Georgia they were entitled to the land. Furthermore, because the Indians were still a threat to the safety of the people of Georgia, he thought he should be commended for building a buffer between the two groups.

Interestingly, had Clarke been an Indian his argument might have worked. According to tribal law, all Indian land did belong to the whole community. Thus, any member was entitled to live on any part of that communal property, just as long as he remembered profits from land sales or cessions belonged to the whole tribe, too.

The men of Trans-Oconee needn't have bothered with the forts. They were not built long enough for Indian skirmishes to begin, or strong enough to combat the Georgia Militia who, under orders from then Governor George Matthews, burned down the forts and drove Clarke and his band from their unentitled land.

Had Clarke responded to earlier orders to leave the area, such harsh treatment would not have been necessary. It took an eviction order by Judge George Walton to point out that even if all the land did belong to Georgia, which was doubtful, that did not mean individual Georgians could grab any portion they wanted for themselves. Because of the continuing fragile relationship between the white man and the remaining Indians, President George Washington was even more alarmed than Walton. Ultimately it was the president who advised the governor to remove Clarke lest there be another outbreak of war with the Creeks, who continued to be resentful of land cessions in the past.

Following the successful outcome of the governor's orders, Clarke's plan to establish his own empire was gone forever. Though he continued to be a land grabber by reputation, a still popular Elijah Clarke managed to acquire a seat in the Georgia Legislature and dabble in further land speculation before retiring to his farm in Wilkes County, where he died on December 15, 1799. His son John, however, would keep the Clark name, now spelled without an "e," at the forefront of Georgia politics for years to come.[5]

Ever since the first settlers came to Georgia there had been two theories on how to distribute her lands—by grant to those who would develop the land and live there themselves, to encourage more people to settle in the state; or by sale to those who could afford to purchase the land, to build up the state treasury and fund Georgia's public buildings and infrastructure.

With the majority of landowners receiving their property by the grant system, Georgia's treasury and thus her infrastructure had never been adequately funded. At least this was the noble reason given by members of the State Legislature for their proposal to sell approximately 35 million acres of Georgia's western lands to four land companies in Georgia and nearby states for $500,000, or about 1½ cents per acre. (Historians differ on the amount of land in question. Because of inaccurate or, sometimes, nonexistent land surveys, the exact size of this area is not known.) Both the land and the land companies this transaction created would soon be identified as "Yazoo," the name of a river flowing through those western lands and into the Mississippi River.

Initially Governor Matthews was as opposed to placing such a large concentration of land in the hands of so few as he was to Elijah Clarke's Trans-Oconee Republic. But after refusing to sign the first Yazoo Land Act in 1794, by the time a similar Act crossed his desk in January 1795, the governor overcame his uneasiness and signed the Act into law.

Matthews was not the only one whose resistance crumbled under pressure from the "Yazooists," as the land speculators were called. James Gunn, one of Georgia's U.S. senators, resigned from Congress to come home and participate in the scheme himself. A large number of legislators, who either were members of the land companies themselves or were given generous bribes of company shares to sway their vote, were also caught up in "the Act."

And what an Act it was! One share of Yazoo stock cost $860 and entitled the shareholder to 25,000 acres of land. Now Georgia's western lands had reached the doubled value of three cents an acre. Subsequently, even a small markup on so large a block of land would earn great profits for the investors, while the price was still so ridiculously low that buyers were standing in line either to purchase the land for themselves or become part of the pyramid scheme, pad the price again, and sell to someone else.

Before long Georgia's other senator resigned his seat in Congress too, but not to accept the half million acres of western land he had been offered to support the Yazoo scheme. An outraged James Jackson came home to put an end to the scandal that threatened to taint his beloved Georgia in the eyes of the nation. Jackson would succeed, but not without help. Stalwart statesman William Few, along with newcomer to the Columbia County political scene, William H. Crawford, and other anti-Yazooists, would work with Jackson to bring the sordid affair to a sensational end.

25

FROM TAINTED LAND TO MORAL GROUND

It was no exaggeration to call the Yazoo land scheme one of the largest real estate transactions in U.S. history, and one of the most corrupt. With the biblical story of the Children of Israel and their Promised Land in mind, the Yazooists advertised Georgia's western lands as "the land of promise." Outraged critics called it "a promised land for the few, but not for the rightful owners, all the 'children' of Georgia."[6] Today in the business world we call such transactions "insider trading." When they occur in government circles, we call it "graft."

Georgia's land speculation, however, did not start with Yazoo. Some of those bounty grants given to veterans for their Revolutionary War service became a kind of speculation, too. Veterans who fought in Georgia but lived in another state, or Georgians who wanted to settle somewhere else following the war, frequently sold their land to finance their relocation. It is also true that some of the veterans, such as those who remained in Georgia but did not want to raise cotton or tobacco, tried their hand at "raising" land. Certainly not all potential buyers or sellers of Georgia's western lands were as unprincipled as the men of Yazoo.

For example, about the time the Yazoo companies were being formed, William Few, in partnership with Augustan John Twiggs, former governors John Wereat and Edward Telfair among others, established the

Georgia Union Company. This group's purpose was the same as that of the Yazoo companies, to buy and sell Georgia's western land and thereby help build up the state treasury. But their plan and its benefit to Georgia were much different. The Union Company offered the state substantially more money for the land than did the Yazooists, and they did not offer anyone a bribe to push their request through the Legislature.

But the Union Company Act did not pass. By then the Yazoo faction had already lobbied—and bribed—enough delegates to secure the necessary votes to turn the Union Company down. With this decision, not only did the state lose at least $300,000 on the initial sale, but had Georgia followed the examples of Congress and other states who were selling smaller sections of their public lands for as much as fifty cents to a dollar an acre, they might have swelled the state treasury by another $50 million.

Lost revenue and delayed infrastructure, however, were not the only losses Georgia suffered because of the Yazoo land fraud. As the price charged by the Yazooists continued to rise, large blocks of the western lands would increasingly be sold out-of-state, including Philadelphia and New York, where the wealthy buyers lived. The bulk of Georgia's poorer citizens would then have to pay an even higher price to buy back parcels of their former public lands.

Ultimately it was the cheated "children of Georgia" who convinced Senator Jackson to come home and mount a campaign to rescind the Yazoo Act.[7] Surely the men of Yazoo did nothing "noble" for their state by replacing the unprofitable land grant system with their get-themselves-rich scheme.

The life of the Yazoo Land Act ended scarcely a year after it began, but its consequences for Georgia and eventually for the U.S. Government would linger for the next twenty years.

"I consider Georgia as having passed a Confiscation Act, by taking [the property of] your children and mine, and unborn generations, to supply the rapacious grasping of a few sharks."[8] The anger in former Senator Jackson's words was exceeded only by the energy he would spend spearheading the drive to overturn the infamous Yazoo Act.

After only a brief campaign, but with strong backing from his home district of Savannah, by November 1795, Jackson easily won a seat in the Georgia Legislature. At the same time the state capital, which had remained in Augusta for the previous ten years, moved to its new facilities in Louisville. Despite excitement over the move, another subject overshadowed everything else that election year: Each candidate vying for office campaigned on the issue of Yazoo, and Yazoo alone. Although several of the Yazooists were returned to office—a few with contrition in their bones—the anti-Yazooists won the most seats. Therefore, it did not take long before the delegates went to work on what also nearly became a one-issue session—rescinding the Yazoo Act, which the same governing body had passed just one year before.

As soon as the new Legislature convened in Louisville on January 11, 1796, new Governor Jared Irwin chose a committee, including Jackson and William Few, to study the circumstances surrounding the Yazoo sale. With Jackson as its chairman, the committee first passed a resolution stating that offering a bribe to a member of the House was "one of the highest of crimes," and accepting such a bribe was "so flagrant an abuse of the sacred trust that it ought to . . . disqualify him from serving therein."[9] This resolution also would become part of the 1798 Georgia Constitution, after committee chairman Jackson became the next governor of the state.

On February 13, after only one month's work and nearly word-for-word as proposed by the committee, the bill commonly known as the Rescinding Act passed by a vote of 44 to 3 in the House, and 14 to 4 in the Senate. Governor Irwin signed the bill into law that very day and set plans in motion for a public ceremony to demonstrate to the people of Georgia the importance of this legislation.

"Within three days," the governor announced, "both houses of the Legislature should expunge from all public books . . . all papers relative to the Yazoo sale [which] shall be publicly burnt in order that no trace of so unconstitutional, vile, and fraudulent a transaction shall remain in the public offices thereof."[10] At the same time, clerks of every superior court in the state were ordered to destroy all Yazoo records in their county's files. Failure to obey this order would result in the immediate suspension of the offending clerk and a $1,000 fine—with one-half the proceeds of the fine going to the informer.

Two days later, and with all the pomp of a royal funeral, the Secretary of State, President (now called "Governor"), Secretary of the Senate, Speaker of the House of Representatives, remaining legislators, and a crowd of spectators all marched outside their new capitol, where a bonfire was being prepared to "bury" forever the offensive documents.

"GOD SAVE THE STATE," cried the Messenger of the House as the records were about to be burned, "AND LONG PRESERVE HER RIGHTS! MAY EVERY ATTEMPT TO INJURE THEM PERISH AS THESE CORRUPT ACTS NOW DO!"[11]

Obviously, enough Yazoo records survived one or two fined or suspended clerk's files—or remained in some newspaper reporter's archives—to inform later generations of both the original Yazoo Act and its rescinding legislation. Other details survived too, especially those concerning the famous fire, albeit with less than credible authenticity.

Few Georgians familiar with the Yazoo affair will fail to add the tale of a man with snowy hair and beard who stepped from the crowd and offered to start the fire with a magnifying glass. "The fire to consume such a monstrous iniquity should only come from heaven," the stranger declared.[12] Supposedly, heat rays from the sun then pierced the glass, and the documents were, indeed, purged from the earth with fire from heaven.

It is no tale, however, that legal entanglements caused by the Yazoo affair could not be destroyed with fire from heaven or earth. During the brief time sales had been allowed to take place, much of the western land was sold—and sold again. Legislation or no legislation, buyers holding bargain-priced land were in no mood to rescind ownership of their property.

Negotiations went on for years between the governments of Georgia and the United States, the Indians who remained in the area, and the new "owners" who ardently believed the land belonged to them. Slowly, amid lingering animosity and one decision or act of legislation at a time, the Yazoo land scheme and the complications it produced would be resolved.

The U.S. Government acted first by declaring in 1798 that the western lands were no longer part of Georgia, but were now the Mississippi Territory. Georgia was not at all happy with this decision. But after struggling for three years with lawsuits from land buyers and questions of Indian rights, the state agreed to cede to the United States all territory she had claimed west of the Chattahoochie River, and to seek the Federal Government's help in acquiring firm title to all remaining land to the east. By 1802 the U.S. Government responded with two promises to Georgia—to pay the state the first $1,250,000 from sales proceeds of her previously held western lands, and to extinguish all Indian claim to the remaining land within her newly established borders.[13]

Georgia's Yazoo problems might have been over by then, but the issue of compensating those who had purchased western land remained unsolved. Congress, including James Jackson who, after serving two years in the Georgia Legislature and one term as governor had returned to the Senate, grappled for several more years with the Yazoo buyers' claims. Finally, in 1810, when their crisis had neither been settled by Congress nor through litigation, the buyers took their case to the Supreme Court. In a stunning move, the nation's highest judicial body agreed with the buyers and promptly annulled Georgia's 1796 Rescinding Act. Under the provisions of the original land sale, the court ruled, the State of Georgia had no right to rescind what the buyers had purchased in good faith.

The cost of the "noble" Yazoo Act of 1795 went up again, not to Georgia this time for the state no longer owned the land in question, but to the federal government, who would pay more than $4,000,000 to satisfy the claims of those least responsible for a real estate transaction gone wrong.

The United States kept her financial promises to Georgia and to the Yazoo land buyers within a reasonable amount of time, but it would take almost twenty-five more years to extinguish all Indian claims to Georgia's almost entitled western land.

26

Custodians of the Land No More

On the heels of the Yazoo Land Fraud, can we, the descendants of those involved, now bear to hear a grievous sequel, that the land our ancestors fought so hard to acquire and pass along to us had been claimed centuries before by others? Must we relive the decade after decade, river by river pushing back of an already established group of people until their final remnant was driven back across the Mississippi River from whence their ancestors came? Does it pain us that the land Yamacraw Chief Tomochichi first shared with James Oglethorpe more than a century before, and his descendants ceded incrementally to later waves of incoming Georgians, was now lost to his people forever?

Human history, including but not limited to our own, has her glorious moments, but also her chapters that cannot be cloaked with pride. On the subject of land acquisition, close to home or across the seven seas, hardly since the Biblical Garden of Eden has the newcomer found property sufficient for his needs that was not already claimed or occupied by someone else. Just as rare is that initial offer by a kindly Indian chief near Georgia's first settlement to share the excess land his people did not need. Normally those who are stronger, or who consider themselves "more civilized," will drive the more vulnerable group away.

Today, we who look with sorrow or disdain on a past we neither witnessed nor understand, hear of land wars still being fought somewhere in the world and long for the day when such disputes are resolved with words and mutual consent rather than by force or at the point of a gun. But until then, when contemplating the distant past, perhaps we can adapt the view of poet Alfred Lord Tennyson who wrote in "The Charge of the Light Brigade": "Their's not to reason why, their's but to do and die."[14]

Ours, too, may not be to question why, but simply to recall the relationship between our ancestors and their Native American neighbors from its beginning to the early decades of the nineteenth century when, at Georgia's urging, the federal government assumed responsibility for removing the remaining Creeks and Cherokees from the state.

By the time James Oglethorpe and his fellow travelers arrived to establish the last of England's thirteen original colonies in the New World, they were neither surprised to find another group of people already here, nor afraid of the reception they would incur. From Plymouth to Pennsylvania, earlier settlers had told a similar story: The natives they met were kind, peaceful, and willing to help newcomers adjust to their new land. We may enjoy the image of "The Pilgrims" sharing a Thanksgiving feast with their Indian neighbors in the 1620's, but if the natives had not learned long before how to cultivate wild corn, beans, potatoes, pumpkins, and other common domestic foods still served in this country today, not only would the Pilgrims have had no Thanksgiving dinner, but they might not have had enough food to survive.

With this knowledge, plus the example of William Penn, who considered himself "armed with royal authority but sensitive to native consent,"[15] Oglethorpe adopted the same peaceful attitude he expected to find. From that first settlement in Savannah to the trading post in the Backcountry, he understood that the survival of Georgia's new occupants would depend on Indian goodwill.

As long as the early settlers were alive, they would remember how the natives came to their aid, taught them to grow and prepare food, traded animal skins for the white man's goods, and granted them portions of their land. But in later generations, after the white man had adapted to his new surroundings, he no longer needed the services of his native neighbors and his viewpoint changed. Now, all he needed was their land.

Although Columbia County had few Indian neighbors by the early nineteenth-century, all the land within her borders once belonged to the tribes of the Creek Nation. Most tribes, including the Kiokees and Yuchis (also spelled "Euchees"), whose memories linger in the names of county streams, roads, a prominent church, and other landmarks, ceded their land to Georgia before the county was formed. More native influence in the county can be traced to the Creek and Cherokee trails that became Washington, Wrightsboro, and Columbia roads. These trails would also determine the early route of the railroad, since rail lines were often built alongside well-traveled roads. But as in the rest of Georgia, people in Columbia County who wished to trade their small farms for larger cotton plantations also needed more space. When land to the north and west became available, those residents would cross county lines, too.

As time dragged on, following the federal government's 1802 promise to remove the Indians from Georgia, it was obvious the two sides had differing opinions about what that promise meant. Georgians considered the agreement binding and imminent, but the federal government preferred to act slowly in hopes of persuading the Indians to leave voluntarily. With land set aside in the Oklahoma territory for their use, and portions already occupied by a large number of Creeks and some of the Cherokees who once lived in Georgia, the government's "persuasion" included statements like this: "You are too near your white neighbors to live in peace. . . . Your game is destroyed. . . . You will become extinct. . . . Beyond the great River Mississippi . . . your [white] father has provided a country for you, and he advises you to remove to it."[16]

These arguments may have lacked credibility from the beginning, but they were nearly impossible to sustain after 1828, when gold was discovered in North Georgia, where most of the Cherokees lived. Predictably, somebody now suggested a new argument for the Indian removal: since the Cherokees had not been concerned with wealth before, why would they be interested in gold now?[17]

Even if such a supposition were true, the Cherokees did not want to leave the only home most of them had ever known. Besides, by now their citizens owned property, planted crops, governed themselves, and had adopted so many of the white man's ways that they didn't see why the two races could not continue to live together. Also, thanks to the enlightened Cherokee Chief Sequoyah, for the first time in Native American history or in any of their more than two thousand known dialects, this tribe had its own syllabary (alphabet of letters and symbols) and written language. They could read, write, and even publish their own reading material.[18]

For nearly three decades, and after the efforts of a succession of Georgia governors and U.S. presidents, persuasion and diplomacy for removing the last of the Indians from the Southeast had not worked. But Georgia still needed the Indian land, and the U.S. still had a promise to keep. Now it was time to change course.

The discovery of gold may have hastened the Cherokee removal from Georgia, but it was likely the election of Andrew Jackson to the presidency that brought this critical chapter in American history to a close. Jackson had dealt with the Indians before, and theirs was no peaceful encounter.

Before he became America's seventh president, General Andrew Jackson came to prominence as an Indian fighter in the Mississippi Territory, and America's greatest hero in the War of 1812.[19] That war, considered by many to be a postscript to the American Revolution, was waged between the United States and Great Britain, but rivalry between two divisions of the Creek Nation at the same time created a war within a war. The Upper Creeks, also known as Red Sticks, saw the war as a chance to regain their ceded lands and sided with the British, while the Lower Creeks remained friendly to the United States and fought under Jackson's command. But before the decisive victory at the Battle of New Orleans in 1815 that ended the war with the British, increased tensions among the Creeks also involved Jackson in that nation's Civil War.

Following news that the Creek War had spilled over into attacks on white settlers, including the massacre of five hundred people at Fort Mims, Alabama, all those "savage tales" that greeted earlier groups of arriving Georgians were now universally believed. In a series of editorials, the *Augusta Chronicle* joined other Georgia newspapers in denouncing the growing threat: "The Creek Confederacy has long been manifesting a deadly antipathy towards the United States. . . . When the tomahawk and the scalping knife are drawn in the cabins of our peaceful and unsuspecting citizens it is time to call loudly for vengeance. . . . Let us at once secure the peace and tranquility of our own frontier by driving [the Creeks] across the Mississippi."[20]

With the federal government's blessing, Jackson accepted the *Chronicle's* challenge and traveled to Alabama's Tallapoosa River to avenge the Fort Mims massacre. It did not take long. Jackson and his men met the Red Sticks at Horseshoe Bend, and killed them by the hundreds.[21] But, although friendly Creeks and a contingent of Cherokees had often fought by his side, following the Fort Mims massacre and bloody response, Jackson's anger was kindled forever against the Indian race.

In 1814, soon after the battle at Horseshoe Bend, Jackson called a meeting of all the Creeks to discuss peace within their nation. As the meeting wore on, Jackson revealed a second motive for calling the tribe together—to force them to give up large areas of their land in South Georgia and eastern Alabama. What seemed like a cruel, ungrateful move to the Creeks, Jackson justified by saying his government was only seeking payment for a war the United States had fought on their behalf.

Many of the Creeks accepted this new and stronger urging to move west. Those who stayed behind were allowed to live on the remaining Creek land in Alabama, but with the understanding that the United States would no longer honor a long-standing agreement between them— the right of the Creeks to call themselves a Sovereign Nation. Soon a similar ruling concerning the Cherokees would become the final catalyst for moving this tribe, too, across the Mississippi.

At least four pivotal events occurring between 1828 and 1830 led directly to the Cherokee removal: gold drew an influx of new settlers to

North Georgia; Andrew Jackson became president; the U.S. Congress passed the Indian Removal Bill; and an impatient Georgia legislature declared the Cherokee Nation, its constitution and laws, null and void. From then on the Cherokees—and the missionaries sympathetic to the Cherokee cause—would be subject to the laws of Georgia just like everyone else.

The Cherokees now had two reasons to appeal to the federal government for help: Their territory was being overrun with gold miners, and they were outraged that Georgia had abolished their nation. The federal government responded by sending in troops to drive the miners off Cherokee lands, and the Cherokees, aided by missionaries who had been jailed for refusing to obey Georgia laws over their own, took their complaint to the United States Supreme Court.

Georgia reacted angrily to federal interference and asked President Jackson to remove his troops. In turn, the president decided the gold-miner issue was a state matter rather than a federal responsibility, and honored Georgia's request. But on the Supreme Court case, Chief Justice John Marshall, the same judge who had ruled in favor of the Yazoo land buyers twenty years before, ruled against Georgia once again. The missionaries had broken no law and should be set free, he said, and Georgia laws did not apply in the extant Cherokee Nation.

Case closed? Not on your life. Tempers flared in all directions. Georgia Governor Wilson Lumpkin ignored the court's order, and President Jackson, no friend of the Cherokees or the Chief Justice said, "John Marshall has made his decision; now let him enforce it."[22]

Following the Supreme Court decision, Cherokee reaction went from celebration to utter sorrow as the defiant Governor Lumpkin ordered surveyors to begin dividing the Cherokee land into ten new counties, and each to be subdivided into smaller plots for distribution to the citizens of Georgia.

The Cherokees tried to resist, even offering to abide by Georgia law and give up some of their land, but it was too late. In 1835, and without the knowledge of the rest of the tribe, a small group of Cherokees met with federal officials and agreed to give up all their land east of the

Mississippi for far less money than the land was worth. As Chief John Ross was heard to say, "Our gold alone is worth more than this."[23] The Senate ratified the treaty the next year and gave the Cherokees two years to vacate their land.

By the middle of 1838, five thousand Cherokees had moved west voluntarily, but some fifteen thousand in Georgia and more in nearby states were still reluctant to leave. During the next few months U.S. Army troops, who were welcomed in Georgia this time, began forcing the Cherokees to begin the long trek west. Fatigue, disease and, ultimately, the winter weather took a terrible toll. An estimated four thousand people died en route to their promised land across the Mississippi River, leading historians and all who hear this sad tale to call their journey, "The Trail of Tears."

But land frauds and man's inhumanity to man, though they intertwine with the Columbia County story, are only a portion of her past. All of Georgia and most neighboring states were also involved in these less than complimentary chapters of early American history. In fact, with considerable evidence we could say it was the leadership of Columbia County that opposed both the speculation of Georgia's western lands and the forced removal of the Indians.

Though we cannot claim total innocence, it is more than appropriate now to shine our spotlight on some of those leaders who not only spent their lives correcting wrongs and serving their local communities, but also helped guide their new state and nation from birth to maturity among the governments of their country and the world. From local leaders to state legislators and members of Congress, from educators to a governor of the state and almost a president of the country, Columbia County has a long list of remarkable heroes about whom her descendants can be grateful and very proud.

PART IV

MORE THAN HER SHARE OF HEROES

27

ABRAHAM BALDWIN: EDUCATOR,
STATESMAN, AND ENEMY OF NONE

When Connecticut-born Abraham Baldwin arrived in the
Backcountry of Georgia in 1784, and a scant three years later
joined his neighbor William Few as the only signers of the United States
Constitution from the state, Columbia County did not exist. Technically
both men lived in Richmond County. But when that county was divided
in 1790 to create Columbia County, neither man changed his place of
residence. Today we might say only their zip code changed. Abraham
Baldwin and William Few were then residents of Columbia County.[1]

Judging from his impressive résumé, Abraham Baldwin sounds like a
child prodigy, or at least someone who was profoundly shaped by the circumstances of his youth. Motherless from the age of four until his father,
Michael Baldwin, remarried ten years later, young Abraham assumed a
near adult role for much of that time, and he would continue to care for
his seven half-siblings following his father's death. The elder Baldwin was
a blacksmith, an honorable profession even if it did not generate much
wealth. But it was likely his own lack of education that prompted Michael
to move his family from Guilford, Connecticut, where Abraham was
born, to New Haven so his children could study at Yale.

Abraham more than fulfilled his father's ambition. After graduating in 1772 at age eighteen, he remained at Yale another three years to study theology. Although he was then licensed to preach, he put that profession on hold and stayed on at Yale as a tutor until he joined the Revolutionary Army as a chaplain in 1779. Still, when Yale invited him back to the school as a professor of divinity in 1781, he declined the offer because he was no longer convinced the ministry was the life he wanted to pursue. Baldwin did return to Yale, however, not to teach but to become a student again and study law. By the time the war ended he had concluded his studies, passed the bar exam, and become licensed to practice his newest chosen profession.

The two years Baldwin served in the Revolutionary Army may have been the pivotal years of his life. It was there that he worked with General Nathanael Greene, the man who led the final assault against the British in Augusta and who, in appreciation for his military service, was awarded a confiscated Loyalist estate in Savannah at the close of the war. General Greene moved to Savannah in 1783, about the time Baldwin was looking for a place to practice law that offered more opportunities than were available to him in Connecticut. When Greene suggested Baldwin come to Georgia, the young lawyer took that advice and moved to Savannah, too.

The transplanted New Englander was immediately smitten with the Southern state he would call home for the rest of his life. Just as immediately the people of Georgia accepted Baldwin as one of their own, and he soon became immersed in the political affairs of his new state. When the state capital moved from Savannah to Augusta in 1785, Baldwin decided to move with the capital and settle on two hundred acres of granted land near present-day Appling. He was now thirty years of age.

During the next year Baldwin established his law practice and accepted an appointment to the state legislature. From that time on he would represent Georgia in some area of public service for as long as he lived. Although he received praise for a number of accomplishments at both the state and national level, the incident by which he is most remembered happened early in his political career.

Baldwin had scarcely begun his term in the state legislature when he became one of Georgia's delegates to the Continental Congress. From there, along with Georgians William Pierce, William Houstoun, and William Few, he was appointed to the 1787 Constitutional Convention in Philadelphia, where he would make his memorable contribution to the foundation of the country.

In the summer of 1776, when the Continental Congress met in Philadelphia to consider becoming an independent nation, it took the fifty-six delegates just under four weeks to draft, adopt, and sign the Declaration of Independence. Eleven years later, following a long war and years of discussion in and out of Congress, it would take a similar number of delegates almost four months to draw up a constitution. With every state but Rhode Island represented, the Constitutional Convention gathered in Philadelphia on May 25, 1787, to work out the details of governing their new nation.

For some states the Articles of Confederation, the initial attempt following the Declaration of Independence to construct a working constitution, were sufficient. Remembering the strong monarchy they left behind, these states might have been happy without a central government at all. But others recognized weaknesses in the earlier document on such issues as taxes, trade, interstate disputes, and divisions of responsibility between the state and national governments that might hamper the future of the country if left unresolved. These differences had already been debated so often that by the time Congress adopted the resolution to hold the convention, it was the understanding of some that the only reason for the meeting was, once again, to amend the Articles of Confederation.

Members of both camps arrived at the convention ready to air their views. One side planned to lobby for stronger government at the state level while the other side prepared to point out the need "to render the constitution of [the federal] government adequate to the exigencies of the Union."[2]

For weeks this mixture of national, political elites and advocates of local and state interests met in private, in committee, and jointly with all delegates present. They debated long and tediously on each point, made decisions one day that were amended the next, and worked toward a compromise on all matters of disagreement. But of one thing they were in agreement almost from the start—to discard the Articles of Confederation and frame an entirely new constitution.

The first idea to emerge was the Virginia Plan, because it was written largely by James Madison from that state. This plan, establishing a supreme national government with three separate but equal branches—legislative, executive, and judicial—met with nearly everyone's approval, until it came to deciding how to construct that coequal legislative branch. According to Madison, the legislature would be made up of two houses, with population or some other proportional measure used to determine the number of members from each state in both houses.

Not so, said delegates from the smaller states, who believed that, under this plan, their representation would fall far below that of the more populous states. James Paterson from the small state of New Jersey then presented the New Jersey Plan, which called for a one-house Congress that would include an equal number of members from each state. By June 19 this plan too was rejected, and it would take another month of contentious debate—and the wisdom of a delegate from Georgia—before this divisive matter was settled in what is still called the Great Compromise.

Tensions ran high in Independence Hall on July 2, when a roll-call vote on the composition of the proposed legislative branch was scheduled. Neither the large states nor the small states appeared willing to compromise their positions. Furthermore, if the concerns of the small states were not addressed, their delegates had threatened to walk out of the convention and, essentially, shut the constitution process down. Since Georgia was a large state, everyone assumed her delegates would vote against the wishes of the smaller states.

Georgia was also the last state to vote and, as fate would have it, the vote was tied by the time Houstoun and Baldwin—the only delegates present that day—cast their votes. Houstoun went first and, as expected, voted with the larger states. Baldwin, however, perhaps with some empathy for his former—and smaller—state of Connecticut, stunned his colleagues by voting against his fellow Georgian and in favor of the other side.

With the vote still tied and weeks of wrangling behind them, how would they ever come to a decision now? But what Baldwin had done was buy the delegates more time. If he had voted with Houstoun, the convention would have been over. Now the two sides could return to the bargaining table and try again to reach an agreement.

Baldwin had also accomplished something else. When the delegates realized how close they came to failing this important task, tensions abated and cooler heads were ready to return to work. Two weeks later, on July 16, the Great Compromise concerning the legislative branch of government was adopted. There would be two houses, just as the Virginia Plan suggested, but representation in only one house would be determined by population. The other house would include two members from each state regardless of size, just as the small states had requested.

Other sections of the document still needed refining, but the most difficult work of the convention was over. On September 17, 1787, the thirty-eight delegates present adopted the new Constitution of the United States of America, which to this date is the longest-lived national constitution in the history of the world. Among the signers of that momentous document were Abraham Baldwin and William Few from—soon to become—Columbia County, Georgia.

Baldwin was then appointed to the Grand Board, whose members would fine-tune the wording of the text and coordinate the transition from the Articles of Confederation to the Constitution. In 1789 he became a member of the very Congress he helped form, serving in the House of Representatives for the next ten years before moving to the Senate, where he remained until his death.

Surprisingly, however, despite his remarkable congressional career, Abraham Baldwin's greatest contribution to Georgia may not have been in the arenas of politics and law at all, but in education; and the Connecticut Yankee's desire to practice law outside his home state may not have been the only reason he moved to Georgia.

With Nathaneal Greene and then Georgia Governor Lyman Hall, also former residents of Connecticut, it is likely they knew of Baldwin's education credentials. Thus, when Governor Hall was looking for someone to help establish a seminary (college) of higher learning in Georgia, some have suggested that the governor and the general worked together to coax the educator south. Evidence of Baldwin's greater involvement in education than in law includes: scant records of legal work past his first year or two in Georgia, and the fact that prior to the birth of Columbia County or the incorporation of the City of Augusta, he was appointed to the Richmond County Commission, whose duties were to "exercise over the town . . . and the [Richmond] Academy such authority as the General Assembly appointing them saw fit to delegate."[3] Baldwin also is known to have submitted a plan to Governor Hall for common (now called elementary) and secondary education throughout the state, but it was in the establishment of the University of Georgia for which educator Baldwin still is best known.

Among his other pursuits, Baldwin had hardly arrived in the state before he was appointed to the Board of Trustees to manage forty thousand acres of land set aside by the General Assembly to be used or sold to finance the establishment of a Seminary of Learning in Georgia. By 1785, after becoming chairman of the board, Baldwin completed a written charter for "Franklin College," initially named for Benjamin Franklin, but later called the University of Georgia, the name by which it is best known today. Baldwin's efforts, which he based on his alma mater, Connecticut's Yale University, was the first recorded charter for a state university in the nation. (Yale, Harvard, and William and Mary were earlier universities, but they were not under the auspices of any state.) As the General Assembly also decided, the university would be constructed in Louisville, the proposed site of the next capital of Georgia.

As soon as the initial college charter was adopted, Baldwin set about acquiring a site, arranging for construction of the buildings, and selecting a faculty and students. But he needn't have hurried. Renewed clashes between Georgia and the Creek Indians in the Louisville area put a stop to the proceedings, and progress on the Seminary of Learning lay dormant for the next fifteen years.

By 1800, when plans for the college were revived, the trustees recommended changing the location from Louisville to a new town on the Oconee River called Athens. The campus would be located on land donated by Georgia's eighth governor, John Milledge, and financed from the sale of the original land set aside for that purpose. Baldwin was considered acting president of the university from the time the charter was adopted until the school opened in 1801. But since he was serving in Congress by then and, thus, was too busy to serve the university too, he resigned the position. In his place and upon his recommendation, Josiah Meigs, one of his former students at Yale, became the first active president of the college.

Abraham Baldwin remained a bachelor all his life. As some say, he was never married to anyone but his work. The only recorded references to his family are of the education of his siblings and their children, and a close relationship with his sister Ruth and her husband, Joel Barlow. He had many friends and was known to enjoy life, but he did not enjoy it long. He was only fifty-two years old when he died in Washington, D.C., on March 4, 1807, one day after the final session of the Ninth Congress. Friends said it was typical of him to wait until his work was finished to die.

It was a cold, rainy day when Baldwin's funeral procession left the capitol for the Rock Creek Cemetery on the banks of the Potomac River five miles away, yet everyone who was able made the journey with him. He was buried next to his friend and fellow Georgian, James Jackson, who had died the year before, and whose career and contribution to the state had also lain side by side with his own. On the death of such an able and respected man, one member of the procession was heard to say, "Never did I see such solemnity and regret." Baldwin died, it is believed, without an enemy.[4]

But he did not die without a memory. In 1803 the area surrounding Milledgeville, Georgia's capital from 1807 to 1868, was named Baldwin County, and a century later the town of Tifton became the site of Abraham Baldwin Agricultural College, in tribute to his valuable contribution to the field of education in the state. There is also a street near the university in Athens that bears his name.

Upon the death of Abraham Baldwin, Georgia sent another remarkable man to Congress to take his place. Get comfortable, for it will take three chapters to tell the story of the next great man from Columbia County, William Harris Crawford.

28

WILLIAM HARRIS CRAWFORD:

COLUMBIA COUNTY'S

"MAN FOR ALL SEASONS"

He was not born in Columbia County, and he would live there less than twenty years. But few events in early county, state, or national history escaped the influence of part-time native son and, many say, her most famous citizen, William Harris Crawford, a "man for all seasons."[5] To date, no other county resident has served in the cabinet of two American presidents or been nominated for the presidency itself. Also, as far as we know, no one else with even a temporary Columbia County address ever met or elegantly impressed then president of France, Napoleon Bonaparte.

The ancestral line that produced so fine a statesman as William Crawford began in Lanark County, Scotland, also the home of legendary Scot Sir Walter Raleigh, to whom it is believed the Crawfords were related. Despite allusions to noble birth and for reasons similar to those of the Mayflower Pilgrims a generation before, by the middle of the seventeenth century the family of John Crawford left home, privilege, and the political turmoil of Oliver Cromwell's Commonwealth behind to join other Europeans in search of a fresh start in the New World. The Crawfords settled in the Jamestown area of Virginia where, in 1772, their celebrated descendant William Crawford, the sixth of Joel and Fanny Harris Crawford's eleven children, was born.

Near the close of the Revolutionary War, when William was still a boy and new land became available in the Georgia Backcountry, Joel Crawford moved his family to the Kiokee settlement which, within the decade, would become the center of Columbia County. Right away young William attracted attention for his tall, handsome frame and keen intellect, the latter despite having received almost no formal education prior to that time.

Education, however, would always be part of young William's life. Following years of home schooling enhanced by an avid desire to learn, he enrolled at Carmel Academy (also called Mt. Carmel) as soon as Moses Waddell's premier Columbia County school opened, and he became an exceptional student in classic literature and languages. It was said that William could speak the ancient languages of Latin and Greek better than he spoke English.

Following graduation, William remained at Carmel for another two years as a teacher. Two of his students, John C. Calhoun from nearby South Carolina and Thomas W. Cobb from Columbia County, would later become prominent lawyers and politicians just as he would. William then transferred to the Academy of Richmond County in Augusta, where he taught English while studying law under headmaster Charles Tait, with whom he would establish a lifelong friendship.

William Crawford, however, acquired something more than education during those formative, Columbia County years. In the words of Georgia Governor and historian, George Gilmer, when faced with the inevitable decisions of life and career, "Crawford's clear and conscientious sense of right and wrong kept him on the straight course."[6] Those "clear and conscientious" principles carried him to enormous heights—and one day may have cost him the presidency of the United States.

William Crawford's star might not have shined as bright or so soon had it not been for the infamous Yazoo Land Fraud that dominated Georgia politics just as he was beginning his professional career. Senator

James Jackson, who had resigned his seat in Congress to fight against the scandal, was miles away in Savannah and needed someone from the Backcountry to work with him. With Crawford already on the record as "anti-Yazoo," and his intellectual reputation firmly in place, Jackson could think of no one better to fill that position than he. However, although the overturning of Yazoo would become a stepping-stone to higher office, Crawford's refusal to enter such a scheme in the first place earned him the opposition of what historian Spencer King calls, "the united clique." In King's opinion "Crawford's talents and integrity were very much in the way of their success."[7]

Politically speaking, when the nineteenth century began most Georgians followed the Jeffersonian Doctrine, calling themselves Jeffersonians, or Democratic-Republicans, even though their underlying philosophy was little different from that of the Federalists, the major political party in the nation at the time. But Georgians, who were always fearful of an overly strong federal government, wanted no part of the Federalist name. It hardly mattered what they were called anyway, because the name seldom described a unified party. Political in-fighting in Georgia was blatant for more than a generation following the sharp divisions created by Yazoo.

Consequently Georgia's political loyalties were more likely determined by strong leaders at the head of each faction than by the issues they espoused. In post-Yazoo Georgia, the two predominant political groups were the Crawfordites and the Clarkites, based on the rivalry between William Crawford and John Clark, the son of Revolutionary War hero Elijah Clarke. (Unlike his father, John preferred spelling the family name without what he considered the pretentious "e.")

Like their leader, the Crawfordites tended to be well educated, above average in wealth or position, and Virginia-born, while the less educated Clarkites identified with the frontiersman or small farmer and had family roots in North Carolina. With more small farmers in the Backcountry than plantation owners, more Clarkites than Crawfordites lived there all during those rival years. The lines between the two camps were not strictly drawn, however, since a number of the original Yazooists were wealthy planters and Clark followers, too. Still, for the next thirty years, nothing distinguished the Georgia politician from his rival quite as much as his loyalty to the man at the top of his political wing—the principled Crawford or the feisty Clark.

Dueling has never been legal in any civilized society, but in certain cultures and historic times, including the early years of our own country, this barbaric practice was both widespread and condoned. Murder, it seems, was a lesser crime during this period than either insulting a man's honor or letting such an offense go unchallenged. So when attorney and Crawford friend Charles Tait learned that Clarkite attorney Peter Van Allen did not consider him a gentleman, Tait countered this breach of manners with a reply in kind.

"I shall not attempt to vie with you in the low arts of scurrility and abuse [by] calling you an insidious rascal . . . nor shall I tell you how much you are condemned by all honest men."[8] Still, to emphasize his disdain for Van Allen, Tait challenged his fellow attorney to a duel. Since it was customary for both the challenger and the challenged to choose a "second" to deliver messages and handle details of the duel, Tait selected William Crawford for this task. Van Allen took plenty of time to reply, before refusing to accept Tait's challenge.

During the next few weeks a number of angry letters, written by the attorneys themselves or by their seconds, either were delivered to the recipient or published in the *Augusta Chronicle* for all to read. Finally, after Tait insulted Van Allen by saying he had retreated into "the Temple of Cowardice,"[9] Van Allen asked Crawford to arrange the much-delayed duel with Tait. But on the morning of the scheduled event, Tait didn't show up. An irate Van Allen then took out his venom on Crawford and challenged *him* to a duel. Crawford accepted, and felled the Clarkite attorney with his second shot.

Later William Crawford would have two more opportunities to defend his honor, both with his archrival, John Clark. The first quarrel developed following the 1803 election for judge of the Western Circuit between Clark's brother-in-law, John Griffin, and the aforementioned Tait. With Clark and Crawford each supporting his chosen candidate, charges flew from both sides against the campaign tactics of the other. Finally, after Tait won the election and Clark suggested that Crawford's law practice was now benefiting from the favors of the new judge, an angry Crawford challenged Clark to a duel.

The much publicized event might have taken place as scheduled had cooler heads not intervened. Realizing what a loss the death of either man could be to the political leadership of the state, supporters from both sides asked then Governor John Milledge to appoint a Court of Honor to settle the dispute. With Clark and Crawford in agreement, Milledge complied. When the five-man court finished their deliberations, they publicly declared both men "brave and intrepid," before decreeing that the combatants "relinquish their animosity, and take each other by the hand as friends and fellow citizens."[10]

It was a grudging handshake, but the animosity did cool for a while—until Judge Tait issued what the opposition considered a shameful decision from the bench, and Clark called for his impeachment. Unfortunately for Clark, Crawford had more influence in the legislature than he did, and the impeachment motion failed. Clark's anger then flared again, and it was his turn to challenge Crawford to a duel.

This time not even the governor could talk the two men out of their fight. Thus, on the appointed day and with two doctors standing by, one favorable to each side, a brief duel took place. Clark quickly wounded Crawford in the wrist, and Crawford refused to continue the fight. His damaged wrist would plague Crawford for the rest of his life, while another "plague" rested equally as long on the otherwise unscathed Clark. No matter how notable Clark's own career became, including two terms as governor of Georgia, it never measured up to that of his rival. For the rest of *his* life John Clark would rue the day he had not killed William Crawford.

Clark, the former soldier and superior fighter, remained an avid duelist even as Crawford supported legislation to outlaw the practice. In 1809 Georgia did pass a law against dueling, which forbade anyone in any way connected with a duel from holding office in the state. But, as historian Coulter writes, "So imbedded was the custom that for more than half a century a few duels were still being fought."[11]

In 1799, the same year William Few left Columbia County for New York, William Crawford also moved north, but only to Georgia's Oglethorpe County. There he would practice law and indulge in what became a lifelong hobby—experimenting with a variety of grasses and fruit trees to discover which were best suited to the Georgia climate and soil.

Crawford soon became the largest landowner in Oglethorpe County, but he would never be called a planter because he owned too few slaves. Unlike most of his peers in politics or in planting, Crawford was opposed to importing slaves to America in the first place. He also supported a movement to return blacks to their African homeland, a surprising opinion since he later opposed moving Georgia's Indian population to the west. By analyzing this philosophy, however, it would appear that William Crawford believed the black man and the red man were just as entitled to their homeland as America's newly independent citizens were entitled to theirs. This opinion would become another side note to the principled Crawford, and yet another nail in his political coffin when his final competition for national office heated up.

But first, the former Columbia Countian would spend a quarter century winning hearts and praise all the way from Georgia to the nation's capital, and Napoleon's court.

29

ONE OF THE ABLEST MEN
WHO EVER LIVED IN GEORGIA

His wagons were hardly unpacked before Oglethorpe County's new resident-lawyer was chosen to represent his new neighbors in the Georgia legislature. William Harris Crawford served with distinction in this capacity until 1807, when he became the prime candidate to succeed recently deceased Abraham Baldwin in the U.S. Senate. Crawford also had other successes during his early nineteenth-century years: establishing a thriving law practice; building "Woodlawn," the plantation he would own for the rest of this life; and marrying his longtime sweetheart, Susanna Girardin (also spelled Gerardin), one of his former students at the Academy of Richmond County in Augusta. The union of William and Susanna produced eight children and multiple descendants, some of whom reside in Columbia County to this day.

If William Crawford's political rise was swift in Georgia, it was meteoric in the Senate. Besides the still unresolved Indian dilemma in his native southeast, Crawford immediately began grappling with other national and international issues, including the country's complicated banking system and growing tensions with Great Britain over territorial rights and shipping on the high seas. Also, as the youngest member thus far to become President Pro Tempore of the Senate, he attracted the attention of then President Thomas Jefferson, as well as future presidents James Madison and James Monroe, whose terms in national office coincided with his.

It was Jefferson who first considered Crawford presidential material, a theme soon echoed by Madison and Monroe, both of whom he would serve as cabinet member and confidante. While working for the latter president, Crawford is said to have played an important role in forming the Monroe Doctrine, the 1823 plan declaring the American continents off limits for further colonization by any European power, and the cornerstone of American foreign policy to this day.

In 1811 Crawford was returned unchallenged to the Senate, but he did not complete his term. When the fragile, post-revolution relationship between America and Great Britain exploded into war the following year, President Madison urged him to leave the Senate and become his secretary of war. Crawford turned that offer down, but a year later when the president asked him to become America's minister to France, he agreed to serve. With tensions between Great Britain and France also heightened during this period, America was caught in the crossfire. Her ships were already subject to seizure by the British; now they were being seized in French ports as well. Crawford's mission was two-fold—to recover payment for lost cargo and ships, and to establish a treaty on shipping and trade between America and France with no loss of advantage to the United States.

Crawford spent almost two years in France, much of the time in difficult negotiations with the French government and all the time homesick for Georgia. Clearly France was more impressed with the giant of a man from America than the visitor was of his host country. Hardly a taller man than Crawford could be found in all of France, understandably leading the much shorter Napoleon Bonaparte to say, "William Crawford is the only person to whom I ever felt constrained to bow."[12]

Four months into Crawford's visit to his country, the French president also told the American, "I have great regard for the United States and I will do all in my power to make the relationship between our two countries as friendly and beneficial as possible."[13] However, despite Napoleon's reassurance, negotiations continued to drag on, no doubt hindered because the French foreign minister spoke no English and Crawford spoke no French.

But not all the American minister's term in France was spent in treaty negotiations. Culling from the memoirs of Crawford's cousin and Columbia County physician, Dr. Nathan Crawford, historian Lucien Lamar Knight relates the following incident during which the Crawford diplomat might have wished the Crawford family doctor were practicing medicine in France instead of Georgia.

It could have been the water, the French food, or the stress, but at some point Crawford became ill with a gastric distress diagnosed as bilious fever. Impatient with his lengthy recovery, Crawford asked his French servant if there were such things in the city as hog jowl and turnip salad (presumably the vegetable's leafy top).

"Oh, yes," replied the servant, "but in Paris we feed turnip salad to the cows."

"Never mind," Crawford said. "You get me a peck of turnip salad, a hog's jowl and a pot big enough to hold them both. Then get me some cornmeal bread, well-baked, and I will show you how a gentleman can enjoy himself."

After the stunned servant complied with his request, Crawford prepared the meal himself, ate to the last bite and crumb and, Knight concludes, "proceeded at once to get well." Crawford said that was the first substantial meal he had eaten since he left Georgia, and he blamed his illness on the fact that, since he had been in France, he had nearly starved to death.[14]

Amid the backdrop of increased European tensions, Crawford continued his slow and frequently discouraging mission. He did recover some compensation for the lost cargo and ships, and he helped negotiate the Treaty of Ghent that determined the outcome of the War of 1812. But ongoing, internal problems in France would hinder the satisfactory treaty between the two countries he spent so long trying to reconcile. In the spring of 1814 Napoleon's empire crumbled, leading to the emperor's exile on the Mediterranean Island of Elba and the return of former King Louis XVIII to France. Though Crawford continued negotiations with the new French government, those efforts also met with little success.

Finally, following the end of the war with England in December 1814, and Napoleon's surprising escape from Elba and return to France, Crawford made plans to come home. After a succession of delays, including a longer than expected stopover in England to assist in further postwar negotiations, on August 1, 1815, Crawford once again set foot on American soil. Though he had failed to secure the anticipated treaty with France, it was generally agreed that under the political circumstances at the time no one could have accomplished such a mission. Still, Crawford gained considerable respect for his efforts, and his political career continued to rise.

Incidentally, by the time the distinguished Georgian arrived home from France, Napoleon Bonaparte had left the country too, following a shorter than expected stopover at Waterloo.

With his work in France complete, Crawford considered either retiring from public life or returning to the Senate. He did not plan to pick up a newspaper in England weeks before he sailed for home and learn that he had been confirmed by the Senate as President Madison's secretary of war, the very appointment he had refused three years before. Madison later explained he had expected Crawford home months earlier, at which time he hoped to persuade the returning diplomat in person to accept the cabinet-level position. But in the interest of time, and perhaps with more than a grain of optimism, he went ahead with the confirmation process anyway.

There are several reasons why, just six days after returning to the United States, Crawford overcame his reluctance and agreed to become Madison's secretary of war:

1. The nation was at peace. The War of 1812 was in progress three years earlier, and Crawford had felt inadequate to handle the department in wartime.
2. Madison's formerly troubled cabinet was also at peace. Though no stranger to controversy himself, throughout his political career

Crawford worked tirelessly for harmony and competence at all
levels of government.

3. Despite the accolades he received for his French diplomacy,
Crawford himself did not believe his efforts were commendable.
Ultimately he accepted the cabinet position in gratitude for the
president's continued confidence in his work.

Crawford spent a few days settling into his new office before leaving for Georgia and a much-needed rest. Early in November, this time
with his family in tow, he returned to Washington, where the reunited
Crawford's would remain for nearly ten years.

Crawford's tenure as secretary of war was stellar, controversial,
and short. The War of 1812 had revealed some glaring deficiencies in
America's ability to defend herself and, to the delight of some and the dismay of his ever-present critics, Crawford set about to reform the department in charge. Politically it might have been to his advantage to serve
as war secretary during wartime after all, since one of the largest contro-
versies he now faced concerned manpower levels of a peacetime military.
The harder Congress worked to slash defense funding after the war, the
more Crawford and the president argued for a military ready to become
an immediate fighting force should such a need arise.

Crawford appears to have won that fight. Congress responded posi-
tively to his budget requests, and two years later his successor, John C.
Calhoun, would say the former secretary "combined simplicity with effi-
ciency in the reorganization of the department so well that I made only
a few changes."[15]

Defense, however, was not the only task on the agenda for the new
secretary of war. Managing the U.S. Military Academy at West Point
and chairing the Department of Indian Affairs were among a myriad of
other duties under his command. With projects as varied as revamping
the curriculum and deciding what the cadets should be fed, Crawford's
reorganization thumbprint was soon apparent at the military school.

But it was likely his handling of Indian affairs that attracted the most
criticism while he was at the war department. Crawford's opinion that the

Indians be allowed to keep their land was already enough to anger those who wanted the controversial land for themselves, but when he uttered his famous phrase that the Indians should also be allowed "to intermarry . . . and become integrated into the white man's culture,"[16] he blew the political fissure wide open. Crawford would not be on the presidential ballot for another eight years, but many who heard those lightning-rod words would never forget them, nor vote for a man with a view like that. The man who charmed Napoleon and won the confidence of three presidents could not always override the opinions of his peers, and he would not abandon his.

Crawford was not the only politician to hold this view and, in the decades following the Civil War, integration rather than removal is exactly what happened to the black race. Although a few Negro slaves were returned to Africa, the once popular deportation movement never caught on to the degree that the American Indians were first encouraged, and then forced to move west.

Crawford had been war secretary less than a year when President Madison asked him to change jobs again. Others could fill the war secretary's position, Madison said, but he believed Crawford's expertise was more needed as secretary of the Treasury. Again, Crawford was reluctant to accept the president's new offer. But after a short vacation back in Georgia to ponder his decision, he accepted the position he would keep for the remainder of Madison's presidency, and through both terms of the next president, James Monroe.

By 1816 the U.S. Treasury Department was the largest government entity in Washington. Besides all things financial, Treasury was also responsible for customs, land offices, coastal and lighthouse services, the internal revenue service, post office, national mint, and more. A department that large also had the most personnel and, Crawford would quickly learn, the most problems.

With the perennial battle between branches of government for fair and adequate funding, plus an ongoing controversy between the federal Bank of the United States (BUS) and numerous state banks, the new Treasury secretary faced enormous challenges. In time he would get to those major issues, but not before making major changes in the operation of his department.

When William Crawford arrived at Treasury, he found cumbersome work methods, poor divisions of responsibility and, worst of all, inadequate accounting procedures for the multiple duties his department was required to perform. But before long, the man with a proven fondness for detail had streamlined the accounting systems, removed overlapping duties and services, and reduced the backlog of overdue accounts by requiring that they be settled within one year instead of three years as previously allowed. By the time Crawford left the department nine years later, fewer employees were doing more work on a smaller budget than when the Treasury Department was formed, and the procedures he put in place would be followed without major change for the next hundred years.

Crawford's Treasury status plus his Georgia roots also prompted him to urge Congress to follow through on their promise to compensate Georgia for the western lands she had relinquished to the federal government following the Yazoo affair, and to finish removing the Indians from the state. Even so, this was a bittersweet effort for the secretary. Although he favored—and secured—compensation for the western lands, he was caught between the president, who preferred to use patience rather than force in removing the Indians, and his impatient constituents waiting for their promised land.

Old disputes also were revived when rival John Clark, who was now governor of Georgia, joined forces with Indian foe Andrew Jackson and pressured him to use his influence on Georgia's behalf. Since Crawford sided more with the president on the Indian issue than with Georgia, this was a difficult task. Though he tried to resolve the festering issue, he would be out of office long before 1838, when the last of the Georgia Cherokees finally left the state.

But no challenge consumed more of Crawford's time and political capital while he was at the Treasury Department than that of solving the controversy between the Bank of the United States and what historian Mooney called, "the more than 400 wildcat banks and their worthless paper money running rampant in most states."[17] Crawford may not have made this statement himself, but he certainly would have agreed with Mooney's assessment of the nation's monetary condition at the time.

In the end, nothing was more important to him as secretary of the Treasury than establishing a uniform banking and currency system throughout the country. With each state setting its own banking rules and minting its own currency, financial transactions between state and federal banks were extremely complicated, and they were nearly impossible across state lines. Even Georgia minted her own money, complete with pictures of her favorite statesmen, including William Crawford himself, although such paper bills were rarely acceptable outside Georgia and, according to Article I, Section 10 of the U.S. Constitution, they were illegal.

What may sound like a simple matter today, enacting legislation to charter a new federal bank and closing the renegade state banks down, was not that simple two hundred years ago. The federal bank Crawford believed would stabilize the national monetary system was not the first BUS the government had established, but the second. Through a mixture of faulty management and corruption the first bank had failed, and now the second bank was in danger of failing too. Add to this instability the still strong opinion, especially among Southern states, that the federal government should not be more powerful than the states, and you had almost a civil war between states' rights and national sovereignty over the country's purse.

Eventually Crawford succeeded in stabilizing this important segment of America's government, but not without angering those who resisted his policies. Some of his critics even accused him of mismanaging public funds and being part of the very corruption scandals that had hampered the banking process from the beginning.

With Monroe's presidency and, thus, his duties at Treasury coming to a close, William Crawford was about to jump literally out of the frying pan and into the fire. For most of 1824, one of Georgia's ablest public servants would wage two battles at the same time—his nomination for the presidency of the United States, and his own health.

30

THE LEGACY OF WILLIAM CRAWFORD

William Harris Crawford may be the only person in American history to serve eighteen years in national office and be nominated twice for the presidency—without waging a significant political campaign.

To recap: Crawford was in his fourth year as Oglethorpe County's representative to the state legislature when, on the first ballot and by both houses of his peers, he was chosen to fill the U.S. Senate seat left vacant by the death of Abraham Baldwin. Five years later, shortly after being reappointed to Congress for a second term, he was selected by his new colleagues as President Pro Tempore of the Senate, also on the first ballot. Within the next four years and under two presidents, he became minister to France, secretary of war, and secretary of the treasury. Then, in 1816 and his ninth year of national service, Crawford's name was placed in nomination by his party's congressional caucus for the presidency of the United States.

The popular politician may have harbored thoughts of becoming president someday, but 1816 was not the year. In his opinion, then Secretary of State James Monroe was the logical choice for both the nomination and the presidency. At forty-four, Crawford was still a young man. His aspirations could wait, at least until 1824. Still, without campaigning and without his consent, when the votes were tallied, Monroe had won the nomination by only eleven votes: sixty-five for the nominee and fifty-four for non-candidate Crawford.

But a lot would happen between 1816 and 1824, and historians are still divided on whether Crawford lost the presidency that year for political reasons or because of poor health. Tradition favors the latter, claiming that several months before the 1824 election Crawford suffered a paralytic stroke. However, although he did become seriously ill with symptoms that were both debilitating and stroke-like, Crawford had actually contracted the skin disease erysipelas, an acute streptococcal infection similar to scarlet fever. A careful study of the 1824 election also reveals that Crawford's political problems may have been more serious than his health.

With an eye toward the presidency as early as the summer of 1823, Crawford and his family remained in Washington that year rather than return to Georgia for their usual vacation. By the end of the summer, however, Crawford was feeling ill with what he thought was inflammatory rheumatism. When he exhibited the classic symptoms of the skin disease—large, red blotches on his face so severe that his eyelids were swollen shut, his tongue thickened, and his hearing was impaired—his doctor incorrectly prescribed a plant-based treatment that made him worse. Now, with Crawford's hands and feet nearly paralyzed, the doctor tried to remedy his first error with another common treatment at the time and "bled" his patient with leeches more than twenty times.

Miraculously, by November Crawford had recovered sufficiently to begin working from home, even though his vision was still so impaired he needed assistance from his daughter and a clerk in order to conduct Treasury business. A few months later he was able to return to his office and to attend cabinet meetings. Unfortunately Crawford's healing momentum stopped the following May, when he suffered a relapse, another symptom of the skin disease.

Reluctantly President Monroe wondered if this time his Treasury secretary should be replaced. Not so, said Secretary of State John Quincy Adams, who noted that "the business of the Treasury has been transacted with as much accuracy and fidelity as is compatible with Mr. Crawford's indisposition." Adams recommended that, "If no inconvenience had oc-curred, it was best not to make a temporary appointment."[18]

Crawford considered taking himself out of the presidential race, but his friends would not hear of it, and they offered to do his campaigning for him. To some degree in a world before the birth of nonstop news, with Crawford out of sight almost until Election Day, much of the country did not know he was ill anyway.

Or was he denied the presidency for political reasons? With eighteen years of public service behind him, Crawford now had a sizable public record—and a reputation for having strong principles and opinions from which he rarely if ever wavered. Understandably, he also had a sizable list of political enemies whose principles and opinions on how to run a state, a department, or a country differed greatly from his. Any one of the fol-lowing incidents or a combination of them all might well have been the reason William Crawford did not win the presidential election of 1824:

—By opposing both the Yazoo Land Fraud and the Indian removal, he alienated many of his Georgia constituents, especially his rival, Governor John Clark, who formed an impressive coalition with Indian fighter Andrew Jackson, one of Crawford's opponents for the presidency.

—As secretary of the Treasury he was often at odds with those who preferred their own, poorly managed state banks to the federal bank he convinced Congress and the president to establish. In the process, as he worked to weed out corruption on all banking levels, he was accused of corruption himself.

—In both 1816 and 1824, as the congressional caucus method of choosing a president came under increasing disfavor, he was considered the candidate of the politicians rather than the choice of the people.[19]

—In addition to Andrew Jackson, Crawford also found himself on different sides of key political issues with two other powerful politicians, John C. Calhoun and Henry Clay, who had their eyes on the presidency as well.

Although he had missed the presidential campaign entirely, Crawford was back at work when the votes for the four surviving candidates—Andrew Jackson, John Quincy Adams, Henry Clay, and himself—were counted in November. With forty-one electoral votes, he came in third, behind frontrunner Jackson with ninety-nine and Adams with eighty-four. Since no candidate received a majority of the votes, the election was thrown into the House of Representatives, where fourth-place Clay threw his thirty-seven votes to Adams, thereby declaring the former secretary of state the winner. (Although Calhoun did not survive the nominating process for president, he was chosen as Adams' vice president.)

Crawford displayed little bitterness over the outcome of the election, and he apparently had no regrets. As he wrote later, "I do now believe that had I been elected, my remains would now be reposing in the national burial ground near the eastern branch of the Potomac."[20] His only ambition now, he said, was "to educate his five sons so as to render them useful citizens to the Republic . . . and see his daughters advantageously settled in Society."[21]

President Adams, who as secretary of state had defended his colleague when he was too ill to perform his Cabinet duties, now asked Crawford to stay on at Treasury during his administration, too. But Crawford was tired. Weakened by his illness, yet buoyed by a sense of accomplishment after so many years in Washington, he felt it was time to go home to his beloved Woodlawn. Flowering trees adorning his plantation made a spectacular backdrop to the tumultuous homecoming he received from his Oglethorpe County neighbors when he returned in the spring of 1825.

But William Crawford's political career was far from over. Contrary to those who were determined to write his obituary, after spending the rest of that year and most of the next puttering about his orchards and regaining his strength, our "man for all seasons" was able to resume his duties as trustee of the State College in Athens, and contemplate a return to the U.S. Senate. Instead, in 1827 he accepted the position of Superior Court judge for the northern circuit of Georgia where, except for considering a run for the vice presidency in 1828 and toying with an appointment to the U.S. Supreme Court, he remained for the rest of his life.

On September 12, 1834, Crawford spent a happy day with his daughter and newest grandchild. Three days later he was dead—stricken, the death certificate said, by "an affection of the heart." Perhaps William Crawford had finally had his stroke.

Newspapers across the country noted his passing in heavy, black headlines, calling his speeches remarkable for their strength, and his votes honest and independent. The *National Intelligencer* may have said it best when they wrote, "He was bold and fearless in his course, he shunned no responsibility, he compromised no principle."[22]

Others would now carry on the Crawford name and reputation, including second son Nathaniel, who went by his middle name "Macon" and was valedictorian of the 1829 graduating class at Georgia College (UGA). This son gained prominence as an educator and theologian, and became the fifth president of Mercer College—coincidentally, in *Macon*, Georgia. Mention has already been made of cousin Nathan Crawford, a prominent physician and surgeon who practiced medicine in Columbia County. Still another pair of cousins, Columbia County plantation owner Peter Crawford and his son George, came close to duplicating their famous cousin's political career.

Even today there are nearly two hundred Crawford entries in the Columbia County area telephone book, and that list does not include female descendants whose family connections continue under other surnames. Of course not everyone with Crawford ancestry was a direct descendant of William Crawford, but it is likely that most of them stemmed from the same Lanark, Scotland/Jamestown, Virginia ancestral line. One female Crawford, however, bears a fitting resemblance to her distant cousin and earns mention here.

Frank Armstrong Crawford was given a non-feminine name because of a pact between her father, Robert Leighton Crawford, and his devoted friend, Frank Armstrong, that each would name his first child after the other. Fortunately for Mr. Armstrong, his first child was a boy, but poor, little Miss Crawford became the unwitting recipient of her principled father's whim.

Nevertheless, Frank Crawford never lived up to her masculine name. Instead, the charming young Southern girl became the proverbial "belle of the ball" who, in 1869, married New Yorker Commodore Cornelius

Vanderbilt in "the most beautiful event of the social season."[23] But the socialite bride never forgot her own people. Realizing that, following the Civil War, most Northern philanthropy toward the South went to endow black schools and colleges while many Southern white youth were housed in rundown, poorly equipped institutions, she convinced her husband to extend his generosity to white children, too. Thus, the sum of $1,000,000 was made available to establish Vanderbilt University, in the *Southern* city of Nashville, Tennessee.

William Crawford, the principled man who served his state and nation, taught students in Columbia and Richmond counties, and lived to improve the education not only of his own children but all the youth of Georgia, would have been proud of "Miss Frank," no matter what she was called.

Today, in and out of Columbia and Oglethorpe counties, parks, squares, streets, two Georgia towns—Crawford and Crawfordville—and a county are named for the man who for years was considered the state's "First Citizen." More recently, in 1955, the Georgia Assembly voted to establish the Hall of Fame for Illustrious Georgians in the rotunda of the State Capitol in Atlanta. Four years later, the bust of William Harris Crawford was among the first of the illustrious few to be placed in that revered hall.

The Crawford legacy now turns to that father and son combination, Peter and George Crawford, who also served their county, state, and nation with distinction.

31

PETER AND GEORGE CRAWFORD:

FROM THE COURTHOUSE

TO THE STATE HOUSE

Joel Crawford and his soon-to-be famous son William were not the only Virginia-born Crawfords to move to Georgia following the land cession of 1773. Joel's brother Charles and their nephew Peter, who would take part in the Revolutionary War, also joined the growing Crawford clan resettling in Columbia County. After the war Peter and his wife, Mary Ann, were then eligible for a "bounty grant," a portion of that available land set aside by the State of Georgia to reward those who had fought for American independence.

The Crawford grant was located between the current Columbia Road and Fort Gordon. Had Interstate 20 been in existence two hundred years ago, the highway would have cut the property in two. Eventually the Crawford property became one of the area's largest and most profitable plantations, and its occupants prominent members of the community they now called home.

Peter was a practicing lawyer by the time he arrived in Georgia, and it would not be long before he began the political career that lasted most of his life. He became Columbia County's first clerk of Superior Court, a post he held for many years, and served ten terms as the county's representative to the Georgia General Assembly. But, although Peter Crawford's influence on local and state politics was substantial, his greatest achievement appears to be the influence he had on his son, George W. Crawford, who was born in Columbia County on December 22, 1798, and whose political accomplishments would be greater than his own.

George's story begins in his father's well-stocked library, where the son received much of his early education before going north to Princeton and graduating from that institution in 1820. For the next two years he studied law with Richard Henry Wilde in Augusta and in 1822 opened his own law practice in that city. In 1827 he was appointed attorney general for Georgia's Middle Judicial District to fill an unexpired term, and was reelected to the office in his own right until 1831.

But George Crawford did more than follow in his father's professional footsteps. Between his law practice and continued interest in the family plantation, before long he was the wealthiest of all the Crawfords. Later, when he was at the peak of his own political career, he would make a magnanimous gesture with part of his wealth that made an enormous impact on all of Georgia, and cemented the devotion her people had for this generous man.

Devotion, however, was nothing new to George Crawford. Besides receiving much of his education from his father, and continuing many of his personal and political pursuits, the son displayed an almost immeasurable loyalty to the older man. Therefore, early in 1828, while he was attorney general and Peter Crawford was declining in health, George was incensed to read a defamatory, unsigned letter in the *Augusta Chronicle* against his father. The writer's stinging words were aimed at Peter's strong, political views, which the aging politician still frequently aired. But in the son's eyes, the assault was on the man himself.

George tried without success to learn who had written the letter. Years later it was reported that the author was a woman, which may have been why the newspaper was reluctant to release the name. But for reasons still unknown—an affinity with the writer's views perhaps—Thomas E.

Burnside, a Columbia County educator, took responsibility for the letter, and was immediately challenged to a duel by Peter Crawford's angry son.

Although dueling was outlawed in Georgia in 1809, the practice may have waned after that date, but law or no law, for the honor-bound citizens of Georgia and elsewhere that long-entrenched method of settling disputes had never stopped. The respectable way to defend one's honor now was to meet an opponent across a state line where dueling was still legal. That is why on January 25, 1828, Crawford, Burnside, and their respective seconds traveled—on the same stage—from Columbia County, Georgia, to Fort Mitchell, Alabama, for the well-publicized fight.

Other than their political views, Burnside and Crawford had much in common. They were of similar age, each was well respected in his profession, and both men had a wife and small children. Burnside's family may have been the reason he told a friend he would not have agreed to the duel at all, except for an unwritten—and usually followed—law that would place his career in jeopardy if he refused.

After reaching Fort Mitchell and before retiring for the night, Burnside composed the following letter:

Dear Wife and Mother,

Tomorrow I fight. I do it on principle. Whatever may be my fate, I believe I am right. On this ground I have acted and will act. I believe I will succeed, but if I do not I am prepared for the consequences. Kiss the children and tell them, if I fall, my last thought was of them.

Yours most affectionately,
Thomas E. Burnside[24]

Burnside did indeed fall, dying instantly from Crawford's third shot, which pierced his chest just above the heart. More than two weeks passed before the Burnside family learned there would be no returning husband and father, nor body to bury or mourn beside. Thoughtful friends among the assembled crowd buried him in a nearby cemetery the next day.

Physically Crawford was unscathed, but a lifetime would not be long enough to lose his remorse over the tragedy he caused. He had broken no law, and his career was not damaged in any way. Still, in a continuing act of contrition, he made annual payments to the Burnside family for most of his life. Mrs. Burnside, however, never knew where the money came from. Crawford's gifts were always delivered through an intermediary and, like the letter that provoked the duel in the first place, the donor remained anonymous.

The Crawford-Burnside duel finally put teeth in the legislature's attempt to outlaw dueling in Georgia. This time the law decreed that anyone who had taken part in a duel in any way—as fighter, second, or physician, in Georgia or out-of-state—would never again be allowed to hold state or municipal office. Though not immediately successful, it would not be long before this barbaric practice, like the migration of the country as a whole in the nineteenth century, moved west.

Crawford resumed his life much as it was before the duel, completing his four years as attorney general and then resigning to concentrate on his law practice. In 1837, the same year he moved to Richmond County and built a large estate home in the newly established community of Belair, he was elected to the state legislature, where he remained until 1842, when he was appointed to Congress to fill a brief, unexpired term. The next year he returned to Georgia, ran for governor, and easily won the first of two successive (two-year) gubernatorial terms. George Crawford had become Georgia's only Whig governor, and the only person in Columbia County history to this date to occupy the state's highest chair.

Governor Crawford inherited a budgetary mess. In fact, his victory at the polls was considered both a protest against the growing Democratic surge across the country, and the belief that Whigs were more frugal in financial matters than Democrats. The governor's first move in addressing this urgent problem stunned his own people and reverberated across the country. He pledged $150,000 of his own fortune as security to ease the state's badly impaired credit, "and Georgia's good name was redeemed due to the patriotic purse of George Crawford."[25]

Throughout his governorship Crawford continued his crusade to improve Georgia's economic plight. In the first year alone he reduced the budget by $66,000, while working simultaneously to liquidate the inefficient Central Bank, establish sound currency, and pay off much of the state's indebtedness. He also is credited with accelerating construction of the state-owned Western and Atlantic Railroad and, after years of controversy about how it should be done, establishing the first State Supreme Court. The railroad delay had been caused by Georgia's inability to obtain credit, but Crawford secured financing from private donors—probably including himself—and used slave labor to complete the project. And, by finally launching the Supreme Court, he brought uniformity to judicial decision-making across the state for the first time.

When his second term ended in 1847, Crawford once again retired to his law practice and a new venture, investing in real estate across Georgia and Texas. But his success in the governor's chair had brought him to the attention of the national Whig Party, and in 1849 he became secretary of war under Whig President Zachary Taylor. Unlike his cousin William, however, his would not be a lengthy Crawford stay on the national scene. Upon President Taylor's untimely death from cholera the next year, this Crawford returned to Georgia and to the private world where he expected to remain for the rest of his life. But privacy would elude him again, first for personal reasons and, in another decade, for circumstances beyond the borders of his community, the state, or his ability to control.

Perhaps it was the all too frequent lot of the successful, or that, like the proverbial good deed, no good leader goes unpunished. But when Crawford resigned from President Taylor's Cabinet, even for the stated reason that he had only gone to Washington to work with that president, suspicions were aroused that a rumor concerning the former governor was true after all. Crawford had never discontinued his law practice while he held public office, and one of his cases had taken seventeen years to resolve. This very public case was known as "The Galphin Claim," for which he was paid a fee of $115,000—coincidentally, about the time he left his Cabinet position. The alleged charges of corruption were later found to be false, and he was completely exonerated. But the suspicions continued, and the experience dampened George Crawford's enthusiasm for further public service.

Still, most Georgians remained fond of their former governor, and though he was reluctant to leave private life to do their bidding, when tensions peaked across the South over issues of slavery, economics, and states' rights, Crawford once again accepted the reins of public office. In January 1861, as delegates from each of Georgia's existing 132 counties gathered at the state capital in Milledgeville to consider seceding from the United States, George W. Crawford was their unanimous choice to serve as president of Georgia's Secession Convention.

Details of this convention and the former governor's role in the approaching Civil War will be covered later when we discuss the war's effect on the people of Columbia County. For now there is one more, essentially private part of the George Crawford story that must be told.

Early in the twentieth century, as University of Georgia Professor Alfred Akerman was researching information about Columbia County, he stumbled across an old, briar-infested burial ground just south of Columbia Road in Evans. With some effort Professor Ackerman was able to make out this inscription on one of the tombstones:

> In memory of PETER CRAWFORD, a native of Virginia . . . a citizen of Georgia. Highly gifted mentally and physically, he closed a long life of distinguished usefulness. As clerk of the Superior Court and Senator . . . in the Legislature of the State during nearly the whole period of his manhood, these records attest the value of his services. Under a sense of right he was inflexible. The widow and the orphan bestowed on him the honorable title: Their Friend. Born February 7, 1765. Died October 16, 1830. My father."[26]

Removing weeds and debris nearby, the professor found what appeared to be a companion to the epitaph he had just read:

> In memory of MARY ANN, wife of PETER CRAWFORD. A cherished wife, mother of a large family . . . for many years the survivor of her partner, the center and light of a large, social circle. As a Christian, she bestowed her charities with gentleness . . . as a woman, she was

steadfast. . . . Her fourscore years only weakened the tie that binds life to body; all else was clear and calm. Born May 9, 1769. Died January 22, 1852.[27]

No additional line identifies Mary Ann Crawford as "my mother," but there is little doubt that George W. Crawford composed this memorial, too.

Nearly a century after the university professor came across this burial ground, Michael and Rebecca Bresnahan, owners of a new home in the Maple Creek subdivision off Columbia Road, made a similar discovery. By this time the stones that they found a short distance from their back door had suffered further from vandalism and neglect, but the new owners were still able to recognize them as the grave markers for Peter and Mary Ann Crawford, the parents of Governor George Crawford and the original owners of their land. In 2005, and with the help of a local Girl Scout troop, the Bresnahans substantially improved the condition of the Crawford cemetery and made it available for public viewing.

As for the governor, the lawyer, and the loyal son, there is no glowing epitaph marking his grave. Following his death in July 1872, and a well-attended funeral service at Augusta's St. Paul's Church, he was buried in the city's Summerville Cemetery near the grave of John Milledge, another Georgia governor. An iron railing was placed around the unadorned grave, with no marker except the name GEORGE W. CRAWFORD attached to the gate. Sometime in the 1960's, one of Crawford's descendants added that missing marker to the still unadorned grave.

It would be impossible to list all the early settlers of Columbia County or to include every accomplishment or worthy contribution each one made. But in the next chapter we will highlight a few of them, and tell why, in varied and unique ways, they were heroes, too.

32

OTHERS WHO LEFT THEIR MARK

ON COLUMBIA COUNTY

Cobb, Cobb, and More Cobbs

We already know about four Columbia County residents for whom Georgia towns or counties are named: William and Daniel Appling—town and county; Abraham Baldwin—county (and also a college); and William Crawford—two towns and a county. Still another family, whose name is intertwined with the first county courthouse, raised a son who increased that list to five. Thomas W. Cobb, grandson and namesake of Colonel Thomas Cobb, plantation owner and Revolutionary War veteran, was the reason one of the largest counties in Georgia is named Cobb.

These two Thomases are the best-known Columbia County Cobbs, although John Cobb, who was a brother of the elder Thomas, settled in nearby Jefferson County (Louisville) and was the father of two more famous Georgians, Thomas R. R. Cobb and Howell Cobb. We can assume that the latter family visited their Columbia County relatives on occasion, which may explain why some records say they were from Columbia County, too. Further complicating the record, John Cobb later moved to Athens, Georgia, so his sons could attend the university there, and called his new home "Cobbham," the very name of a community that sprang up around his brother's plantation spanning the current McDuffie-Columbia County line. The Thomas with the double middle initials would become known for drafting the constitution of the Confederacy and dying in the battle of Fredericksburg during the Civil War, while his brother Howell owned a large cotton plantation and served as governor of Georgia shortly before the Civil War began. Thomas R. R. Cobb is also one of the four generals memorialized on the Confederate War Monument on Broad Street in Augusta.

"Grandpa" Thomas, who was originally from Virginia, was the kind of man of whom legends are born. Not only was his property the largest plantation in the county immediately following the Revolutionary War, but it was either the site or in the vicinity of the original county courthouse. Also, since he was between 110 and 115 years of age when he died, he must have been at least fifty years old when the war began, and sixty when he arrived in Columbia County. At the time of his death, he was said to be the second oldest man on record in the state.

L. L. Knight provides some insight on Cobb's long life by calling him "an efficient manager of a plantation (in Georgia and Virginia) for 80–90 years," and noting that he wrote his presumed last will and testament in 1831, "at the age of five score years and nine, in full possession of his faculties if debilitated in body."[28] Knight also reveals why this Cobb may have been the oldest and most able suitor on anyone's record: "When the old man was 90 years of age he became possessed of matrimonial intentions. Accordingly, he mounted his nag and rode 25 miles . . . to visit the lady in question. On arrival he was met at the gate by a servant who offered to help him alight. But the old man waived him aside. 'Tut, tut!' said he; 'get away! I've come a-courtin.'"

There is no record of these "matrimonial intentions" resulting in a marriage, only evidence of an old gentleman's prowess should such an event occur.

The elder Thomas Cobb outlived his children and most of his grandchildren, including the other Thomas who died in 1830 at age forty-six. Despite his short life, however, Thomas W. Cobb may be better remembered outside Columbia County than was his grandfather. He was born in Columbia County in 1784, studied law under William Crawford, and served three terms in Congress—two in the House of Representatives and one in the Senate. His highest calling, however, was as a jurist. Following his congressional service, Judge Cobb was elected to the Superior Court bench in Georgia, where he remained until his death.

It appears that the elder Thomas favored this grandson above other members of the family, which may explain why he left an extra portion of his estate to two of his great-grandchildren, the children of Judge Thomas W. Cobb.

Moses Waddell

Columbia County's first recognized schoolmaster has been mentioned so many times in previous chapters it may seem redundant to devote another section to the educator here. But though most early county leaders received some or all of their education from this learned man, his poignant, personal story has not yet been told.

Moses Waddell did not start out to be a teacher, become one of the most renowned educators of his day or, perhaps, set the mold for Columbia County's high educational standards to this day. Though born into a poor, North Carolina family in 1770, he was fortunate to live near a school where Latin and other classic subjects were taught. He also was an avid student, becoming so proficient in several of his classes that by the age of fourteen he was able to assist his teachers by instructing other students.

But being of "a contemplative and religious nature," after teaching school for a short time Waddell entered the Presbyterian Hampden-Sydney College in Virginia in 1790 to prepare for the ministry. While there he also became engaged to Elizabeth (or Eliza) Woodson Pleasants, but the course of true love for the young couple would not run smooth.

When Waddell told Mr. and Mrs. Pleasants he intended to move to Georgia and become a missionary-schoolteacher there, his prospective in-laws were much opposed to having their daughter go off to "the wilds of Georgia," and the couple was forced to abandon their marriage.[29]

Waddell continued with his plans anyway, leaving college and Elizabeth behind in 1793 and stopping for a short time in South Carolina to begin his mission work there. While in South Carolina he boarded at the home of Patrick Calhoun, whose son John became his student and whose daughter Catherine would later be his wife.

Waddell came to Columbia County the next year and set up a school he called Mount Carmel (sometimes called Carmel Academy or Columbia County Academy) about two and a half miles from the center of Appling. In 1795 he married Miss Calhoun, whose family apparently had no qualms about her moving across the Savannah River to "wild" Georgia. Sadly, Catherine only survived the marriage a little more than a year. The twenty-two-year-old bride, known as "Miss Kitty," died while giving birth to her first child. The infant, a girl, also died.

The bereaved educator poured his life into his school, establishing a fine reputation for Mount Carmel and himself and teaching students like William Crawford and John Calhoun, who would have fine reputations someday themselves. He also continued his religious interests while he lived in Columbia County, as he would throughout his life. The very name of his school has a Biblical origin,[30] making Mount Carmel School an obvious mixture of his two professions. In 1796 Waddell was listed among the trustees charged with finding a site for an "Augusta Meeting House." Considering his connection to the Presbyterian denomination, this effort may have been the prelude to Augusta's First Presbyterian Church, which was established in 1804.

A few years after Kitty Waddell's death, the widower reestablished his friendship with Elizabeth Pleasants, and in 1800 she became his second wife. A year later, whether to be closer to Elizabeth's protective parents or for a change in scenery, the Waddells moved to Vienna, South Carolina, near the present-day city of Abbeville. When the couple resettled on a plantation near Willington a few miles away, Waddell moved his school

there, too, and it became known as the Willington School. He also established a relationship with the Presbyterian Church back across the river
in Petersburg, Georgia, where he preached "every 6th Sunday," conducted
weddings and funerals, and "traded in the Petersburg stores."[31]

Waddell's reputation as an educator, which grew rapidly at Mount
Carmel and increased at Willington, drew him to the attention of the
University of Georgia Trustees and in 1819 he accepted their invitation to
become the university's fifth president. By all accounts, Moses Waddell
also excelled at the university. Historians Knight and Coulter include
these tributes: "Undoubtedly the greatest president of Franklin College,"[32]
and "No one else approached Waddell in scholarship or excellence of
instruction. . . . No more perfect combination of teacher and preacher
than was to be found in Moses Waddell . . . In those days, it was understood that education without religion was hardly worthwhile."[33]

Apparently trouble had so dogged the tenures of his four predecessors that, according to long-time University Trustee and later Governor
George Gilmer, "When Waddell took charge there were neither funds,
professors, nor students . . . [but] in a few years under his direction,
Franklin College became the most flourishing literary institution in the
Southern States."[34] True to form, from time to time Waddell also filled
the pulpit of the local Presbyterian Church.

L. L. Knight calls Waddell a rigid disciplinarian who "believed in the
birch," presumably a paddle, and was known to advocate "flogging fresh-
men" and "recitations before breakfast." He also believed, and the trustees
concurred, that the students should eat "a strict, healthy diet, substantial
but by no means extravagant," except on Wednesdays when they were
allowed to add dessert to their substantial lunch.[35]

By 1829 and his tenth year at the school, Waddell decided he had
done all he could for the university, and he resigned. The trustees adopted
a resolution expressing high appreciation for his service as president and
urged him to stay. But he was rigid about his own life, too, and he was
determined to leave. His retirement began following commencement
exercises that year, after which "the entire student body marched to his
house to bid him farewell."[36]

Waddell returned to Willington for a while, but was soon struck by ill health. He died in Athens at the home of his son, and is buried in the little cemetery on Jackson Street facing the college he served so well.

Dr. Ignatius Few, Jr.

William Few, Sr., whose Quaker ancestors came to America in the seventeenth-century with Pennsylvania founder William Penn, had four sons. Before the outbreak of the Revolutionary War, the Few's migrated to the colony of North Carolina, where son James took part in an uprising against the administration of Royal Governor Tryon. James was hanged for his offenses against the Crown, but hailed by Patriots as the first martyr of the American Revolution. Soon, following the family's move to Wrightsboro, Georgia, brothers William, Benjamin, and Ignatius would all take up the cause of independence in their fallen brother's place.

As noted earlier, following the war William, Jr., gained political prominence and was instrumental in the founding of Columbia County, and Benjamin helped build the area's initial infrastructure before leaving the state to live in Alabama. Remaining son Ignatius married Mary Candler, daughter of fellow Revolutionary War soldier and Wrightsboro resident William Candler, and became a planter. The couple settled in Cobbham (Winfield today) on the bounty grant that Ignatius received for his war service, and which he called Mt. Carmel. In 1789 their youngest son, Ignatius, Jr., was born.

By this time the elder Ignatius had come under the influence of "pious Methodist itinerants,"[37] and frequently invited the circuit-riding preachers to spend time at his home. Ignatius, Jr., was still a teenager when he inquired of visitor Bishop Francis Asbury about his soul, although the inquiry did not make much of an impression at the time. In fact, the lad was considered an infidel for much of his early life.

Young Ignatius had a keen mind for learning, and an equally keen uncle who had recently moved to New York. Uncle William invited his nephew to come north and further his education there, which he did, remaining until he completed a law degree at Princeton University.

Ignatius then returned to Georgia an avowed "free-thinker" and began to practice law. But both his career and his philosophy of life took an abrupt turn when he was stricken with a lengthy illness.

The "free-thinker" spent much of his recovery time in contemplation, including a return to that discussion he once had with the Methodist bishop who visited his home. When he was well again, Ignatius Few, Jr., left his law practice, became a Methodist minister and, perhaps in the style of his famous Uncle William, championed the cause of a Methodist college in Georgia.

The first site chosen for the school was in Columbia County on land behind Few's boyhood home, by then known as Rose Hill. This site, however, was abandoned when it was considered too near the proposed route of the railroad and too close to the city of Augusta, which some feared would be a distraction. Although there was already a struggling Methodist manual-labor high school in Covington, Georgia, the now Dr. Few succeeded in changing the denomination's emphasis from secondary to college level education. This decision became final in 1836, when the charter for Emory College was granted.

Plans were made to build the institution on 1,400 acres of land two miles north of the former high school in a new village called Oxford. The college was named for Methodist Bishop John Emory, and the village for England's Oxford University, where Methodism's founders, John and Charles Wesley, were educated. The first president of the new school was the man long considered to be its founder, Dr. Ignatius A. Few, Jr.

It would take another year before the cornerstone of the new school was laid, and two more years before the school opened in 1839. But that was long enough for Dr. Few to give Emory the benefit of his leadership before his ill health returned. Following the founder's unfortunate resignation later that year, former Augustan Judge Augustus B. Longstreet became the second president of the college.

Sometime later, another man with Few connections and Columbia County roots would become president of Emory and, afterward, bishop of the Methodist-Episcopal Church. Warren Akin Candler, a descendant of Dr. Few's father-in-law, William Candler, also left his stamp on the college his family had led and prayed into existence. The school's first library was named Candler Hall in his honor, as was the current Candler School of Theology. In an interesting side note, Warren Candler was the brother of Asa Griggs Candler, the first president of Coca-Cola.

There is no "Few Hall" on campus named for the school's founder, but an impressive monument still stands prominently there and bears the following inscription: "I. A. Few, founder and first president of Emory College. . . . In early life an infidel, he became a Christian from conviction, and for many years of deep affliction walked by faith in the Son of God."

Because Dr. Few was also a Mason, fellow members of the brotherhood added this moving inscription to the east side of the monument:

> The Grand Lodge of Georgia erects this monument in token of high regard for a deceased brother, Ignatius A. Few. . . . As a Mason he possessed all the noble traits of character which constitute the worthy brother of this ancient and honorable order. As a minister of the gospel he exemplified the beautiful description of the poet:
>
> "His theme divine, his office sacred, his credentials clear,
> By him the violated law spoke out its thunders;
> And by him in strains as sweet as angels use,
> The gospel whispered peace."[38]

Dr. Ignatius A. Few, Jr., born in Columbia County, died at the age of fifty-six, and is buried at the heights of the Oconee River in Athens, Georgia.

Jesse Mercer, Billington McCarthy Sanders, and Nathaniel Macon Crawford

What are the odds that, with approximately ninety counties in Georgia by the early 1800's, the founders and first presidents of all three major institutions of higher learning in the state would be from Columbia County?

Politician, signer of the U.S. Constitution, and educator Abraham Baldwin wrote the charter and served as first president of the University of Georgia (then called Franklin College); and Ignatius Few, Jr., displayed the same credentials for Emory University. Now, as we consider the origin of Mercer University, we discover that, indeed, the three dominant colleges in Georgia all trace their founding and early leadership to men from Columbia County.

Jesse Mercer, for whom the Baptist school is named, was born in North Carolina. But sometime after his pioneer-minister father Silas Mercer moved the family to Georgia, where he served churches in the vicinity of Columbia County, the elder Mercer baptized seventeen-year-old Jesse into the membership of Kiokee Baptist Church in Appling. Three years later Jesse began a lifelong career in his father's footsteps by pastoring churches, conducting mission work among the Creek Indians, and becoming the recognized leader of the Georgia Baptist Convention. Later, during his fifth decade of life, Mercer presided over the ordination of the man who would found a college in his honor.

Billington McCarthy Sanders was born in 1789—coincidentally, the same year as his colleague Ignatius Few, Jr.—in what would become Columbia County, Georgia, the following year. By the time Billington was ten years old, his parents Ephraim and Nancy Sanders had both died, and he was raised by another county resident and family friend, Ambrose Jones. Sanders received his early education in local schools, and his early Christian training under Abraham Marshall (son of Daniel Marshall) at Kiokee Baptist Church, where both his father and Mr. Jones had served as church clerks.

After attending both the University of Georgia and South Carolina College, Sanders briefly taught school before settling into the life of a farmer and part-time preacher. Gradually, however, his passion for preaching increased until, in 1825, he gave up farming and was ordained to the Christian ministry.

In 1831 the Georgia Baptists asked Sanders to lead the planning committee for a denominational college and theological seminary. Two years later the ambitious Sanders opened Mercer Institute at Penfield, Georgia,

"Hanging Out the Wash." Courtesy Lynell Widener.

"Old Evans Post Office." Courtesy Lynell Widener.

Kiokee Baptist Church, 1808, with courthouse and monument

"Appling Village," including Daniel Marshall Monument and 1856 Columbia County Courthouse. Courtesy Lynell Widener.

"with two double log cabins, each with a garret for dwelling, dining, and studying for both teachers and students." Initially the school had thirty-nine students and a staff of three: Sanders as president, teacher, and steward; his wife as codirector; and one assistant to aid them both. Five years later the institute had grown to ninety-five students housed in "seven good buildings," and in 1838 the name was changed to Mercer University. Sanders resigned the presidency the following year to return to the pastoral ministry and take part in the leadership of the Georgia Baptist Convention, but he continued to serve as the school's (unpaid) treasurer and member of the board of trustees for many years more.

When he died in 1854, Billington Sanders left an impressive legacy—including twenty-two children born to two wives—and his accolades were legion. Said a friend: "He is good at everything. He is a good preacher, a good pastor, a good teacher, a good farmer, a good carpenter, a good brick mason—good at whatever he undertakes." In contemplating the man who established Mercer, another remarked: "He left the comforts of home, sacrificed his farm, and went into the crude new quarters of a log cabin."

His willingness to live in humble circumstances reflected the personal philosophy of Billington Sanders—"to do without what we cannot pay for" and "to consider it honorable to volunteer even for the most humiliating labor." With these principles, Mercer University's first president taught his students more than academics, and endowed his administration with more than the outward signs of success. In his final address as president, Sanders emphasized "substance rather than show, and the value of faculty far more than buildings."[39]

Fifteen years later, following the tenures of two more presidents, Mercer would call another man with Columbia County connections to become the school's fourth president. Nathaniel Macon Crawford may have been born in Oglethorpe County, but he was the son of William H. Crawford, Columbia County's reigning "favorite son." Young Crawford also fulfilled his share of his famous father's wish, "to see his sons well educated and his daughters well established in society." "Macon," as he was called, was valedictorian of his graduating class at the University of

Georgia, before studying law and being admitted to the bar. It was not long, however, before he realized he was more interested in teaching than in law, and he became a mathematics professor at Oglethorpe College, a Presbyterian institution.

But after studying the New Testament, and perhaps under the influence of his Baptist wife, he left his Presbyterian roots and teaching profession behind and became a Baptist minister. He was ordained in 1844 and served churches in Georgia and South Carolina before deciding three years later that teaching, not preaching, was his primary ministry. For the next seven years Professor Crawford taught Biblical Literature at Mercer University. He was elevated to the presidency in 1854, but he resigned the next year due to differences among the faculty. However, he did not stay away long. Two years later he was coaxed back to Mercer, where he remained as president for eight more years.

Nathaniel Crawford is remembered as a lifelong student who achieved excellence in linguistics, mathematics, philosophy, and theology. He is also described as "a man of learning, talent, and popularity." Georgia Baptists laud him, too, for his contributions as a teacher, counselor, and college executive.

David Bushnell

Humility, secrecy, and an act by the State of Georgia to create a new county out of the portion of Columbia County where he lived, all helped to obscure for years the addition of David Bushnell to the list of prominent, early residents of Columbia County. Bushnell, who after 1793 was known in Warren County as the respected physician and teacher Dr. David Bush, invented the world's first combat submarine. But it would take three more decades and the good doctor's death for his community to learn that a famous inventor had been in their midst.

Frail, bookish David Bushnell was born on a farm in Saybrook, Connecticut, in 1740. Like all frontier children, David, his brother Ezra, and three sisters were their father's principle farmhands during their youth, but farming was not in David's blood. So when his father died and, by tradition, left his property to his sons, he sold his half to Ezra and used the money to fulfill a long-held dream of going to college. He was almost thirty years old when he entered nearby Yale and began the first formal education of his life.

But the education of David Bushnell took place against the backdrop of the approaching Revolutionary War, which greatly affected his course of study. Always the scientific mind, he experimented with gunpowder while at Yale, specifically trying to make the powder explode under water. His early attempts were so successful that by 1775, when the war began and he was graduating from college, he had developed a fully functioning 150-pound, gunpowder-packed submarine mine. Now he needed a suitable vessel for moving the potential weapon, also underwater.

David returned to Saybrook where, with the help of his brother, all the money he could scrape together, and encouragement from the Army of Connecticut and another inventor, Benjamin Franklin, he worked through the next year to construct the small, walnut-shaped vessel he called *The American Turtle*. Made of two hollowed-out logs and resembling two turtle shells sealed together, the seven-foot vessel with its assortment of knob and pedal-operated mechanisms for breathing, moving, surfacing, and submerging, was just large enough for one man. Make that one *strong* man, which meant David would never be able to pilot the *Turtle* himself. Enter brother Ezra, who not only was in fine physical condition but also knew how to operate the vessel.

By late summer 1776, when more than three hundred British ships had formed a blockade around New York Harbor, the Bushnell brothers believed the *Turtle* was ready to leave its secluded shed near the mouth of the Connecticut River and make a surprise visit to that blockade. Alas, shortly before the submarine's maiden voyage was to begin, Ezra came down with typhoid fever.

After a hasty search, Sergeant Ezra Lee of the Connecticut Army was chosen, and perhaps too hastily trained, to take the other Ezra's place. Still, on the dark night of September 6, 1776, two longboats towed the *Turtle* and its single occupant out into Long Island Sound and toward the heavily fortified blockade to the south. When the ships were in sight, the oarsmen cut the vessel free and wished Sergeant Lee Godspeed in his attempt to attach one of Bushnell's mines to the bottom of one of the British ships.

It was a harrowing ride, but after fighting choppy water for hours, Lee finally guided the *Turtle* to the HMS *Eagle* and began pounding the screw atop the mine into the ship's hull. But no matter how many times he tried, Lee kept striking the metal strips around the ship rather than the anticipated wood, and it was impossible for the screw to penetrate the hull.

After resurfacing every thirty minutes for more air, and sensing his imminent discovery from lowering tides and the approaching dawn, Lee knew he had to abort his mission. But whether by luck, pluck, or a bungling gone good, as soon as the *Turtle* had cleared the row of ships Lee released the mine, triggering the timing device that moments later would detonate the charge.

What a blast! Though Benjamin Franklin had told Bushnell he thought the 150 pounds of gunpowder in his mine excessive, that explosion in New York Harbor in the early morning of September 7, 1776, was exactly the right formula to frighten the entire British fleet into moving their ships farther out to sea. The British could be thankful no casualties occurred in the unexpected skirmish, but the Americans and an unassuming inventor knew their experiment ended the damaging blockade and signaled the beginning of a new form of warfare yet to come. As Bushnell continued experimenting with his submarine concept, sometimes succeeding, sometimes not, General George Washington was heard to say of the idea and the man, "That was an effort of genius."

When the war ended, interest and financial backing in Bushnell's work ended too, and he needed to find another line of work. This time he would draw upon his extensive education, both from Yale and his lifelong pursuit of knowledge, and accept an invitation from his friend Abraham Baldwin to come to Georgia, where he would teach and practice medicine. Several sources indicate he taught school in Columbia County—some say in the community of Leah—before moving to Warrenton, where it is known he established an academy and practiced medicine, all under the assumed name of Dr. David Bush.

The publicity-shy Dr. Bush—or Bushnell—remained in Georgia until his death in 1824, without anyone except Abraham Baldwin knowing the doctor and the inventor were one and the same person. His secret might have been kept forever had his attorney, Peter Crawford, not discovered the information when probating his will. The authentic David Bushnell had bequeathed all his possessions and financial holdings to the University of Georgia, unless any living heirs were found in Connecticut. Although the eighty-four-year-old inventor-doctor had never married and his siblings had already died, heirs of his brother Ezra were found and their uncle's worldly goods—including drawings and a small model of the *Turtle*—were divided among them.

David Bushnell's possessions may not have remained in Georgia, but the residents of Columbia County and nearby Warrenton will always share in his legacy. Combat submarines are far more advanced today than was that first little *American Turtle* two centuries and dozens of wars ago. But much of the basic technology first devised by a nearly anonymous inventor in our midst is still used in the most sophisticated submarines today.

By no means do the preceding chapters or the stories they tell represent a complete list of people who left their mark on Columbia County or influenced a wider world. Neither is the county's first half-century defined only by individuals or the accomplishments of a few. Groups of people working together within and beyond county lines would now further harness the river, welcome the railroad through her growing cities and towns, and of necessity build another, larger courthouse.

PART V

FROM DEPOT TO COURTHOUSE:

BY RIVER, ROAD, AND RAIL

The Depot, Harlem, Georgia. Courtesy Lynell Widener.

33

Nature's Roadway

The measure of wealth on the southeastern frontier was always that plot of land a settler called his own. But whether granted, inherited, or purchased outright, the place where early nineteenth-century residents lived, raised livestock, or planted increasing amounts of cotton would gradually diminish in value without better means of traveling to and from that hallowed ground.

At first the navigable portions of the Savannah River plus former Indian trails overland created a functional "highway system" through Columbia County—until population boomed, river depths rose and fell to dangerous levels with each rainfall or drought, and those primitive roads either filled with potholes, washouts, and debris, or alternated between mud, dust, and barriers too difficult to maneuver around. Add equipment breakdown and the amount of time needed for transporting people, products, and supplies from origin to destination, and you have the perennial motivation of mankind for something better than the status quo.

No matter how treacherous or rainfall-dependent the river, however, that so-called "nature's roadway" was still the preferred route through the Backcountry. But it would take years before Georgia, South Carolina, and sometimes the federal government could agree on a border between the two states. Obviously such a boundary was necessary in order to determine whose responsibility it was to keep the river free of debris, hidden boulders, or the occasional dam erected by an overreaching landowner or fisherman.

Congress would not declare the middle of the river the official border between Georgia and South Carolina until 1922, but it did not take nearly that long for each state to understand the importance of maintaining as clear a channel as possible through such a vital lifeline. Various cleanup plans, commissions, and fines were enacted until a workable solution beneficial to residents on both sides of the river was finally in place.

Attention also turned to better watercraft, something more efficient than the common flat-bottomed oar or pole-driven boats that moved slowly, carried little cargo and, worst of all, were difficult to row or carry upstream. For a while cotton growers solved the latter problem by floating their crop downriver in wooden "cotton boxes," which then were broken apart and resold as lumber. Otherwise, sturdy men had to push, carry, or paddle the empty boats 131 miles back upriver from Savannah to Augusta and beyond.

Necessity is the mother of invention we are told, which is why two new and very different types of boats conceived in the Georgia Backcountry helped to advance early American river transportation. In 1808, and for want of a year, Augusta civic leader and inventor William Longstreet might have built the first steamboat in the country—had his New York counterpart, Robert Fulton, not set sail on the Hudson River with his steam-powered *Clermont* in 1807.

But Longstreet's invention was cumbersome, moved only slightly faster than the former man-powered boats and, in fact, needed some of that man, pole, and even horse or mule power running on riverside "tow paths" to help pull or steer the weighty boats along. Soon, however, others adapted Longstreet's idea until, by the end of the next decade, two boats owned by the Georgia Steamboat Company and large enough to hold five hundred bales of cotton apiece were making regular runs between Augusta and Savannah.

Unfortunately the steamboats were only useful in deep water, and it was impossible to move them through the rapids above Augusta. Thus, for planters farther north to benefit from river shipping, another type of boat had to be devised. Enter the tapered, flat-bottomed Petersburg boat, built of varying sizes up to eighty feet long, and capable of skirting boulders and other narrow passageways along the often treacherous river.

Named for a now extinct town in Elbert County, where the Broad River joins the Savannah some fifty miles above Augusta, each Petersburg boat could carry up to sixty bales of cotton plus small amounts of grain and other goods sandwiched in between, and companies could afford to own more than two boats at a time. With a pilot and four-to-six-man crew aboard, the boats began their journey in Petersburg and made designated stops all the way to Augusta. Cargo bound for Savannah, Europe, or the West Indies was then transferred to a waiting steamboat for the final leg of its journey to the sea.

Depending on the weather and number of stops, travel from Petersburg to Augusta took two-to-three days. The return trip required at least a day longer than that, and often became a brutal or deadly task for the crew. Add to this difficulty the number of planters above Augusta or away from the river who had to cope with more problems overland, such as small, easily overturned wagons lumbering over frequently impassable roads, and we can understand why our ancestors clamored for a still better way to travel or move their goods. Once again the timing coincided with a new invention, and almost everyone was ready for the railroad.

34

ALL ABOARD!

Public rail transportation did not begin in this country or in Europe until well into the nineteenth century. But the railroad concept was in use as early as the 1500's, when European miners discovered it was easier to move their coal or iron ore out of the mines in small, horse-drawn carts along thin, wooden rails, than for man or beast to carry it to the surface one hod or scuttle at a time.

By the 1700's English coal-mining companies were also building short, wooden railroad tracks above ground, except that the rails were now covered with iron strips. But as Americans would learn a century later, wooden rails are subject to swelling after a rainstorm, or curling in the hot sun. Since these fluctuations plus wear-and-tear caused the iron strips to separate from the wood, it became necessary to construct the tracks completely of iron and attach them to imbedded wooden logs (ties), the method used worldwide today.

Incidentally, the universal distance of four feet, eight and a half inches (1.44 meters) between the parallel rails corresponds to the length of the average axle on a horse-drawn wagon, an accommodation to the "engines" that propelled the first trains.[1]

Besides settling the problem of rail composition, attention also turned to something more effective than natural "horsepower" to move the trains. With steam-powered boats already in operation, railroad pioneers agreed that if steam worked on water, it should work just as well on land. The British were the first to develop a steam locomotive, which by 1825 evolved into the world's first public railroad.

America entered the era of rail transportation in 1830, when the Baltimore & Ohio Railroad Company became the first to offer service in North America. The company's first trains were not powered by steam, however, but with horses aided by sails mounted on top of the rail cars—until inventor Peter Cooper developed the small, one-and-one-half horsepower steam locomotive, Tom Thumb, which roared to life on the Baltimore & Ohio tracks later that year.

About the time Mr. Cooper's steam engine was making its debut a few miles to the north, the newly formed South Carolina Railroad Company was preparing to launch America's first steam-powered, passenger train. Excitement reigned on Christmas Day in 1830, when the small locomotive, Best Friend of Charleston, and two passenger cars left the coastal city and chugged successfully through several nearby towns. The primitive train repeated this same run on schedule for the next six months—until a fireman sat on a safety valve to silence an irritating hiss and the engine blew up.[2] Not to be deterred, the South Carolina Company quickly repaired their "Best Friend" and within two years extended her tracks all the way to Hamburg, just across the river from Augusta.

Would the next stop *be* Augusta? Before long Georgia also would enter the "iron horse" revolution, but not until a number of objections were resolved. If the railroad came across the river, Georgia merchants feared, Charleston then would have direct access to Georgia's rich cotton bounty and thus bypass the markets in Augusta and Savannah. Savannah also objected when the early Georgia Railroad proposed extending its east-west lines to the Lowcountry, where city leaders anxiously protected their lucrative river traffic against the faster, more reliable railroad.

Using a similar argument, the planters also complained. The railroad would be costly to use as well as to build, they said, and they wanted to continue shipping cotton down the less expensive river. Besides, they had another idea for improving transportation routes: digging canals between the major rivers to maximize the "river road." But the canal idea quickly lost favor, after it was discovered that the sandy soil in much of the state was too porous to hold water.

Other anti-railroad sentiment arose in Lexington and Oglethorpe counties, where trains were forbidden to come within four miles of a town. Concerned residents worried that the engines would emit too much soot and the noise would frighten livestock, causing cows to give less milk, hens to lay fewer eggs, and valuable horses to run away. Then, as the early trains began to appear, night runs were halted in some towns after two men were killed when a rainstorm washed out a section of track and the engineer could not see the damage in time to stop the train.

Not to be left out, churches objected to Sunday trains, presumably because of the noise or the temptation for some of their members to enjoy an out-of-town, Sunday excursion rather than attend church. And the residents of Wrightsborough so strongly opposed allowing the railroad through their town that the route was changed to the future town of Thomson instead. The consequences of this latter decision are obvious to this day. Although a few families had remained in the Quaker town after most people moved to Ohio twenty years before, Thomson, named for the railroad's chief engineer, John Edgar Thomson, is a thriving city today, while Wrightsborough barely exists.

Despite the objections of a disenchanted few, pro-railroad sentiment was unstoppable, and the coming of the railroad through east-central Georgia would figure strongly in the area's development from that time on. Railroad construction created an influx of new labor, new towns sprang up wherever tracks were laid, and the railroad's main line cut across Columbia County from one side to the other. Before the start of the Civil War, the state's 1,400 miles of track would anchor the best rail system in the South, with all lines passing through a strategic western town first called Terminus, then Marthasville, and finally Atlanta.

Perhaps no one was more interested in bringing the railroad to the Georgia Backcountry than area entrepreneurs James Camak, William Williams, and William Dearing. No doubt these gentlemen were familiar with the long trip to Savannah by jostling stagecoach, slow steamboat, or harrowing pole boat ride—and waiting a similar amount of time for needed supplies to arrive by wagon, barge, or stage. But their patience wore thin one wintry day in 1832, when a shipment of machinery originating in England and sent slowly upriver by flatboat, failed to arrive because the mule-drawn wagon carrying the cargo inland became mired in rain-soaked Georgia clay.

It would be weeks before the stalled wagon could be moved from its muddy grip, but not nearly that long before Camak, Williams, and Dearing joined other Backcountry businessmen in obtaining a charter for a railroad they first called "Union Railroad," then simply "Georgia Railroad."

Local citizens could not have known how much they owed a little rain, a lot of Georgia clay, and the exasperation of a handful of inconvenienced men. Despite widespread enthusiasm for the railroad, without private monies to fund the expensive project it could have been another decade before their railroad dream came true. Georgia's financial condition during this period was so fragile it was nearly impossible for the state to obtain credit—until 1843 when Columbia County native, George Crawford, became governor and augmented the state treasury with his financial expertise and some of his own funds. Before Crawford left office in 1847, his administration would complete the western leg (The Western and Atlantic) of the state's rail system, but the task was made infinitely easier because of private enterprise some ten-to-fifteen years before.

Meanwhile, in 1833, when the Georgia Legislature granted a charter "to incorporate the Georgia Railroad Company [to] construct a railroad from the city of Augusta . . . to the towns of Eatonton, Madison, and Athens,"[3] the company's board of directors was given authority to grant an initial stock offering of 15,000 shares at $100 a share. Many of those formerly disenchanted planters joined other enthusiastic investors in making this new venture a success. Two years later, when their capital reached $2,000,000, the company name was changed to "The Georgia Railroad and Banking Company," based on a proposal that when the railroad construction was complete, the company would continue to exist for banking purposes.

Although work began on the Augusta to Athens branch of the railroad in 1833, it would be four years before the first trains were in operation. Property had to be condemned, routes determined, and experience gained for this new type of construction. But steady progress continued along both the initial east-west route, and on newer branches fanning across the more populous areas of the state throughout the next decade.

Of particular interest to Columbia County were the towns where the trains stopped or passed through. Ten miles after leaving Augusta, the train stopped in the small Richmond County community of Belair, located near today's intersection of Wrightsboro Road, the Jimmie Dyess Parkway, and the Columbia County line. Once inside Columbia County, the train then stopped in Berzelia and Campania, communities between the current cities of Grovetown and Harlem, and the small lumber town appropriately named "Sawdust." (Later in the nineteenth-century, when these small communities ceased to exist, new and larger depots would be erected in both Grovetown and Harlem.) With the birth of McDuffie County still twenty-five to thirty years away, the Columbia County towns of Dearing, Boneville, Thomson, and Mesena were next, followed by Camak just inside the Warren County line.[4]

No one should be surprised that the towns of Dearing and Camak were named for two of the men whose delayed shipment more than a decade before played such a strong role in the coming of the railroad. William Dearing also was a physician and mayor of Augusta, while James Camak, an attorney and first president of the Georgia Railroad Company, is still revered by the citizens of his namesake town, especially during Camak's Railroad Days Festival in the spring of each year.

Although freight transportation was the primary motivation for building the railroad, once folks overcame their aversion to the noise or fear of running off the tracks, passengers were eager to pay their two cents a mile to travel between towns on business or pleasure. Sometime later, after the city of Harlem was established, a small passenger train called The Picayune offered daily rides for commuters between Harlem and Augusta. Also, once passenger traffic increased, community leaders capitalized on their new attraction by moving post offices, town meetings,

184

local events and, by the end of the century, Western Union and Railway Express offices into their railroad depots, the new social center of a railroad town.

Passenger traffic continued through Columbia County and across the state for more than a hundred years. But with the rise of the auto and the end of World War II, the last major event requiring movement of large groups of people at one time, passenger service gradually declined. Except for an occasional, prearranged excursion, or permission to "hop" a ride on a freight train, regular passenger service on Georgia's trains ended during the 1960's. If anything, freight service has taken up the slack. Today, no one whose customary travel route includes crossing one or more sets of railroad tracks will be surprised to learn that approximately eighteen trains a day still pass through Columbia County. Some of them are a mile long.

35

A New Route to Augusta, and a
Popular Playground at Home

As predicted, the railroad revolutionized the movement of goods and people through the Backcountry. But residents were also moving— to Alabama, Mississippi, and Texas—in search of new land or prosperity, and something more than transportation was needed to strengthen the faltering economy of the 1840's. Henry Cumming, prominent Augusta resident and law partner of George Crawford, had an idea.

Canals may not have been feasible statewide, but along Georgia's fall line, where the rocky piedmont joins the softer bedrock of the upper coastal plain, Cumming not only believed a canal extending from the Savannah River was possible, but that such a channel would provide enough water power to attract much-needed industry to the area. Based on his study of older, European canals, and inspection of those that were newly built or under construction in the United States, Cumming had a good understanding of the subject. He also knew where to turn for advice about building a similar waterway nearer home.

John Edgar Thomson, chief engineer for the nearly completed Georgia Railroad, was ready to return to his native Pennsylvania when Cumming approached him, not only for advice, but also for help in planning the proposed canal. That is why in November 1844, instead of packing for Pennsylvania, Thomson was traveling upriver from Augusta with Cumming and a handful of other community leaders to determine if a canal could be built along the river and, if so, the mid-river channel Bull Sluice, just over the Columbia County line, was the best place to begin.

Yes to all the above, including Thomson's two-year extension in Georgia to survey the land and map the canal's route. Besides his professional skills, the highly respected engineer's prestige also helped sell the canal idea to the public.

Still, like the railroad in its early stages, the canal had its critics. As usual, the initial outcry concerned the price tag. With the area already depressed, investors' funds still tied up in the railroad, and no one experienced enough in canal building to project even a close estimate of the cost, many were unwilling to jump onto another expensive bandwagon quite so soon. Others either objected to the canal's route or feared spoiling the landscape and creating a potential for flooding. Some people also pointed out the injustice of creating something so costly that would benefit only wealthy business owners at every taxpayer's expense.

Although the above objections reappeared during each phase of the canal's development, they would eventually subside. But one more controversy had to be resolved before the project could begin. Realizing the purpose of the canal was to attract industry to the area, those who were steeped in the plantation culture of the South wanted no part of the manufacturing mentality they associated with the North. In a clash of ideals that would culminate less than twenty years later in a national civil war, these critics could not forget the prevailing image of Northern sweatshops and their reportedly ill-treated employees who, they believed, were worse off than the Southern slave so disdained by the North.

Cumming himself helped overcome this final obstacle by appealing to an emerging, regional ideal. Southern independence from Europe or the more industrialized North could be achieved, he said, when goods manufactured in the South reduced the need to purchase elsewhere what they could make less expensively themselves.

Cumming's diplomacy was apparently as well received as his initial canal idea. Now that all major obstacles were removed, work on the approved canal began in the spring of 1845, barely six months after the Cumming-Thomson party took that exploratory hike from Augusta to Bull Sluice.

With a labor force that included former railroad employees, newly arrived Irish immigrants, additional crews from around the state, and available slaves, work on all twelve sections of the canal began to take shape. Of the two sections in Columbia County, section one, comprising the head gates, lock, and a diversion dam to redirect water from the river into the canal, was of primary importance and among the first to be completed. Eighteen months later, on November 23, 1846, water flowed through the canal for the first time from the head gates to the end of level one at Augusta's Thirteenth Street basin seven miles away. Though more difficult to build, levels two and three inside the city itself were completed by 1848, making the entire canal about nine miles long.[5]

Because they built it, did the anticipated industry come? Did it ever! Thanks to a fifty-two-foot drop in elevation from the head gates to the city of Augusta, the downward flow through the canal provided exactly the water power Henry Cumming had envisioned five years before. Within a few years at least seventy factories, mills, and related businesses were benefiting from that power, and providing jobs and goods to benefit the local economy besides. Before long, one more cog in the local industrial revolution would attract the largest manufacturing effort of all to the banks of the new canal.

A little more than a decade after completion of the canal, war clouds loomed again over a still young America. No longer was the economy uppermost in Southern minds. Their survival as citizens of the United States—or perhaps of a new nation—concerned them now. More than factories versus plantations separated the South from her Northern neighbors in 1861, as the new Confederate States of America was born.

No one with the slightest memory of that earlier breach between the American colonies and Great Britain expected the division of the now American States to occur without bloodshed. But not even Henry

Cumming could have known what an important role the Augusta Canal would play as his new nation prepared for war.

In July 1861, three months after the firing on Fort Sumter that signaled the start of the American Civil War, Confederate States President, Jefferson Davis, commissioned Colonel George Washington Rains to build a powder works complex large enough to supply the munitions needed by his new army. Paradoxically, because of Augusta's accessibility to manpower and supplies via the railroad, and her inaccessibility to enemy attack due to her inland location along a not entirely navigable river, Rains was first attracted to the east-central Georgia city. But it was the canal with its spacious banks and abundance of water power for turning factory turbines that clinched the decision to build the vital Confederate States Powder Works in Augusta, Georgia.

By 1862 twenty-six buildings spaced far enough apart to limit damage in case of an explosion lined a two-mile stretch on both sides of the canal. Before the war ended three years later, the enormous facility supplied the Confederate Army with weaponry as diverse as cannons and cartridges, pistols and percussion caps, grenades, and nearly three million pounds of gunpowder, plus every conceivable component necessary for battle in between. The war may not have ended as he wished, but as he watched his factories close down a proud Rains was heard to say, "No Confederate soldier ever lost a fight for lack of ammunition."[6]

The waterwheels of the once productive Powder Works stopped turning on May 3, 1865, when both the massive complex and the city of Augusta were surrendered to Union General Emory Upton following the war. By the time the city bought the abandoned buildings from the federal government in 1872, they were unfit for use and had to be torn down. In ensuing years the property was resold, and in time a smaller number of new mills erected in their place. One structure, however, survived. Colonel Rains, who remained in Augusta to teach at the Medical College of Georgia, asked that the 168-foot chimney still towering over the canal and a modern array of primarily textile mills "be allowed to remain forever as a fitting monument to the dead heroes who sleep on the unnumbered battlefields of the South."[7]

Although the primary purpose of the canal was to power the very industry that resurrected a local economy and armed a country for war, there were other benefits from Cummings' idea as well. From the beginning and to this day, the City of Augusta has drawn its water supply from the canal, and pleasure seekers have flocked there to fish, paddle canoes, and hike or peddle bicycles on the adjoining tow path. More recently, residents have been able to ride reconstructed Petersburg boats along this tranquil waterway between the head gates and the city.

Augusta capitalized on the canal's recreational popularity early in the twentieth-century by adding a dance pavilion and barbecue pit just below the head gates in Columbia County, and traffic along the canal was bustling to and from that destination for more than fifty years. But when these buildings deteriorated and the surrounding area fell into disarray, for safety reasons the city padlocked the gates to the property they still owned to keep the public out. Fortunately the gates would not stay locked for long.

In the early 1990's, following a lengthy study about where to locate a new park and community center in the Martinez-Evans area, the Columbia County Commission looked beyond the overgrowth and debris near the head gates and saw what that thirty-three-acre site could become. With some cleaning up, restoration of existing facilities, and the addition of an attractive, new community center atop the eighty-foot bluff overlooking the river and canal, the commissioners considered the possibility of building their park and community center there. Upon request, Augusta agreed to lease the site to Columbia County for fifty years, in exchange for the county's promise to restore the dilapidated dance pavilion and barbecue pit, and to do everything possible to maintain the pristine quality of the upper canal.

In typical Columbia County (or human nature) tradition, not everyone was happy with the proposed community center plan. To some the old mantra, "it's not centrally located," was the chief objection. More common, however, were the environmental concerns, including contamination of the canal, loss of trees and endangered plant life, and the possible disturbance of Indian graves beneath the huge bluff. After learning that the bluff was man-made with fill from the river when the diversion dam was extended across the river in 1875—long after Indians were known to have lived in the area—and following repeated promises to be environmentally sensitive, the commission proceeded with their park and community center plan.

Though some critics continued to frown on the project during the building process, from the time the naturally landscaped grounds, parking areas under a canopy of still standing trees, and the aesthetic Savannah Rapids Pavilion Community Center were completed in 1993, hardly a protest could be heard against the suddenly popular facility. Well into the first decade of the twenty-first century, the versatile center with its breathtaking view, improved access to the canal, and tranquil setting beneath moss-draped oaks and pines continues to draw enthusiastic individuals, families, and dozens of private and community recreation and events to the no longer locked and abandoned grounds.

Following creation of the Augusta Canal Authority in 1989, and the 1999 conversion of part of the old Enterprise Mill on Greene Street into a Canal Interpretive Center, heightened activity also occurred on the lower sections of the canal. In 1996, thanks to the cumulative efforts of U.S. Representatives Doug Barnard and Charlie Norwood, and Senator Paul Coverdell, Congress named the Augusta Canal one of eighteen National Heritage Areas in the country, and the only one in Georgia. With this designation, special funds are now available for continued upkeep and improvements to the canal.

The Columbia County section of the canal also has benefited from the National Heritage designation. With their portion of the additional funds, restoration of the dance pavilion and head gates has been completed, and the former lockkeeper's cottage has become the county's first ever, state-certified Visitor Center. Blue signs along Riverwatch Parkway, Stevens Creek, and Evans-to-Locks Roads direct you there.

36

A New Courthouse

for a Growing County

Mystery surrounds what happened to Columbia County's 1812 Courthouse. Did a storm pass by? Did the builder use an inferior quality of Georgia clay for his self-made brick, or had forty plus years taken its toll on the best of nineteenth-century materials? Or, similar to an even faster-growing Columbia County at the beginning of the twenty-first century, was the thirty-by-fifty foot building just too small for transacting increased county business?

For whatever reason the 1812 building needed to be replaced, midway between completion of the Augusta Canal and the start of the Civil War, the county again made plans to build a new courthouse. But for once, despite deliberations over cost, builder, and specifications in general or minute detail, one problem the county has faced when erecting each of her other courthouses was not present in 1855. This time not a soul complained that the site was not centrally located. Columbia County's third courthouse would be built over the core of the 1812 building on William Appling's five-acre tract in the center of a town and county seat that still bear his name.

Unlike the earlier Appling structure that was built more for function than for style, the new building would reflect a growing rivalry between counties for the courthouse with the finest appearance. Therefore, the county commissioners made a wise choice in selecting John Trowbridge— "an architect and house carpenter . . . a man of great energy, of character, of nice taste in his profession, and fully equal to the task you propose"— to make Columbia County a proud contender in the annals of courthouse competition.[8]

Judging by the building's simple, carpenter design, the "tasteful" Mr. Trowbridge must have agreed with those who believe "there is no greatness where there is not simplicity."[9] The two-story, fifty-by-sixty-foot rectangle, plus a small extension on the south side of the building surrounding the front entrance, earned its external "greatness" through symmetry, brick and stucco façade, imposing twenty-four "light" (pane) windows, ornate Italianate brackets under the eaves, and elegant, wooden front doors. Additional aesthetic touches can be found inside the building in the crossed hallways on the first floor, twin stairways (added in 1979) that merge into one at the landing near the second floor, and a pressed-tin ceiling above the spacious, new courtroom upstairs.

In contrast to the 1812 building, which placed the courtroom downstairs and offices on the second floor, the new courthouse would have space for the clerk of courts, ordinary (probate judge today), tax assessor, and other county offices on the first floor and the courtroom upstairs. But the greatest contrast between the two buildings must have been their size. By increasing the outer dimensions of the new courthouse from thirty-by-fifty to fifty-by-sixty feet, the interior space of the two-story building doubled from three thousand to six thousand square feet. Courthouse employees and county residents alike must have enjoyed a festive ribbon cutting when those elegant doors opened for the first time in 1856.

Those who have no memory of this courthouse before the latter part of the twentieth-century may not recognize it by the above description, and some explanation is in order. Although the building has stood on the same site for more than 150 years, during that time a number of changes have occurred both to the courthouse and to the surrounding landscape.

Georgia Route 221, the road that passes through Appling today, followed a different route in 1856. If you were approaching the center of town from Harlem or Columbia Road before the 1930's, you would have followed a road that curved left before reaching the courthouse, angled right again behind the building, crossed Mattie and Jake Pollard, Sr's front lawn, and joined the current highway near the intersection of Appling-Harlem Road and Scott's Ferry Road. Thus it is easy to understand why the original front door of the courthouse was on the south side of the building. The entrance faced the road then, just as the newer east entrance faces the rerouted road today.

Unfortunately the county's third courthouse did not always lead a charmed life. For example in 1875, barely twenty years after John Trowbridge began layering brick, mortar, and ornamental touches for the new building, a devastating tornado swept through town and nearly destroyed in minutes what took months to build. One end of the building was completely blown in, and the roof lifted from the building and dropped into a pile of timbers on a nearby lawn. There is little record of the restoration process or how long it took, except that sturdy steel rods now restrain all the walls from future implosion, and the reconstructed roof is anchored to its reinforced, brick base, never—so far—to blow off again.

As the years turned into another century, more and more county functions found a home in the courthouse. At one time, in addition to rooms for court and commission personnel, space was also made available for the sheriff, coroner, school superintendent and Board of Education, county registrar, and more. But by the 1930's, about the time the new road came through the center of Appling, even the doubly large courthouse was running out of space.

This time, rather than erect a new courthouse, the County Commission decided to build additional space next door for the clerk of courts and the probate judge. This building, including the vault where important, historic records are kept, is still in use, even as the much larger 2002 Courthouse Annex in Evans handles the bulk of county business today. Other facilities also remain at the county seat. The small jail across the street from the courthouse, another 1930's project, has become the office of the Columbia County Historical Society, and the sheriff and tax collector each maintain a satellite office nearby to serve residents from the western section of the county. Prior to their move to Evans in 2006, the offices of the Superintendent of Schools and Board of Education were located just north of the old jail, while the county garage continues to maintain their buildings between and slightly behind the former school offices and jail.

Through the years several historic and memorial touches have been added to the Appling Courthouse. Especially noticeable are the county's war memorials, including three marble plaques behind the judge's bench listing the county's casualties in the Civil War and both world wars, and a stone monument to the Korean War dead on the front lawn. Otherwise, not much changed in or around the courthouse until the county's population explosion began in earnest during the last quarter of the twentieth century.

Apparently not much maintenance or repair work occurred in those mid-twentieth-century decades, either—until 1979, when Superior Court Judge Franklin H. Pierce threatened to fine—and jail—all five county commissioners for allowing the courthouse to fall into disarray. In their defense, the commissioners blamed their inaction on lack of funds and low priority. The courthouse was not used enough, they said, to warrant the tax increase it would have taken to comply with the judge's demands.

But Judge Pierce was adamant that the work be done. Besides a leaking roof, peeling paint, and other cosmetic problems, the building had not been modernized. There was no insulation, no air-conditioning, nothing more than substandard restrooms and, according to a state fire marshal, there was good reason for the building to be condemned. With only one exit from the upper floor, the marshal ordered the building closed until the repairs and both an elevator and second stairway were installed.

Through appeal, a promise to release sales tax money to fund the repairs, and the posting of each other's bond, the commissioners managed to stay out of jail while the work they quickly authorized was being done.

Not since the tornado swept through town a century before had the courthouse undergone such a facelift. New roofing, paint and carpet, central heat and air, restrooms and insulation all were completed as required by Judge Pierce, and an elevator and that extra stairway installed to satisfy the fire marshal. Before completing this double new access to the second floor, however, an extension had to be added to the north side of the building. Pleasantly this extension also restored the building's lost symmetry when the front entrance was moved from the south side to its current location.

Following these projects, the Appling Courthouse reopened for business in 1980, the same year Judge Pierce rescinded his citation against the commissioners, and Columbia County's attractive again courthouse was placed on the National Register of Historic Places.

But now, between the rapidly increasing population of the county and a more inviting place to conduct court business, more and more activity took place at the former "low priority" courthouse—so much so that, by the mid 1990's, a new round of complaints began to be heard.

"The Appling Courthouse is too small . . . too far from Augusta where most of the attorneys have their offices . . . there's no place to park." Also, reminiscent of George Walton's reluctance more than two hundred years earlier to locate the Richmond County seat "way out in the woods," with more people now living in the Martinez-Evans area than "way out in Appling," guess what? The courthouse was not centrally located anymore.

Not everyone agreed. Longtime county residents who still lived in Winfield, Leah, and especially Appling were saddened at the thought of giving up the only courthouse they had ever known. Besides, for them it was just as long a drive to Augusta for jobs and business transactions as it was for court participants to travel the other way. But most of all, it was the historic value of their nationally recognized courthouse that formed their opinion either to enlarge the existing building or build a new one on or near William Appling's two-hundred-year-old lot.

To some degree, the Columbia County Legislative Delegation agreed with the latter group. They knew that county seats are determined by the state and that the county courthouse had to be located there. The courthouse could not be moved without changing the county seat, which would be an enormous undertaking, including a change to the state constitution.

In early 1998, however, the legislators were able to do something else—pass a bill that allowed both Superior Court and Grand Jury proceedings to be held in a Courthouse Annex when the county seat is located in an unincorporated area. Although Appling was approved for incorporation in 1816, according to G. B. ("Jake") Pollard, Jr., the former Columbia County clerk and state senator, the townspeople saw no need for another layer of government beyond their existing county government. Consequently they did not follow through on the incorporation process. Now, in order for Appling to remain the county seat, all that was required under the new law was for a probate judge's office to remain on the existing premises, and the Superior Court to hold at least two sessions a year in the courthouse located there.

At last the commissioners had a workable solution to this latest courthouse controversy, but could they sell that solution to the voters? If the people agreed with them, they would build that Courthouse Annex in a location to be determined by the voters, comply with the law to hold court at least twice a year in Appling and, most important, thoroughly refurbish the existing historic courthouse and encourage the building's continued use for a variety of community purposes.

Following a series of public meetings to outline their plan, including the necessary one-mill tax increase to fund this project and at the same time expand the county's also outgrown detention center, the voters were asked to make their wishes known at a special election the following July. The courthouse portion of the referendum was in two parts: Would the voters approve the Courthouse Annex and, if so, where should it be built? By this time the site selection had been narrowed to an area next to the expanding detention center on Columbia Road in Appling and a lot adjacent to the existing County Government Center in Evans.

The referendum to build the annex (also called "Justice Center") passed overwhelmingly, and a majority of the assenting voters chose to place the building in Evans. After acquiring the land, choosing the architect and builder, and finalizing the building's specifications, commissioners, members of the judiciary, and a crowd of spectators gathered in the vacant lot on February 18, 2000, to break ground. Two and a half years later, on August 30, 2002, an even larger group of people gathered for the ribbon cutting of Columbia County's new 72,000 square-foot brick and white columned Courthouse Annex. Three months later, on November 30, citizens and dignitaries alike returned for a dedication ceremony, with United States Supreme Court Justice Anthony M. Kennedy giving the dedicatory address.

It would take three more years, but on November 4, 2005, the county held another ribbon cutting to reopen the fully restored and further modernized Appling Courthouse. In addition to the twice annual Superior Court proceedings, the attractive building also hosts occasional County Commission meetings, displays public notices at the front entrance, prepares to accept a branch library, county museum, or other suggested use, and opens her elegant doors once again to the public she serves.

Before we leave this chapter, one final courthouse subject needs to be addressed: Is Columbia County's Appling Courthouse the oldest, continuing courthouse in Georgia as many claim, or not? Well, yes and no.

If by "oldest courthouse" we mean the current building, with its doubled size over the courthouse of 1812, the obvious answer is "no." But if we mean a continuous courthouse presence on the same site in the same county seat, transacting the same county business, the answer, in principle, is "yes." Though we can only surmise the reason for replacing the earlier Appling building, we can be certain that courthouse business in the thriving county continued somewhere, whether in the original jail across the street (not the 1930's building, but one where the satellite tax collector's office stands now), in someone's home, or parceled out to several locations not far from the courthouse site, all during the transition process.

Purists will answer the age-old question "no." On the other hand, those who are governed by "the spirit of the law" will likely answer "yes." After all, courthouse business must have been disrupted during the 1875 tornado cleanup and subsequent renovations without any claim that this courthouse was not in "continuous use" during those temporary interruptions.

Whatever the ruling on this question turns out to be, Columbia County's fully restored and busily engaged Appling Courthouse today shows no sign of stopping its "continuous use" for the foreseeable future, if not a century to come.

Now that much of the chronology and the stories of those who made these events happen have been documented, we turn to another group of people who, some might say, were not on anyone's list of prominent citizens, but without whom the complete story of Columbia County could not be told. Today their descendants are called African-Americans. Early residents called them Negroes, free blacks, and slaves.

PART VI

FROM AFRICA TO THE BACKCOUNTRY

OF GEORGIA:

THE AFRICAN-AMERICAN HISTORY

OF COLUMBIA COUNTY AGAINST THE

BACKDROP OF THE CIVIL WAR

First Mount Carmel Baptist Church (organized October 13, 1873).
Courtesy Lynell Widener.

37

First They Were Slaves

"Do Lord, O do Lord, O do remember me,
Way beyond the blue."[1]

If James Oglethorpe had had his way there would have been no Emancipation Proclamation in 1863, or thirteenth Amendment to the U.S. Constitution abolishing slavery completely in 1865, because there would have been no slaves to ban or free—at least in Georgia. In the idealistic founder's mind, "Widespread economic vitality cannot be achieved in a society dominated by slave labor."[2] Although he shared the belief of many that slavery was "against the Gospel," Oglethorpe's primary reason for opposing the practice was to foster a strong work ethic among the colonists themselves. But his idea to ban slavery altogether was neither shared by the other colonies nor, as he would soon learn, the arriving Georgians.

The institution of slavery has existed almost since the origin of mankind, and long before the American colonies were established or Oglethorpe and his fellow Trustees forbade the practice in Georgia. For example, on the African continent, where most of the early slaves lived before they were brought to the western world, the Egyptians used slave labor to build such lavish structures as the ancient sphinx and pyramids. At the same time, warring tribesmen often turned their captives into forced laborers for their own use or to exchange with traveling traders for needed goods. Initially these primarily Spanish, Dutch, and Portuguese traders resold their slaves in Europe, but when Europeans began migrating to the American colonies some of the traders turned their ships toward the New World, too.

With timber to cut, land to clear, and crops to plant and maintain, slavery was thought to be a necessity in the colonies, especially on large plantations in Virginia and the Carolinas. Later, when the South Carolina planters extended their holdings across the Savannah River, slaves were found in the future colony of Georgia long before the slavery ban was in place.

It's not surprising then that Oglethorpe's utopian plan for a colony without slaves would be short-lived. Barely five years after their 1733 landing on Yamacraw Bluff, rice and indigo planters along the Georgia coast noticed how much more prosperous the slave-owning South Carolina growers were, and they pleaded with the Georgia Trustees to relax their prohibition against slaves. The Trustees were unmoved that time, but the settlers continued to plead their case.

It would take another dozen years, but by 1750 a majority of the Trustees gave in to the colonists' demands, dropped their ban on slavery, and opened the port of Savannah to incoming slave ships. Almost immediately slave auction blocks appeared in Savannah and not long afterward in Augusta. More than 500 slaves entered the colony that first year alone, and by 1766 the number had increased to 3,500. On the eve of the American Revolution nearly half the state's 33,000 residents were slaves, and Georgia's economy was almost totally dependent on slave labor.[3]

The Georgia founder remained a Trustee following his return to England in 1743, but he continued to oppose slavery for the rest of his life. Therefore, when the ban on slavery was removed he ceased attending Trustee meetings, and he never again set foot in his beloved Georgia. But Oglethorpe and his principled stance would not be forgotten, and he never knew how many Americans agreed with him. Neither would he live to see the day when slavery was banished forever, not only in Georgia but in all of America.

Slavery was a divisive issue for the American colonies from the start, pitting those who believed the institution was not only necessary but ordained by God, against those who sought with equal passion to oppose it.[4] And no subject was more troublesome during the crafting of the Declaration of Independence and the Constitution than this one.

Reconciling slavery with the phrase "all men are created equal" was a particular problem for Thomas Jefferson, a reluctant owner of inherited slaves and the principal author of the Declaration of Independence. But opposition from Southern delegates to the Continental Congress led to the exclusion of his antislavery paragraph from the document and the first of many compromises the Founders made on this issue alone. Even Jefferson agreed that establishing the Union was more important in July 1776 than waiting until every difference of opinion was resolved. Besides, he was among those who believed, if left alone, slavery would disappear from the new country on its own, as already had happened in other parts of the world.[5]

The problem of slavery may have been resolved in the Declaration of Independence, but satisfying all points of view during the writing of the Constitution was a far greater task. Eleven years had elapsed since 1776, the Southern plantation system was much more entrenched, and seeds of the antislavery, Abolition Movement were already underway. Thus the few weeks necessary to complete the Declaration of Independence paled in comparison to the nearly eighteen months required to write, rewrite, and ratify the constitution in all thirteen states. Naturally there were other problems to overcome during that lengthy ordeal. But neither the composition of the branches of government nor the balance of power between state and federal governments was as troublesome for the delegates to the Constitutional Convention as deciding how this new government would handle slavery.

Georgia delegate and Columbia County resident Abraham Baldwin, who had helped construct the famous legislative compromise, now faced a new challenge. In a prelude to the later practice of "gerrymandering"

205

perhaps,[6] Baldwin joined other Southern delegates in determining how the slave population would be factored into the number of people served by each member of the House of Representatives. By this time the convention had agreed there would be one representative for each 30,000 residents in that member's state,[7] but a problem arose when they disagreed on how this number should be derived. The slavery issue now took a critical turn.

As the property of their owners, slaves were neither citizens nor voters. Yet with ninety percent of all slaves living in the South by the time of the Revolutionary War,[8] and a majority of new immigrants settling in the Northern states, the South would be decidedly underrepresented in Congress unless slaves were counted, too. Besides, if there were fewer slaves in the North, Southern delegates feared it would not be long before the northern plurality in Congress overrode their wishes and simply outlawed slavery. On the other hand, with slaves numbering from a third to half the population of the South, neither were Northerners willing for the South to gain a congressional advantage by counting their slaves.

When Northern delegates did not want slaves counted at all and Southerners wanted them counted as whole persons, few delegates were interested in another compromise. Furthermore, a number of Northern delegates still wanted an article in the Constitution forbidding slavery altogether, while four Southern delegates, including Baldwin, vowed they would not sign a constitution that failed to offer some provision for including slaves in the population figures of their states.

Suggestions—and tempers—rose and fell, including an outburst by one Massachusetts delegate that if the South wanted to count their slave property, then the North should be allowed to count their horses and cows.[9]

Although a provision was included in the Constitution not to ban slave *importation and migration* for another twenty years,[10] banning slavery itself did not appear in the final document, nor would livestock ever be represented in the Congress of the United States. However, an ingenious method of slave representation did satisfy both the non-slaveholding states and those whose population was nearly as black as it was white.

Each state would be allowed to count three-fifths of her total number of slaves, a formula which, at the time, made congressional representation as nearly equal as possible in both Northern and Southern states.

It also must be said that while the morality of slavery continued to be debated on both sides of the ideological divide, slaves were always more plentiful where they were most needed. Large-scale agriculture was not as prevalent in the North as it was in the South, and slaves were thought to be most useful in an agricultural setting. As the South expanded her larger farms and plantations, the North built factories. Since Negroes were not considered skilled enough for factory work, Northern slave owners gradually sold their slaves or set them free. Free blacks also existed in the South, but their numbers and opportunities were noticeably less there than they were in the North.

Wherever they lived, however, free blacks were a category all their own. They may have been free from forced labor, but because of their race and local law they still were prevented from becoming citizens. Consequently, voting, owning property, holding public office, acquiring an education, and other rights granted automatically to the white population were denied the black man whether he was a slave or free. With some exceptions, such as those who had received training or education before 1829, when such bans were put in place,[11] a capable free black might become the manager of a restaurant or other establishment, but he could not be the owner.

Thus, rather than enjoy a higher social status than the slaves as we might expect, it was precisely because they were not slaves that free blacks rarely enjoyed security for their daily needs. Since slave owners were also likely to own places of employment, it was less expensive to assign laboring jobs to their slaves than to hire free blacks. Also, in addition to this obstacle, what jobs were available nearly always were offered to white workers before they were offered to them. Free blacks, Thurmond writes, "hovered between bondage and citizenship."[12]

But whether bond or free, like the immigrant immortalized at the base of the Statue of Liberty, the southern Negro "yearned to breathe free,"[13] totally free. History destroys the lore that the black man "knew his place," or that it was his natural condition to be subservient to the white man. The high percentage of both attempted and successful escapes disproves the theory that slaves were content with their lot. Yet it was because of this "yearning" that alternate forces beyond their control worked simultaneously either to grant them that freedom or, for as long as possible, to keep it from them.

Voluntary release by the slave owner and his own escape were not the only ways a slave could become free. Those with special skills—blacksmiths, brick masons, domestics, and the like—might be allowed to "hire out" and earn enough money to buy their freedom. This avenue, however, was only possible if both the slave owner and the state where he lived allowed it. Not all states did. By 1818, when a growing number of owners chose to free their slaves either by this method or upon their deaths, Georgia was among the states passing legislation to restrict the practice.[14]

Tense forces were at play. Southern slave owners, politicians, and all who saw their future tied to slave labor clashed not only with organized abolitionists, but also with a growing number of white citizens who, with or without slaves, believed with James Oglethorpe that slavery was both morally wrong and harmful to the Southern way of life. This latter group may have been the larger of the two, but the former wielded more power. In the end it was that powerful minority that held both the Negro and his white sympathizers hostage to a system neither was able to change.

Thus the Negro would bide his time, while remaining trapped in a growing conflict between those who fought to keep him enslaved and those who toiled to set him free. No dozen-year duration for this impasse, but decades of turmoil until a clash over conscience, economics, and states' rights accelerated toward America's second major war.

At the same time, and against overwhelming odds, a surprising number of former slaves and the formerly freed not only survived this era but prospered, and more than a few of those once thought unskilled and incapable of managing life on their own would make lasting contributions to their communities, including Columbia County. Following a discussion of the war that ended their slavery, we will meet some of them.

38

RUMBLINGS OF WAR

"Go down, Moses, way down in Egypt's land;
Tell old Pharaoh to let my people go!"

Just as James Oglethorpe had no idea his dream of a slave-free Georgia would one day come true, by 1860 neither did the state's more than 400,000 slaves know it would take a war to fulfill that same dream for them. Oglethorpe spent only a decade in Georgia, and died long before the slavery issue grew so contentious it nearly sliced America permanently in two. But thousands of Negroes, who had known nothing of freedom since their ancestors began arriving in the New World more than two centuries before, would soon be caught up in the pinnacle of that contention, the American Civil War.[15] Their freedom would come, but at a terrible cost to the slaves, their former owners, the Southern economy and undeniably the entire country.

In 1790, when Columbia County was born, one fourth of Georgia's population above Augusta were slaves. With the advent of the cotton gin in 1793, planters and small farmers alike poured into the Backcountry to take advantage of the area's fertile, piedmont soil and its most prolific crop, short staple cotton. Slaves poured in too, at two and three times the rate of the arriving whites. By 1830, after Columbia County's population had reached 12,606, barely 4,000 of those residents were white. More than 8,000 were black slaves.[16]

Understandably, with these statistics and the presence of the principal cotton market for the Georgia and South Carolina Backcountry in Augusta, area cotton production soared. Except for the local Quaker settlement and other abolitionists, a majority of Southern whites now accepted slavery. None of this economic success, they believed, would have been possible without slave labor. At the same time, if the proponents of slavery encountered opposition for their views, they became more passionate in their defense. Prominent leaders, including Crawfordville's Alexander Stephens (soon to be vice president of the Confederacy) and Governors George Gilmer and Howell Cobb, reminded their communities of long-standing reasons why slavery was an approved practice: "Subordination is the normal condition of the Negro. . . . Our fathers left this system to us; we've grown up with it. . . . The Negroes were slaves in Africa; we didn't make them that way. . . . We've created a bond between master and slave; we care for them like our own family."[17]

Some pro-slavery arguments included elevating the American slave from the despotism of his African roots, while others either reflected a growing hostility toward Northern factory owners who, it was rumored, treated their workers worse than Southerners treated slaves, or bordered on the divine. Besides the common view that the North did not need slaves in their more industrialized society, Gilmer once claimed the reason there are so few slaves in the North is that it's too cold there for the former Africans and, conversely, too hot in Southern cotton fields for former Europeans to perform such labor themselves. The outspoken governor also reminded his critics that "The Negroes of the South have had the Gospel preached to them . . . and they are now able to Christianize their countrymen."[18]

Gilmer's belief that, except for the climate and lack of need, the North would have had slaves too, and his calling attention to Southern efforts to provide for the slaves' spiritual welfare, contain more than a kernel of truth.

While the practice of slave *owning* in the Northern states may have been all but extinct by the middle of the nineteenth century, slave *trading*—or smuggling—continued to occur in the North long after the 1808 ban on slave importation and migration went into effect. Northerners also benefited from the Fugitive Slave Act of 1850. When everyone from federal marshals to ordinary citizens was required by law to return runaway slaves to their owners, the promise of generous rewards for their efforts attracted bounty hunters in the North as well as the South. With a prime field hand now valued at $1,800 and skilled craftsmen worth still more, capturing slaves could be a very lucrative business.

Furthermore, although both Northern anger and abolition activity increased as the Civil War drew near, it was often true that those who opposed slavery did not necessarily accept Negroes as neighbors or friends.[19] Southern cries of hypocrisy against the North also included Northern markets for Southern goods. For example, although Northern textile mills could have imported raw material from India or Great Britain, their owners chose profit over principle by purchasing less expensive Southern cotton, grown almost entirely by slaves. Historically speaking, the North may have had more "good guys" where slavery was concerned but, as these examples show, not all the "sins" of slavery occurred in the South.

Regarding Gilmer's argument that owners cared for the souls of their slaves as well as their bodies, who among us can hear an African-American "spiritual" today without sensing the religious nature of the former slaves? Whether this trait was inborn or the result of their owner's influence may be unclear, but it is known that worship, church attendance, and sacred singing played an important role in early American slave life.

We also know that, in addition to laws governing slaves, some regulations were directed toward the slave owner. Under one such rule, slaves could be made to work long hours every day of the week, except Sunday. That day was free time, family time and, almost universally, "church time." The slaves might worship in a courtyard near their cabins, gather inside a chapel built especially for them on plantation grounds, or sit in a reserved section of their owner's church. In the latter case, for many slaves in Columbia County that meeting place was Kiokee Baptist Church.

In their books on the history of Kiokee, James D. Mosteller and Waldo P. Harris III compiled detailed information on slave presence and participation in the life of this historic church.[20] Not surprisingly, the early buildings, including the still standing, two-hundred-year-old brick structure on Tubman Road in Appling, were built with slave labor. But it may be a surprise to learn that between the early nineteenth century and the Civil War, slaves outnumbered white members of this congregation by as much as six to one. The authors illustrate this ratio with their numbers for 1863 when, out of a membership of 215, 181 were black slaves, and only 34 were white.[21]

Stories abound of slave owners who were kind to their slaves and provided for them well. But when comparing even the best of slave circumstances to the ordinary lot of their white neighbors, no argument was strong enough to convince the slave or a growing number of white citizens in the North or South that the phrase "all men are created equal" applied only to the white man. From the Confederate guns that pounded Fort Sumter in April 1861, to Union General William T. Sherman's wide swath through Georgia nearly four years later, a terrible price was about to be paid to achieve that equality, and weld a fractured nation back together.

39

Caught in the Cross Fire

"It's me, it's me, it's me, O Lord,
Standing in the need of prayer."

War again? Barely eighty years after the American colonies fought a lengthy battle for independence from Great Britain? Was there no other way to settle the growing hostility between northern and southern states than this? We know the answers to these questions and grieve for our forebears who made the agonizing decision to return to the battlefield, sparing no cost to recapture what each envisioned that independence to mean.

With the election of Abraham Lincoln to the presidency in November 1860, and the presumption that long-festering issues of slavery and states' rights would now doom the South to the dictates of a largely Republican North, the possibility of seceding from the Union loomed high in discussions all across the South. Columbia County was well represented when talk turned to action, as delegates to Georgia's Secession Convention in Milledgeville on January 16, 1861, chose native son George W. Crawford to chair this important body. (Although Crawford lived in Augusta much of his adult life, he was a native and long-time resident of Columbia County.) Three days later Georgia voted 208 to 89 to secede from the

Union and in early February voted also to join six neighboring states in forming the Confederate States of America. After the Confederate attack on Fort Sumter the following April and Lincoln's call for Union arms in response, four additional states from the upper South joined the Confederacy. The dreaded, but expected, Civil War had begun.

Columbia County sent many sons into the fray. Thanks to the meticulous efforts of Thomas E. Holley, Civil War historian from Thomson, Georgia, we have a detailed record of three local infantry companies, including names, personal histories, time and field of service. We also learn who survived the war and who fell on the battlefield never to come home again. Brief excerpts from these records appear below, but the complete stories are available from the author or for reference in the Columbia County libraries.[22]

Thomson Guards: Company F

(Note: Thomson was part of Columbia County until McDuffie County was created in 1870.)

"Ruthless! Bloody War! The saddest of all evils . . . 'Tis writ upon the stern, solemn face of the warrior . . . 'Tis writ upon the sad countenance of mothers, wives . . . whose homes and hearts have been made desolate. How many of the brave and good—the noble—have fallen!"[23]

The guns of Fort Sumter had hardly ceased before Captain William Johnston declared his Thomson Guards "ready, willing and anxious to respond to the call of His Excellency [President of the Confederacy, Jefferson Davis] whenever the safety, liberty, and defense of their Country require their services."[24] On May 29, 1861, 104 planters, overseers, merchants and their sons left Thomson, Georgia, for that "call" in Richmond, Virginia. On June 3, the tightly-knit, hometown group became Company F of the Tenth Infantry Regiment of Georgia Volunteers. By war's end a total of 128 men, including twenty sets of brothers, would participate under this banner in the major battles of the war.

Today the "Guards'" muster roll reads like a local phone book, their memories living on in families such as Blanchard, Cliatt, Fitzgerald,

Holley, Morris, Neal, Paschal, Prather, Reese, Reeves, Smith, Stovall, Sturgis, and many more.

Ramsey Volunteers: Company K

The popular Isaac Ramsey, who spent one term in the Georgia Legislature before coming home to serve his county as sheriff or sheriff's deputy for the next twenty years, is thought to be the source behind the naming of this group of Civil War soldiers from Columbia County. With the Thomson Guards already on the battlefield, Captain Robert Joshua Boyd set up four recruiting stations around the county in July 1861 to organize another company of local men for the Southern cause.

Sons or grandsons of Revolutionary War patriots, including twelve sets of brothers and three father-son groups, were among the eighty-one men who left for Virginia in August 1861—the oldest nearing fifty, the youngest barely in their teens. By September another twenty-one had joined their fellow Volunteers, now known as Company K of the Sixteenth Georgia Infantry Regiment. Their commander, former Governor Howell Cobb, was promoted from colonel to brigadier general the following year.

Four years later Captain Boyd was among the forty-three members of Company K who either died in battle or succumbed to wounds or disease, leaving fifteen widows and forty-eight children behind. General Cobb survived the war, but his brother, General Thomas R. R. Cobb, lost his life at the Battle of Fredericksburg and is memorialized to this day on the Civil War Monument in Augusta.

Hamilton Rangers: Company K

Captain Thomas James Hamilton and the men who formed a third infantry company from Columbia County did not volunteer their services until the conflict was nearing its second year. They may have been among those who believed the war would be swift and victorious without them. But as time and battles raged on, they were part of that second wave willing to join their brothers in a conflict each wanted desperately to win.

Like the Thomson Guards, this group also lived in the southwestern corner of the county, but unlike either the Guards or the Ramsey Volunteers, the Hamilton Rangers tended to be older, more settled in their life's work, and members of some of the county's most prominent families. In fact, Captain Hamilton and his wife paid for all the equipment needed by most of the new recruits who left for Richmond in May 1862. Judging from the Hamilton story, the phrase heard frequently throughout the South that they were engaged in "a rich man's war and a poor man's fight" did not always apply. Some men of means were just as willing to join the "fight," as they were to finance the "war." As part of the Forty-eighth Georgia Infantry Regiment of General Ambrose Wright's Brigade in the Army of Northern Virginia, Company K took part in some of the fiercest battles of the war.

The accolades and casualty lists for Company K were equally high. In his report following the Chancellorsville Campaign in May 1863, General Wright wrote this about the Forty-eighth Georgia: "I cannot . . . close my brief report without expressing my highest admiration for [their] splendid conduct during this eventful week. No man ever led better or braver soldiers. [They] acted with distinguished coolness and courage, driving a vastly superior force of the Yankees for nearly a mile . . . until receiving orders from me to halt."[25]

Of the 131 Rangers who participated in the war, twenty-six were killed in action and twenty more died of wounds or disease. Only twenty-three answered the muster roll during surrender ceremonies at Appomattox Court House on April 9, 1865, and a total of seventeen wives and forty children would never see their husbands or fathers again.

Although he did not die on the battlefield, Captain Hamilton was another casualty of the war. Suffering repeatedly from a lung ailment, the man who had assembled and financed Company K was forced to give up his commission on May 10, 1863, just one year after he and his Rangers began to fight. The company's leading soldier must have wished his body were as strong as his determination to serve his country.

Hamilton succumbed to his illness on October 12, 1867. He was forty-three years old.

Another Civil War record with a local connection has been compiled by Columbia County native Jean Lewis Morris, whose mother Harriet Tiller Lewis and uncles William R. Tiller and Traylor A. Tiller have been lifelong residents of Evans.

"The Civil War Encounters of Gus and Tom" is a fascinating, personal memorial to Mrs. Morris' great, great grandfather—and the Tillers' great grandfather—Augustus ("Gus") Abner Traylor and his brother Thomas ("Tom"), two of five Traylor brothers from Abbeville, South Carolina, who served in the war. Gus and Tom were members of the Seventh Infantry Regiment of South Carolina, which was attached to the Army of Northern Virginia under General Robert E. Lee. Material for this memoir was gleaned from letters the brothers wrote home during the war.

The most poignant part of the brothers' story began on the first day of the Battle of Gettysburg, when Tom received the wound that would end his life one week later. Gus found shelter in a nearby barn where, for a few days, he nursed his wounded brother. Sadly, Gus was captured by Union soldiers and taken to a New York prison two days before Tom died. It would be months before Gus was returned to his company, and perhaps that long before he learned of his brother's fate. Gus was the only one of the five Traylor brothers to survive the war.

One more Columbia County war story reveals the contribution of yet another native son, Henry Lewis Benning, great grandson of the county's celebrated centenarian, Thomas Cobb, and cousin of generals Howell Cobb and Thomas R. R. Cobb. The Benning family later moved to Columbus, Georgia, where, after graduating from Franklin College (U.G.A. today), Henry became a noted attorney, member of the Georgia Supreme Court, and avid secessionist. Following Georgia's secession from the Union and the likelihood of war, he invested heavily in bonds and other financial programs to raise capital for the Confederacy.

Benning, however, would do more than support the war effort with his purse. Before long he was raising his own regiment with the same fervor he had displayed as a court attorney, even to offering his life for a cause that had become his own. In August 1861 now Colonel Benning and his Seventeenth Georgia Infantry Regiment became part of Robert Toombs's Brigade in the Right Wing of the Army of Northern Virginia. Following the Battle of Antietam in 1862, the colonel was promoted to brigadier general and nicknamed "Old Rock" for his courage.[26]

After the war Benning returned to Columbus and resumed his legal career. In October 1918 the "Home of the Infantry" and one of the busiest military bases in the country was established there, and named Fort Benning after him.

There were no "muster rolls" recording names of the county's black sons who contributed to the war effort, but their presence was well known. Before 1863 Negroes could be found in both the Confederate and Union armies, not as soldiers because there had been a federal statute against arming free blacks or slaves since 1792, but as cooks, drivers, and blacksmiths, or laborers to build and maintain military fortifications.[27] With so many Southern white men at war, however, far more slaves were left behind to continue the work of the plantation and care for the owner's family. But after 1862, what happened to the slaves directly affected the progress of the war.

From the beginning of his preelection campaign to the summer of 1862, candidate and then President Lincoln had promised not to ban slavery in any state where the practice still existed. But with the war taking its toll in time and casualties, pressure mounted from Congress and the public for Lincoln to rethink his position on slavery. Thus, following lengthy consultations with Congress and his advisers, the president issued his historic Emancipation Proclamation, declaring all slaves in states still in rebellion on January 1, 1863, "then, thenceforward, and forever free."[28]

As difficult as this decision was for the affected states to understand, the president was within his constitutional rights as military commander-in-chief both to confiscate his enemy's property and to cripple his ability to wage war. Freeing the slaves robbed the Confederacy of its prime labor force to generate income at home or supply men and matériel for the war. At the same time, following passage of an act repealing the 1792 law against arming Negroes, some of that labor force became a military advantage for the Union.

In continued defiance of orders from President Lincoln and a government they no longer considered their own, not every slave owner obeyed this proclamation. Neither did all slaves leave the plantation even when the order was obeyed. But of those who did take advantage of their new-found freedom, an estimated 93,000 enlisted in the Union Army and fought against the masters they once served. By war's end 186,000 former slaves and free blacks in both the North and the South would fight for the Union, and 38,000 would die.[29]

At no time was this exodus from the plantations more apparent in Georgia than during the final months of the war when thousands of former slaves and their families fell in line behind General Sherman's "march to the sea." It also must be noted that this particular manpower shift was not encouraged by Sherman or his Union forces. They had a war to fight, not a humanitarian mission to carry out. If anything, the added burden of all those extra bodies to care for robbed Sherman of the provisions needed for his men and slowed the primary mission down.

To solve this dilemma for both the general and the former slaves, shortly after the fall of Savannah in December 1864, and before the entourage could follow his march northward through the Carolinas, Sherman issued "Special Field Order 15," the infamous decision known to this day as, "Forty Acres and a Mule." With the approval of Secretary Edwin Stanton of the War Department, and the availability of confiscated land nearby, Sherman provided a fresh start for a group of people who had never before had any "acre" to call their own.[30]

Three months later the war was over, President Lincoln had been assassinated, and some twenty-thousand former slaves were marking their forty-acre plots all across the Sea Island land or along the Georgia, Carolina, and Florida coast.[31] But the euphoria the freedmen (former slaves) called their "Day of Jubilee"[32] would be short-lived. Along with their Southern masters and white neighbors, they were about to experience a nightmare which for many would out-peril the war, and last much longer than the four-year conflict just past.

The freedmen were not the only ones caught in the cross fire. The war may have been largely about them and about the right of the Southern plantation society to enslave them. But more than a military loss or a political defeat, an entire way of life had been laid waste for white Southerners, too. Historians call this period "Reconstruction." Along with well-documented negatives of the era, however, great efforts were begun to turn that tragic era into a time of hope and recovery on both sides of the racial aisle.

40

RECONSTRUCTION: THE LONG JOURNEY
TO FREEDOM AND RECOVERY

"There is a balm in Gilead to make the wounded whole;
There is a balm in Gilead, to heal the sin-sick soul."

Only a blissful Pollyanna could have expected life to return to normal as soon as the guns of war lay silent in April 1865. Fighting may have ended on the battlefield, but much of the hostility that led to combat in the first place would wage on in the hearts of those whose lives had been so painfully altered by the previous four years. To the detriment of both the freedmen and the white South, that hostility also waged on in the halls of government in Washington, D.C.

President Lincoln had a reconstruction plan, but he would not live to carry it out. Newly inaugurated Andrew Johnson had a plan too, as did Congress, who not only disagreed with the former vice-president but also with each other. We cannot know if Lincoln's goal of healing the nation's wounds "with malice toward none and charity for all"[33] could have spared the country much of the suffering that followed the war. But events occurring just prior to this historic moment contributed to a less than charitable result.

It is difficult to say whether the unsilenced gun of John Wilkes Booth or the elevation of Andrew Johnson to the presidency had the greater effect on post–Civil War America. Booth defied both civil law and the rules of military engagement when he assassinated Lincoln five days after the war ended, while Republican strategists hoping to guarantee victory in the most recent presidential election had placed politics above persona by choosing pro-Union, Southern *Democrat* Johnson as Lincoln's running mate in 1864. Neither the assassin nor the maneuvering politicians could have imagined the consequences of their decisions. Booth silenced "the best friend the South ever had," General Sherman told a woman cheering Lincoln's death,[34] and the cantankerous relationship between Johnson and the so-called "Radical Republicans" in Congress would markedly hinder any effective plan for Southern recovery.

At first the former Confederates rejoiced over their presumed ally in the White House. But when it became apparent Johnson did not share Lincoln's philosophy of "malice toward none," their joy quickly faded. Johnson may have sympathized with his fellow Southerners to the point of planning for their quick readmission to the Union, but they may not have known about his long-standing resentment of the slaveholders—not because he was against slavery, but because he was a man of moderate means who could not afford slaves.[35]

At least the Confederate *military* could thank their former adversaries, Generals Grant and Sherman, for the leniency they received from an angry president and the members of Congress who shared his view. For example, when a federal grand jury indicted General Robert E. Lee and others for treason, and Johnson ordered Grant to carry out the arrests, the furious general threatened to resign rather than obey what he considered a misguided command. Parole for Confederate military leaders had been part of the terms of surrender, Grant reminded the president, adding that without such a guarantee Lee would not have surrendered and the war would have continued much longer.[36]

Reluctantly the president agreed. Except for modest prison sentences for former President Jefferson Davis, Vice President Alexander Stephens, and Georgia Governor Joseph Brown, few other Confederate leaders received court-ordered punishment for their roles in the just completed war.[37]

It was no secret that Johnson also had little love for the freedmen, as evidenced by such statements as, "This country is for the white men and . . . as long as I am President it shall be governed by white men."[38] Johnson also vetoed much of the legislation designed to aid the freedmen, including rescinding Sherman's much celebrated "Special Field Order 15."[39]

Besides absolving the former Confederates of further punishment, and in a likely concession to his Southern counterparts, President Johnson's amnesty order on May 29, 1865, restored all confiscated Southern lands to their former owners. Since many of the freedmen had already planted crops on the land they thought they owned, the order gave them until the end of the year to leave their farms or be forcibly removed. But long before eviction notices could arrive, thousands of disillusioned freedmen abandoned their crops, packed their meager belongings, and took to the road in search of a new place to belong.

The displaced freedmen were not the only ones who needed assistance. With their property in disarray, Confederate dollars worthless, and three-quarters of their wealth—including $3 million in slaves—gone, destitute planters also were in need of help.[40] No matter how controversial or misguided their attempts, the federal government would spend the bulk of the next five years trying to meet these immense needs for the entire South.

Groundwork for a benevolent organization to ease postwar problems for the freedmen began with a commission created by the War Department soon after Emancipation in 1863. Commission members traveled throughout the South gathering information from both blacks and whites, and presented their report to Congress well before the end of the war. Prompted by repeated requests from the former slaves for land of their own, in addition to food, clothing, and other necessities, commission recommendations included the land confiscation and redistribution idea behind Sherman's resettlement plan. The commission's strongest advice, however, was that whatever plan emerged be temporary. Encouraging the freedmen to become self-reliant as quickly as possible, they said, should be everyone's goal. Optimistic commissioners recommended such a plan last no longer than a year.[41]

Following months of contentious discussion, and the decision to aid Southern white refugees as well as the freedmen, Congress enacted the Bureau of Refugees, Freedmen, and Abandoned Lands (commonly known as the Freedmen's Bureau) in March 1865. Both the initial act to establish the bureau and subsequent bills to renew or adopt further reconstruction legislation would also be passed by Congress, but only after overriding President Johnson's ever-present veto. Many historians suggest that much of the failure of postwar reconstruction can be laid at the feet of an unsympathetic president and the Congress who couldn't bear to follow his lead.[42]

To some degree that failure must be shared by those the bureau was created to help. No matter how many times the freedmen were urged to seek work, even to going back to the plantations as workers earning their own income, some lacked the will to follow these suggestions or walk that self-reliant road. Thus, like falling dominoes, the more the freedmen failed to help themselves, the more white Southerners lacked the desire to assist them. Neither did it take much of that presumed idle behavior to reinforce generations of Southern thinking that the black race was inferior to the white.

But without education or experience in managing their own lives, the freedmen were facing a future as unfamiliar to them as were poverty and uncertainty to their former owners. What did a people whose entire lives had been controlled by someone else know of labor contracts, money management, or even making simple decisions on their own? These were but a few of the problems facing the former slaves—and a succession of understaffed and underfunded Freedmen's Bureau employees whose task was equally new to them.

Much has been written about the agonies of reconstruction for both the black and white South, and volumes exist with anecdotes and analysis from every possible point of view. We read of postwar military occupation by a federal government unsympathetic to the Southern plight; of newly arriving "carpetbaggers" thought to be Northern opportunists dictating their "ways" on the South or lining their pockets with the misfortune of others; and of Southern "scalawags," whose motives were questioned when they cooperated with educators, missionaries, and other benefactors from the North.

Armed with their own ideas of rights and freedom, these traditionally incompatible groups of people approached this complicated period with three distinct points of view: whites to cling to the social and economic status of the past, blacks to pursue their long-held dreams of freedom, and the primarily Northern "intruders," whose stated desire was only to help one side or the other through the reconstruction phase. In short, while each group may be complimented for its effort and intent, everyone was suspicious of everybody else.

Considering all these hurdles, the surprise is not that the conflict would continue off the battlefield, either among those leading the reconstruction or within the families and communities needing aid, but that there could be any postwar recovery at all. But, in time, there was! Between improving efforts by government and benevolent agencies to help, and a growing determination by the displaced to create opportunities for themselves, signs of that recovery may be seen throughout Columbia County to this day. In some cases, because of the scarcity of published records, we learn those stories from the descendants they left behind.

41

A Place of Their Own

"I looked over Jordan, and what did I see?
A band of angels coming after me,
Coming for to carry me home."

Much like the settlers of a new county who were on their own in 1790, now another group of people were essentially beginning their lives again. But Columbia County's newly independent African-American population would have more difficulty making that new start than did their white counterparts seventy-five years before.

Should they go back to the plantation and work for wages rather than servitude, as the Freedmen's Bureau and their own leaders urged them to do? Some would do just that, while others were afraid to follow this advice lest they continue to be treated like slaves. Despite repeated assurance that they now could leave their new jobs if they wished, many of the freedmen chose an uncertain future over what might have been a return to the familiar past.

The planters faced decisions too. Between war casualties, loss of capital, devastation, and devaluation of their property, it was difficult now for anyone to "go back home." Even plantations with minimal war damage could not be maintained without funds for labor and supplies. Sometimes the only solution for a once-prosperous planter was to divide his land into sections and rent the smaller parcels to those willing to work in exchange for food on their tables and a roof over their heads. These reorganized lands then offered new opportunities for both recovering whites and newly independent blacks.

Sharecropping and tenant farming, as these new systems were called, became a compromise between the freedmen's desire for land of their own and the planters' need for labor.[43] While the owner supplied a house and farmland in either case, sharecroppers were also given tools and livestock for working the land plus the privilege of purchasing necessary provisions on credit. All their expenses were then repaid with a "share" of their crops at harvest time. Tenant farmers, who we might say had reached "economic level two," supplied their own animals and equipment, but they too paid for their house, land, and supplies with proceeds from their crops at the end of the growing season. Both arrangements allowed motivated freedmen to return to the only occupation they had ever known, while maintaining some measure of independence from the former plantation system.

As fine as these plans may sound, neither sharecropping nor tenant farming was an automatic pathway to success. Crop failures, inattention to duty, or more accumulated expense than the proceeds of their harvest could repay frequently kept these renter-farmers in perpetual debt. Depending on the mercy of the landowner, the industry of the freedman, or both, some were able to live with their indebtedness while others faced eviction or left voluntarily to seek another line of work.

Still, just as land ownership represented the pinnacle of success for early white settlers, some of the freedmen were now in a position to pursue that higher goal. But it wouldn't be easy. Racial prejudice, neither surrendered at Appomattox[44] nor yielded with ratification of the thirteenth, fourteenth, and fifteenth Amendments to the U.S. Constitution—commonly called "the Negro's Bill of Rights"—would keep the black race socially enslaved for another century.

Consequently, the freedmen found it difficult to find white landowners who would sell to them. If they needed financial help to make such a purchase, it was harder still to find an individual or a bank willing to grant them a loan. Also, those who were able to secure funds often lost their property by failing to pay their loans or taxes on time. According to oral history, such losses were due as much to vague or dishonest loan agreements as they were to default by the debtor.[45] Simply put, in such cases, the frequently illiterate buyers may have been little match for the more sophisticated sellers, who kept all the records themselves.

A fortunate few, however, did receive property either by their own initiative or through inheritance, the latter most likely either from a free black who previously owned the land or from an appreciative former slave owner. Confederate Vice President Alexander Stephens, for example, allowed his slaves to live freely on his land following emancipation and to acquire the property upon his death.[46]

William Sanders, father of Harlem resident Mary Sanders, was one late nineteenth-century freedman who, perhaps from family example or initial inheritance, overcame all obstacles and acquired more than two-hundred acres of land in the Lamkin Grove (also spelled Lampkin) section of Columbia County. Judging by the bundle of fragile, yellowed deeds, contracts, and receipts still in his daughter's possession, Sanders was quite the businessman. He bought numerous parcels of land, often from the Georgia Railroad Company or at an estate sale, or from willing individuals with confidence in a man with a proven record of paying his bills. Sanders also was a shrewd cotton farmer who stored his crop in a nearby Augusta warehouse each fall, and sold it in the spring when it would bring a higher price.

But Sanders was more than a farmer. About the time he married Mary's mother, Lurelia, and perhaps as a wedding gift for her, he cut timber from his own property to build a handsome, still-standing house on South Bell Street in Harlem to be nearer the center of town. He also served as deacon and treasurer of New Holt Baptist Church and in 1909 helped establish the first school for black children in Harlem. His wife, who had attended Augusta's Haines Normal School in Augusta (now Lucy Laney High School), would later teach at the new Harlem school.

Mary Sanders, teacher. Courtesy *Columbia County News-Times*.

Although there is scant information about the level of their own schooling, William and Lurelia Sanders' interest in education must have been the inspiration behind their daughter's lifelong career as a Columbia County educator. After graduating from Pollard Academy, a later Harlem school named for the prominent black carpenter Bertha Bailey Pollard, who helped build the 1909 school,[47] Mary Sanders also became a schoolteacher.[48] Her own education continued piecemeal, course by course and summer by summer, until she met state requirements to teach in the county's new consolidated schools in the 1950's. A decade later, she also was one of the first black principals in the county's newly integrated schools.

After teaching for more than half a century, Mary Sanders still was not finished with education or walking in her parents' footsteps.

Following her retirement in 1998, she became the first black member of the Columbia County Board of Education.

Perry Dunn had little education, but with the examples of his tenant-farming father and grandfather, the man born in the midst of the country's great depression gained enough "learning" to become a lifelong asset to his family and community. Like the Sanders family, the Dunns also settled in Lamkin Grove, where Perry's grandparents worked for Dr. Pierce Gordon Blanchard, father of future Columbia County School Superintendent John Pierce Blanchard. Members of the Dunn family lived in the vicinity of Old Clanton, Tubman, and Euchee Creek roads for more than half a century.

Perry was not much of a farmer—or student. He quit attending Mt. Olive School when he turned fourteen, the same year he received his driver's license and three years after he started "hanging around" his cousin's auto repair shop. He not only knew how to drive a car by then—well enough to convince a friendly state trooper to "forget" he was under age—but he could repair it too.

Fourteen was a magic age for Perry Dunn. That was the year he held his first job at an Augusta dry goods store—and the age of his wife Alice when they married three years later. But before the seventeen-year-old groom took his marriage vows, he had already transferred from the dry goods store to the Augusta Arsenal garage, and a job more suited to the skills he had begun acquiring at age eleven. He would not remain long at the arsenal, but a contact made there would open doors for the industrious young man for much of his life.

Martinez resident Hartwell Morris, Sr., was Perry's supervisor at the arsenal until 1950, when he resigned to open a supermarket and service station at the corner of Berckman and Washington roads in Augusta. Perry not only left with Morris, but before long he had become the manager of the service station. He was barely out of his teens.

Seven years later, when Morris built a new supermarket without a service station in Martinez, Perry and his employer parted ways—but not completely. Friends as well as working partners, whenever Perry stopped by the new store to visit, he recalls, "There was always something for me to do." He ran errands, delivered groceries, fixed whatever needed fixing, and drove the Morris children to school each day. But he was more than a handyman and chauffeur: he was part of the family. When Mr. Morris' father, Howard Morris, died during the still socially segregated days of 1955, Perry drove the grandchildren to his funeral and, at the family's insistence, sat with them in the reserved section of the church.

Working part-time for the Morris family, however, was not all Perry did after their service station closed. He took on another full-time job at the Elliott Reese Garage in the National Hills section of Augusta, worked there as a mechanic for fifteen years, and bought the business when the owner retired in 1972. By the time Perry retired in 1994, he was a master mechanic, and he had been servicing cars for more than fifty years.

Today Perry and Alice live in an attractive home on Washington Road in Evans, not far from the old family neighborhood of Lamkin Grove or Mount Olive Baptist Church, where they have been active ever since they moved back to Columbia County in the late 1950's. They are still friends of the Morris family and the descendants of Dr. Blanchard, Perry's grandfather's first employer. Their four children come "home" to visit every Sunday, and Perry now serves as chauffeur for his own grandchildren. We should not be surprised if "Grandpa" also fixes their cars.

Before the era of motor vehicles, options were still available for freedmen who did not want to sharecrop, tenant farm, or till their own land. Skilled blacksmiths, carpenters, brick masons, midwives, even barbers and former house servants were as much in demand after emancipation as they were before. Some freedmen, however, combined farming with their particular skill and became more successful than those with only one way to make a living.

The following item, which appeared in the *Augusta Chronicle* on January 31, 1866, is as much an advertisement *about* the writers as it is a definition of their skills: "We are prepared to do all manner of wood and iron work, wagon making and repairing included. We have not turned fools because we are free, but know we have to work for our living and are determined to do it. We mean to be sober, industrious, honest, and respectful to white folks, and so we depend on them to give us work." The ad is signed "William and Jim, Colored, one a blacksmith, the other a carpenter, and both living in Appling, Georgia."[49]

Robin Allen was a blacksmith on the Appling plantation of John Tyler Allen—and the likely father-in-law of Harriet Allen, the legendary former slave who is believed to have lived in parts of three centuries (1798–1906) and is buried in a well-marked grave off Scott's Ferry Road. During slavery, Robin and his wife lived on separate plantations. Although their son Washington Allen lived with his mother before his own marriage, he still may have been allowed to learn blacksmithing from his father. At some point, either as a free black or a trusted slave, Robin established his own shop, where he plied several trades in addition to blacksmithing. Upon Robin's death, his shop and business clientele became the responsibility of his son.

Robin Allen's legacy and his son's willingness to carry on his father's work made it possible for Washington and Harriet Allen to become that rare nineteenth-century black couple to earn the respect of both the black and white community.[50]

As inspiring as the above examples might be, it would take more than Northern missionaries, the Freedmen's Bureau, or personal incentive to generate large-scale progress for African-Americans in those early decades following emancipation. Collectively they faced added pressure from "Black Codes," a set of laws enacted by state governments across the post-war South ostensibly for the freedmen's protection, but often little more than a thinly disguised warning that "they never adopt the fatal delusion of social and political equality" with the white race.[51] The freedmen also were subject to rising threats by the vigilante group known as the Ku Klux Klan to drive that warning home. Thus, before these success stories spread from the individual family to the wider community, it would take education and it would take the church.

Meanwhile, if obstacles, injustice, and other barriers to success had been the only picture of life for the freedmen during the latter third of the nineteenth century, there might not be a thriving African-American presence in Columbia County—or anywhere else in America—today. But here and there, both within the black community and out of the hearts of concerned whites, the long process of elevating these once dependent people to prosperity and independence began to appear. In some cases the groundwork had been laid generations before.

42

LEARNING, EMERGING—TOGETHER

"Lift every voice and sing till earth and heaven ring,
Ring with the harmonies of liberty;
Let our rejoicing rise high as the listening skies,
Let it resound loud as the rolling sea. . . ."

—James Weldon Johnson[52]

Much is already known about Daniel Marshall, founder and first pastor of Kiokee Baptist Church in Appling, but this celebrated eighteenth-century preacher was not the only Columbia County Marshall to leave an important spiritual legacy. Possibly, the achievements of Daniel's son, Abraham Marshall, were even greater than his own.[53]

By establishing the first permanent Baptist presence in Georgia, Daniel Marshall helped lay the foundation for the largest Protestant denomination in America today, the Southern Baptist Convention. A generation later, however, Abraham Marshall was instrumental in forming more than three dozen churches, including Springfield Baptist Church in Augusta, the first continuing independent black church of any Christian denomination in America.[54]

Of all Daniel Marshall's ten children, eldest son Abraham was the most ardent follower in his father's footsteps. Though he had little formal schooling, Abraham's grandson once wrote, "his unquenchable zeal in his Master's service compensated for any educational deficiencies."[55] Besides serving from 1784 to 1819 as Kiokee's second pastor, Abraham's vision included preaching, planting new churches, and ordaining pastors "in all directions from his home."[56]

While visiting in nearby Silver Bluff, South Carolina, Abraham Marshall made the acquaintance of Jesse Galphin and a group of Negro Christians who had been meeting there since 1773. Galphin was likely a nominal slave who had earned the freedom to travel away from his Silver Bluff home. He also had been ordained to the ministry by a fellow black preacher. The Galphin connection fostered Marshall's interest in establishing Negro churches, specifically those that could exist without the customary supervision of white pastors or congregations. It also explains why Marshall accompanied Galphin to Savannah in 1788 to ordain Andrew Bryan, the black pastor who founded that city's First African Baptist Church.

Not long after the Savannah excursion, perhaps because his owner had moved across the river to Augusta, Galphin and his Silver Bluff flock began meeting in the Georgia city, too. This was the group that became the nucleus of a church constituted by Abraham Marshall and Elder David Tinsley in 1793, in the section of Augusta known at the time as Springfield.[57]

For more than two hundred years the still active Springfield Baptist Church has reaped a remarkable harvest within the African-American community, especially in the fields of religion and education. Most of Augusta's older black churches are considered "daughters" of Springfield, and much of the foundation for area black education is tied to this historic church. In addition to promoting schools for younger children, with assistance from Augusta's First Baptist Church, the first black school of higher education was established in 1867 with thirty-seven students at Springfield Baptist Church.

Hardly a decade passed before some 250 students had attended this school—by then called Augusta Institute—and studied subjects as

235

varied as basic reading skills, advanced mathematics, philosophy, and the ancient languages of Latin and Greek. The school moved to Atlanta in 1879 and continued operation under the new name of Atlanta Baptist Institute. In 1913 the name was changed again, this time to Morehouse College, known to this day for producing scores of nationally prominent African-American leaders, including civil rights leader and Nobel Peace Prize winner, Martin Luther King, Jr.

As if by divine intervention, about the time the first school of higher education for black students moved to Atlanta, a proposal to establish another such school in Augusta began to take root. Once again we see the growing bonds between education and the church, and between black and white community leaders who shared the same concerns.

The idea for a local college to train African-American teachers and preachers was the brainchild of Lucius Henry Holsey, bishop of an alliance of black churches then called the Colored Methodist Episcopal Church (usually called the CME Church, even after the word "Colored" was changed to "Christian"). Much like area Baptist leaders who helped guide Springfield Baptist and Augusta Institute into existence, the CME Church received support from the Methodist Episcopal Church South (MECS), forerunner of today's United Methodist Church, for a similar, dual-ministry role.

Holsey, a former slave who had displayed a passion for educating members of his race ever since he taught himself to read while it was illegal for others to teach him, first voiced the higher education idea in 1869. But when Augusta Institute left the city scarcely ten years later, leaders from both black and white Methodist churches felt an urgency to act on Holsey's request. Thus, in 1882 three trustees from each group of churches met in Augusta to establish Paine Institute, named for MECS Bishop Robert Paine, who helped organize the CME Church. Two years later, classes at the newly incorporated school began meeting in rented quarters in downtown Augusta. With continued interest and financial assistance from both the local and national MECS, Paine was able to move to its current, Fifteenth Street location in 1886.

Because there were no public secondary schools for area black students at the time, Paine began with a high school component and added a college program as those early students created the need. The school's first four-year degrees were granted in 1901, and two years later Paine Institute became Paine College. The high school remained on campus, however, until the first public secondary school for black students opened in Augusta in 1945.

Paine Institute and Haines Normal School, the previously mentioned private secondary school in Augusta founded by prominent black educator Lucy Laney—with help from the Presbyterian Board of Missions, another example of white support for black schools[58]—were also open to interested Columbia County students. Since there were no public schools in Columbia County for black children of any age before the middle decades of the twentieth century, without these two Richmond County schools one wonders where teachers could have been found to satisfy the expressed need of African-American parents to educate their children. If not by divine intervention this time, then certainly with the efforts of succeeding generations of divinely inspired pastors along with those newly educated, prospective teachers, the desire these families shared with Bishop Holsey to educate members of their own race was fulfilled.

To see an example of early black education in Columbia County, we need only drive to the center of Appling and visit the small, weathered building across the street from the courthouse, not far from the latter, twentieth-century office of the Board of Education. Walnut Grove School, which the Columbia County Historical Society moved, refurbished, and maintains for public display, was one of about thirty one-room elementary schools in use for black children prior to the opening of the county's first "separate but equal" consolidated schools in 1956. These schools were usually located on or near the property of a church with the same name and, prior to state-standardized education and county-levied school taxes, erected and maintained by that neighbor church. Walnut Grove School, for example, was located beside Walnut Grove Baptist church, four miles north of Appling on Ray Owens Road. When this school first appeared in the county superintendent's report in 1932, the building was valued at $1,000 and served the needs of one teacher earning $100 a year to teach forty students in five different grades.

Sarah Washington, who began teaching immediately after she finished high school in 1934, describes her early experience in a similar, one-room school: "Those schools weren't the nice, sealed-up buildings with nice walls and nice floors like we have today. Maybe there were a few windows and a door, but there were cracks everywhere. You could look out and see everything from the sun to the stars through the walls and the roof."[59]

On cold days a stove in the middle of the room compensated for those cracked walls—as long as a parent or trustee remembered to bring in a wagonload of wood. When that did not happen, Sarah recalls, "I had to stop class early in the afternoon and take the students out into the woods to break off limbs so we could keep warm." Teachers had to be equally inventive when it came to the school's nonexistent plumbing.

"The trustees bought us a shiny new bucket and dipper at the beginning of each year, and the students took turns going out to the well or spring every morning to bring in fresh water. And when we needed to go to the restroom, everyone just went outside in a different direction."

Not only were the buildings in primitive condition, but they were virtually empty of furnishings and supplies. "There were no desks, no books, no blackboards, no chalk, not even a teacher's desk—until I bought my own from a pile of junk for a dollar. Before the state stepped in and gave us free books, we teachers had to come up with teaching materials the best way we could. If a parent could afford it, a child would come to school with a five-cent tablet. Otherwise, we would use the back of a letter or the other side of a calendar sheet when we tore it off. Any blank piece of paper would do."

Walnut Grove or its counterpart was the only school experience most black children at that time would ever have. Poverty and lack of transportation often prevented traveling to Augusta to further their education. Sarah Washington was a fortunate exception. Her family had friends in

Augusta, where she could board while attending Haines Normal School. She also had the example of her mother, Belle Avery, who attended Haines before she did, and was the only elementary schoolteacher Sarah ever had.

But even with poor facilities, sporadic attendance and, by today's standards, ill-equipped teachers, Sarah looks at the positives of that educational era: "You felt you were doing something good. We taught children to read, spell, write and do math, and we did it in only four or five months a year. If you got a good high school education and had common sense, you were able to do that."

Like her friend and fellow teacher, Mary Sanders, Sarah completed her college education one course or a summer at a time. During the 1960's she also became the first black principal of an integrated, county school. By the time she retired in 1979, Sarah Washington had been the principal of three different elementary schools in Evans and Martinez, and served the students of Columbia County as a teacher or administrator for forty-five years.

If there were thirty small, black schools in Columbia County between emancipation and integration, at least that many black churches existed here during the same period of time. Not all the churches survived beyond their early years, and new congregations emerged following population shifts and changing ideas on church management or belief. But just as worship was the social center of life for the slaves, so the church continued to be the dominant gathering place and support system for the independent black community.

Stories abound of the origin and ministry of New Holt, the two Mt. Moriahs, 1st and 2nd Mt. Carmel, Mt. Olive, Mt. Enon, Lamkin Grove, and other congregations still precious to the families whose ancestors established the church where they have worshipped for a lifetime. But like individual families and societies within the white community of that era, single black churches were not usually successful unless they too were part of a group designed to strengthen and support the individual congregation.

Thus, by the late 1880's, and primarily through a grouping together of their churches, African-Americans began forming burial or benevolent societies to aid each other financially and emotionally during the more difficult circumstances of life. To sustain such a society, members might pay a fee of 25 to 35 cents a month to belong, which entitled the family to burial and other emergency expenses when that member died.[60]

If this idea sounds like the forerunner of the life insurance industry for African-Americans, it was. In 1898, for example, the concept inspired an enterprising pair of black Richmond County brothers, Solomon and Thomas J. Walker, their pastor and friends, to form the Pilgrim Benevolent Society, later known as the Pilgrim Health and Life Insurance Company. Not only was this endeavor a boon for Augusta-area black clients and employees alike, but it was the first black-owned insurance provider for African-Americans in all of Georgia.

In less than twenty years Pilgrim had acquired 58,000 policyholders and after fifty years of operation paid more than $14 million in benefits. By the time an Atlanta firm purchased the company and moved it to that city in 1991, Pilgrim had enjoyed continuous operation in Augusta for ninety-three years. "Even today," reported *Augusta Chronicle* Business Editor Damon Cline, "Pilgrim remains the most successful and influential black business ever created in Augusta, Georgia."[61]

Rosemont Baptist Association, the largest and most enduring benevolent society in Columbia County, shows no sign of moving anywhere more than a century after its founding in 1902. The Reverend George W. Jones, pastor of the Lamkin Grove Baptist Church for nearly sixty years, conceived the idea and offered a parcel of his own land just south of Pollard's Corner on Washington Road as a satisfactory site. Six years later the Superior Court of Columbia County granted Rosemont's original charter, and the association purchased the approximately 150-acre site for homes and community buildings from Reverend Jones as a permanent location. Second Mount Carmel, the only church actually on the original

Rosemont premises, was established on a two-acre site where it remains to this day. At one time the community also operated Rosemont Elementary School and, for a brief period, held additional classes in their own high school.

The number of churches served by the association has varied through the years, according to the wishes and duration of each particular congregation, and some of the original congregations eventually left to operate on their own. That the churches are primarily Baptist is likely due to the influence of Kiokee Baptist Church, where most members of early black congregations in the county worshipped before they moved to their own buildings. While the existing eight member churches are scattered throughout Appling and nearby communities today, the original Rosemont neighborhood resembles a typical subdivision. Homes of varying age and design are still there, along with 2nd Mt. Carmel's first and second buildings and a modern, multipurpose building erected on Burks Mountain Road in 2004.

What began as a burial-benevolent society has also evolved, with education, care of the elderly, and retirement issues augmenting or replacing the needs of their ancestors a century ago. For example, in the association's 2006 anniversary booklet we find a twenty-page listing of sources for obtaining minority scholarships. Surely education and caring for each other continue to be the primary purposes of this unique Columbia County community.

In contrast to the sporadic good fortune of a William Sanders or a Robin Allen a century ago, success and productivity are no longer the exception among present-day African-Americans. As demonstrated by one Rosemont family in particular, the belief of those long-ago visionaries that educated black children would one day join their white neighbors as teachers, pastors, doctors, and other leaders of their communities has been fulfilled. Twin educators Leslie and Lester Pollard, and their sister, Zelean Pollard Quick, are but a microcosm of the transformation that has revolutionized this race of people from the remnants of slavery to the successful, independent members of society they are today.

Still charming in her ninety-third year, former model, Miss NAACP, and Miss New York Subway, Zelean Pollard Quick knew just how long such a transformation could take. The little girl born in Columbia County to teen-aged parents in 1914, and raised by that young father and his parents when her mother died while she was still a small child, remembers that struggle well. She also knew that any success story rising from a black family in those days required more than caretakers, role models, and the efforts of someone else. The lady who once worked as an elevator operator for the city of New York used an appropriate metaphor to describe what that missing ingredient was for her:

"I elevated myself all the way through," she said. Newspaper clippings, scrapbooks, and the award- and photo-covered walls of her home prove this lady was making nothing up!

Education? Not much, beyond a few months at a time when she lived with family members in Augusta. She did not read well or understand math, but she excelled in history and geography. "I was interested in those things," she explained, "so I learned the facts by heart."

Zelean was almost a teenager herself when her father remarried, and the brothers and sisters she had always wanted began arriving, "a baby every year." But perhaps the increased size of her family, coupled with an emerging streak of independence, was the reason her family accepted an aunt's invitation that she move to New York City and live with her. Beyond an occasional trip home whenever she could afford the bus fare, she would not return to Georgia for more than forty years.

New York City was quite an adventure for the girl from rural Columbia County. To begin with, "I could sit in the front of the bus, and no one told me to move or say, 'Yes, Ma'am.'" But when her well-meaning aunt registered her for school, her sixteen-year-old body was not the right fit for the classes her prior educational experience required her to attend.

"I was so much bigger than the mostly 10–12 year-olds in the class that they made fun of me." Despite her teacher's efforts to tone down the teasing, Zelean's school days were numbered, and she left the New York school with little more than the limited elementary schooling she had received in Georgia.

But did the lack of education slow her down? Not at all. Before long she was taking care of three children, earning a dollar a day plus room and board, and enjoying life more than at any time since she left Georgia. With very few expenses, she was able to send $8 a month home to her family and save most of the rest. When she took a housekeeping job paying $40 a month, she celebrated her "big raise." Zelean expressed her obvious contentment like this: "Every night when I would lie down I would say, I made another dollar and I had a beautiful day."

Maybe it was this attitude that attracted others to her, including the lady hat maker who told her, "You have a face for hats," and hired Zelean to model her merchandise. Wearing those hats elevated her self-confidence, and made her decide she didn't want to do housework forever. So she went back to school—not to academics this time, but to beauty school where, "I didn't have to know how to read." But after a short time—and "the smell of all that grease"—she changed jobs again, becoming a waitress for a woman who had a public dining room in her home, and earning the large sum of $5 to $10 a day plus room and board. It was during this time that the unexpected happened: she met and married a man whose mother was a schoolteacher and another relative was an executive with *National Geographic*. She may have found this connection intimidating, but it would not be long before her well-educated in-laws had reason to look up to her.

Besides modeling, catering to upscale customers at the beauty shop and restaurant paid dividends beyond her ever-increasing income. Zelean ran for Miss NAACP—and won; posed for photographers and became the first black Miss New York Subway. "My picture was everywhere!" she exclaimed. She also received a job offer no one could believe, least of all Zelean herself.

"With all that publicity and invitations to places with a lot of famous people, the editor of the *Newark* (New Jersey) *Herald* asked me to write a column for the newspaper."

But she still could barely read or write. How could she ever do something like that? Her husband and friends urged her to accept the job, and offered their help.

"I would write down the names and a few of the words I wanted to say, and they would correct my spelling and help me put the column together."

The combined efforts of author and ghost writers must have worked, because soon Zelean was writing a similar column for a girls' magazine. Other opportunities also came her way, including more contests and awards. She sighed as she remembered: "Everything I entered, I won." Except, perhaps, her marriage, which ended in divorce after twelve years—but not before one of the happiest moments of her life, the birth of her only daughter. Like the mother, the daughter—also named Zelean— "elevated herself" by becoming a prominent ballerina. As if to continue the family tradition of aiming high, today *her* daughter, Cece Peniston, is an actress and international recording artist who has sung at the White House and in 1989 became the first black Miss Arizona. Daughter Zelean also has a son who is a successful model and musician.

Zelean Pollard Quick came home again in the 1970's and reconnected with her family and church. From then until her death in 2008, she lived with memories of her "beautiful days" and a succession of new blessings which, like the awards of the past, kept flowing her way.

Unlike their older sister, for twin brothers Lester and Leslie Pollard education has been the primary focus of their lives. Thanks to the timing of their birth, those mid-1950's Columbia County consolidated schools were in operation by the time they and their young siblings were in school. Each child went first to Gibbs (Road) Elementary School and then to Blanchard High School, now Columbia Middle School, on Columbia Road. Following high school, the twins became the first members of their family to graduate from college.

After finishing Paine College in 1965, both brothers returned to Blanchard High to teach, but not for long. Although their father had encouraged them to continue their schooling and to become doctors or lawyers, the only significant role models for educated blacks in those days were teachers. "We didn't know any black attorneys," Leslie recalls, which was the primary reason they both returned to school to major in education. Lester earned a master's degree at Atlanta University and his Ph.D. from the University of South Carolina, while Leslie received his advanced degrees from Syracuse University in New York. Their proud father now had two "doctors" in the family, even if they were not in the medical field as he had planned.

Dr. Lester Pollard spent the next few years teaching English at Paine, his alma mater, before moving to Augusta State University, where he remained until his retirement in 2006—at least from teaching. Today he is actively involved in the Rosemont Baptist Association, where he serves as president of the board of directors and editor of their publications.

Dr. Leslie Pollard began his higher education career teaching history at Voorhees College in Denmark, South Carolina, before transferring to Paine and teaching there until his retirement in 2008. Leslie is also the author of the book *Complaint to the Lord: Historical Perspectives on the African American Elderly*, published by Susquehanna University Press in 1996. He plans to continue writing on historical themes, including perhaps a book on the history of Blanchard School, the first public high school for black students in Columbia County.

The Pollard patriarch, Zack Pollard, Sr., had every reason to be proud of his family. He may not have raised his own crop of medical doctors or attorneys, but in addition to the twins, three more of his children became teachers in Richmond and Columbia County schools, and those other professionals he once dreamed of parenting began appearing among his grandchildren. Lester's daughter is a practicing attorney today, and Leslie's son is a Columbia County physician.

Like American playwright Eugene O'Neill's 1956 award-winning play, "Long Day's Journey into Night," the African-American's long journey from slavery to freedom was full of sorrow, pitfalls, misfortune, and unrealized dreams. Although this journey may have been longer than that of their fellow-traveling whites, by measuring their progress not from yesterday or the recent past but from generation to generation, we discover a remarkable progression from the beginning of the African-American story to the state of their lives today.

The journey is not over by any means—for them or for their white counterparts in Columbia County or the entire *human* race. But lessons learned, hurdles cleared, and obstacles overcome have "elevated" this group of people far above their status or condition when "first they were slaves."

PART VII

CONCLUSION:

AN OVERVIEW OF THE TWENTIETH

CENTURY AND THE STATE

OF THE COUNTY TODAY

43

COLUMBIA COUNTY,

"MY, HOW YOU'VE GROWN"

Imagine how astonished the Quakers, Crawfords, Fews, and other early settlers would be if they could visit Columbia County today. Would they even recognize that sparsely settled, timber-covered frontier they found when they first arrived, or could they locate that plot of once unlimited space and rich, piedmont soil so favorable to the crops and livestock they raised here? More importantly, would they like what they see? Would they be proud of what their descendants have done with their legacy?

Before concluding our journey into Columbia County's past, let's travel briefly through the more recent decades and answer those questions as though we were the ones bridging the time warp, not they. Surely we won't travel far before discovering that the county's heroes and significant events did not end after our first wave of settlers died or moved away. From the population momentum during those decades to the "quality of life" description we hear at every turn, we will judge for ourselves why people still are attracted to this small section of earth we call home.

Our astonishment would likely match that of our forebears, however, were we to join them in contrasting the small, eighteenth-century settlements of Brandon, Wrightsboro, and Kioka (Kiokee) with that same part McDuffie County, part northwestern section of Columbia County today. Add the cities of Harlem and Grovetown, and the burgeoning communities of Evans and Martinez, and even we may wonder if we are talking about the same plot of ground. Population charts, compiled from the county's inception to the year 2005, may not dampen our surprise, but they at least will clarify that both generations are indeed talking about Columbia County.

As previously noted, when Richmond County was divided in 1790 to create Columbia County, the population of the backcountry had reached 11,000. A decade later approximately 8,300 people lived in the new county alone. Except for some migration away from the county by the Negro population following the Civil War, and the loss of Thomson and Wrightsboro after McDuffie County was created in 1870, mild growth would occur west of the two-county line for the next 150 years. But as the following figures will show, no one could have predicted what would happen to once rural Columbia County during the past fifty years.[1]

1830	12,606	1980	40,118
1870	13,429	1990	66,031
1900	10,653	2000	89,288
1920	11,718	2002	94,641
1940	9,433	2003	97,122
1960	13,423	2004	100,554
1970	22,327	2005	103,812

To further understand the impact of the above statistics, consider the following statements collected from a variety of late twentieth-century and early twenty-first-century reports in the *Augusta Chronicle*:

—Columbia County rose from the 70th largest county in the state in 1960 to the 44th largest in only one decade (1970).

—From 1980 to 2000 the population of Georgia increased by 19.7%. During the same period of time, Columbia County gained 50,000 people for an increase of 39%, or roughly twice that of the state, with growth in the 1980's alone topping 55%. The county then added 23,000 more people between 1990 and 2000 and in 2001 became the fastest growing county in the Central Savannah River Area (CSRA).

—By the year 2000, the population of Columbia County had experienced a near ten-fold increase since 1950, or from 9,525 to just under 90,000.

—In 2005 the Georgia State Office of Planning and Budget projected 20,000–23,000 new residents in Columbia County per decade for the foreseeable future.

In the next chapter we'll explore the reasons why.

44

THE BEDROOM COMMUNITY OF AUGUSTA

If you were new to east-central Georgia during the mid to latter decades of the twentieth century and needed a job, you looked to Augusta. From large-scale industries, including Proctor and Gamble, Continental Can (now International Paper), Monsanto Chemical, and Columbia Nitrogen, to the medical complex and other business and industry within the city or surrounding Richmond County, there seemed to be no end of opportunity to make a living there. But if you wanted a home outside those city limits plus good schools for your children and a short commute to work, you looked to Columbia County, commonly called the bedroom community of Augusta.

Developers could not build new subdivisions fast enough, and portable classrooms for sudden student overflow became a common sight outside most county schools, even as additional facilities were constantly breaking ground. As traffic increased, so did the need for new roads or upgrades to those already on the map. Older residents still remember when Washington Road was only a two-lane, unpaved road, and candidates won or lost elections based on their support for the "Murray Road Project," the parallel route to Augusta that became Riverwatch Parkway. Both Interstate 20 and the entrance to the Bobby Jones Expressway, so important for travel to and from the county today, were constructed or improved, section by section, from the 1960's to the present day.

Augusta's internal industry, however, was not the only reason more and more people moved to Columbia County during the twentieth century or why, near the end of that time, only 15 to 20 percent of her residents were native to the county or perhaps even to Georgia. Three major developments nearby were responsible for much of that influx, as well as for increased employment opportunities for the entire CSRA and the number of schools and "bedrooms" needed in Columbia County. Almost cities unto themselves, these important new arrivals were the Fort Gordon military installation; the combination flood control, hydropower, and recreation project along the Savannah River Basin, known at the time as Clarks Hill Lake and Dam; and the Savannah River Plant (now Savannah River Site), across the river in South Carolina. All three not only drew an immediate labor supply during lengthy construction periods but, when completed, continued to attract a large number of military, engineering, and specialty personnel to maintain them. Considering the number of Columbia County residents who came here because of one of these establishments, some details of their origin and impact are in order.

Fort Gordon

Remembering that the reason for establishing an outpost in the Georgia Backcountry in the first place was to protect the Indian trade from unscrupulous traders, and the settlers from threats known or unknown, we could say Augusta, complete with her own fort near where St. Paul's Church now stands, has always been a military town. Add Thomas Brown's Revolutionary War stockades near the former Fort Augusta site and, following the war, the federally sponsored Augusta Arsenal in their place, and we find a continuous local military presence from 1736 to the present day.

The arsenal might have remained by the river much longer had not a plague wiped out most of the troops assigned there in 1820. The complex then moved to the presumably healthier "hill" section of the city where soldiers trained for combat, worked hand-in-hand with the Augusta Powderworks factories during the Civil War, and continued to supply weaponry and personnel for the Defense Department until the facility was abandoned in 1955. Two years later the former arsenal grounds became the home of the Junior College of Augusta, which was renamed Augusta College in 1958 and, in 1996, Augusta State University. This prominent and ever-expanding school is still bordered by a road between the campus and Walton Way called Arsenal Avenue.

But long before the arsenal's departure, the area's first full military installation was established near the intersection of Highland Avenue and Wrightsboro Road. With the founding of Camp Hancock to assist America's sudden involvement in World War I, Augusta's military-town description remained intact. Sudden also describes the speed with which a temporary home for nearly 100,000 troops over the next eighteen months was completed. Initially the city and the army had only two months to prepare the site, pipe in the water, and construct necessary facilities before the first contingent of 36,000 recruits arrived in late summer 1917. The next spring, as these soldiers were leaving to join the war effort in Europe, another 60,000 trainees moved in.[2]

When the war ended in November 1918, Camp Hancock also became a temporary resident of Augusta. With the hopes of the world now united in peace, the work of the short-lived military post was over. A decade later the prized property still known as Hancock Field acquired a new purpose and a new name. In honor of Mayor Raleigh Daniel, the city's new airport was renamed Daniel Field.[3]

As the threat of another war in Europe loomed near the end of the 1930's, attention again turned to this area for military support. In fact, with Daniel Field still capable of reviving the services once performed by Camp Hancock, local representatives went to Washington, D.C., in 1939 to bid for another army camp on that site. The trip was more than successful. By September 1940, two thousand men and a hundred planes had arrived for training purposes on Daniel Field. At the same time, additional sites south of the city were acquired for further military use, and the still functioning arsenal was enlarged to include ten giant warehouses where new weaponry produced in the arsenal's modernized shops could be stored.[4]

Unlike World War I, World War II quickly became wider than a European problem with spin-off enemy attacks on American ships en route to Allied ports. Following Japan's attack on Pearl Harbor, Hawaii, and the loss of some 2,300 American lives there on December 7, 1941, more than a few planes and small training sites would be needed in response.

Military construction already underway on both ends of South Augusta's Tobacco Road intensified. Before long a new army camp took shape at the western end, while an airfield to train army pilots began operating at the other. The encampment was soon called Camp Gordon, in honor of former Georgia Governor and Confederate General John B. Gordon, and the airfield named "Bush Field," in memory of aviation instructor Donald C. Bush, who died in an early training accident there. Years later, when World War II was over, Augusta's Daniel Field became a private airport and the city retained the larger Bush Field as her municipal airport. Following completion of a new, modern terminal in 2000, the former Bush Field then became Augusta Regional Airport.

Encompassing 55,600 acres southwest of Augusta and, in a small part, inside the southeastern border of Columbia County, Camp Gordon would become the area's largest and most multifaceted military presence to date. The camp's barracks and administration buildings were only partially completed, however, when the Pearl Harbor bombing took place. Yet within days the newly assigned camp commander and his staff moved from their temporary quarters in downtown Augusta to a hastily assembled "tent city" on Camp Gordon grounds to prepare for an immediate influx of troops ready to be trained in their country's defense.

Before the war ended in 1945, three prominent army divisions would train at Camp Gordon, including the renowned Fourth Infantry Division, whose men were among the first wave of Allied soldiers to land on Normandy's Utah Beach on D-Day 1944. The Division Commander, General Raymond O. Barton, is remembered to this day by the naming of the large parade field near the center of the post after him. The

German-Italian cemetery just inside Gate 2 today is a lingering reminder of another World War II function of Camp Gordon, the internment of foreign prisoners of war and the burial ground of those who died while incarcerated there.

Following the war, Camp Gordon served temporarily as the Army's Separation Center. Approximately 86,000 service personnel were discharged from military duty there before the camp itself was scheduled for deactivation.[5] But this latter decision also proved to be temporary. Before the end of 1948, Camp Gordon's spacious grounds and newly vacated premises acquired two new tenants: the Army's Military Police School (MP) and one unit of the developing Army Signal Corps. In 1956, as world events and the needs of the Defense Department continued to evolve, the former World War II training camp became "Fort Gordon," indicating that this valuable installation was here to stay. Although the MP School moved to Alabama in 1974, conflicts in Korea and Vietnam during the nation's "cold war" with communism, and the 1986 consolidation of all Army Signal Corps training at this location, underscored the importance of that mid-twentieth-century decision to make Fort Gordon permanent.

Aside from her direct military missions, no discussion about Fort Gordon would be complete without mentioning another important component of the post: the Dwight David Eisenhower Army Medical Center (DDEAMC), named for the Army's former five-star general and the country's thirty-fourth president who, in addition to vacationing often in Augusta, made his farewell address to the Army at Fort Gordon on January 7, 1961.

Long before the towering concrete structure opened in 1976, however, Camp Gordon was home to a sprawling "Field [or Station] Hospital" erected along the main entrance road (Chamberlain Avenue today) in 1941 and 1942. To gain a perspective of the earlier hospital's size, if DDEAMC's thirteen floors plus parking areas were laid side by side today, it's doubtful the entire complex would cover the eighty acres required for those former 139 interconnected, single-story wooden buildings intended for temporary, war-casualty use during World War II.

Although the needs of the Army changed and the field hospital was reduced in size, once again the word "temporary" was a misnomer. For more than thirty years personnel and visitors alike continued to walk through three miles of connecting corridors from parking lots to duty stations or patient wards. The gradual downsizing, however, was of great benefit to the community. Today remnants of the old wooden buildings can still be seen across the countryside transformed into schools, churches, storefronts, and even homes. That double-wide trailer you think you see just might be the field hospital's reconstituted "Ward 39," where a returning soldier from Europe, Korea, or Vietnam recuperated from his wounds.

While still a hospital, still a place where active duty personnel, retirees, and their families receive medical care and the war-wounded from Afghanistan and Iraq come for treatment, the aptly named Medical Center today serves both the military and civilian community in a variety of ways. Sometimes called "the Walter Reed of the South," DDEAMC also has become a teaching hospital and medical research center in cooperation with other medical facilities in the CSRA, including the Medical College of Georgia in Augusta.

Besides the Medical Center and Fort Gordon's status as one of the largest military training posts in the country, the impact of this installation on the entire CSRA is almost incalculable. In 2005, shortly before the Defense Department's most recent Base Realignment and Closure initiative (BRAC) caused a community-wide scare, the newly formed military-civilian partnership, the CSRA Alliance for Fort Gordon, sponsored a full-page ad in the *Augusta Chronicle* to explain what the loss of the Post would mean to the area. The ad included the following:

—With a workforce of more than 12,500 military and nearly 5,000 civilians, Fort Gordon is the CSRA's largest employer. The jobs of 28 percent of Richmond County residents and 14 percent in Columbia County are Fort Gordon related.

—Fort Gordon's annual $1.2 billion impact goes directly into area stores, banks, real estate, and other businesses.

—Nearly 13,000 military retirees live in the CSRA, generating $214 million in military retirement income.[6]

Thankfully, either the local impact, the needs of the Army, or both were successful once again in keeping Fort Gordon open. New building projects, including the anticipated 2010 completion of the National Security Agency's Intelligence-Gathering Center, are constantly underway. These new projects plus the old, including the post's own Twin Towers—the Medical Center and the ten-story Signal Towers building that anchors the Signal Center—dominate the CSRA's southwestern skyline, and help give this military installation a permanent, local address.

Incidentally, with a projected three-thousand jobs anticipated for the National Security Agency alone, Columbia County developers will need to keep building new homes—and the Board of Education to set aside land for more schools—before that sizable new "impact" arrives.

Clarks Hill Lake

Before beginning any discussion about the U.S. Army Corps of Engineers' largest inland water project east of the Mississippi River, one important matter needs to be resolved: What is that giant water project's correct name?

Is it Clark Hill without an "s," Clarks Hill with an "s"—with an apostrophe or without—or, following a 1987 Congressional Resolution to drop the variegated Clark-Clarks-Clark's name altogether and rename it after South Carolina's long-term Senator J. Strom Thurmond, is it now and forever Thurmond Lake and Dam?

Well, that depends. When the project was conceived in 1944, both the lake and dam were to be called Clarks Hill, not with an apostrophe to indicate an individual namesake—in this case, possibly John Mulford Clark, a landowner on the South Carolina side where the dam was to be built—but, according to Corps of Engineers policy, after Mr. Clark's geographic location, the community of Clarks Hill. There is, however, more than a similarity between the name of the town, Clarks Hill, and the aforementioned landowner. According to Augusta resident John

Marks, Clarks Hill was named for his great, great, great, grandfather, John Mulford Clark.[7]

This explanation settles both the apostrophe discrepancy and the reason for the naked "s," but is there evidence to support those who believe there should be no "s" on Clark at all? Search the record today and you will find many references to Clark Hill Lake and Dam without the "s," but only because of a typographical error on some staffer's paperwork when the project was initially presented.

But, with all that history, is the name still Clarks Hill or, since 1987, Thurmond? Well, that depends. When the name change was suggested by South Carolina Representative Butler Derrick as a birthday present to Mr. Thurmond, the resolution passed quietly and nearly unanimously by the senator's colleagues in Washington, D.C. Reaction back home, however, especially on the Georgia side of the river, was overwhelmingly *against* the decision.

Buoyed by angry citizens who circulated petitions against the name change, Georgia Representative Doug Barnard introduced legislation to change the name back to Clarks Hill. Barnard's bill never made it out of committee in Congress, but all those thousands of signatures resonated loudly with area legislators in Atlanta. Thus, although the Corps of Engineers and South Carolina mapmakers set the Thurmond name in stone—literally, across the top of the dam—Georgia lawmakers enacted legislation to keep the name Clarks Hill Lake on all their state's maps and signs. Now and then, you can still hear a seasoned South Carolinian using the original name, too. After all, the town of Clarks Hill is still on their side of the river.

Therefore, in a gesture of neighborliness and compromise—and in semi-agreement with the Corps' 2006 brochure, "J. Strom Thurmond Dam and Lake at Clarks Hill"—we will use the names Thurmond Dam and Clarks Hill Lake for the remainder of this discussion.[8]

But there is no controversy on either side of the river about the importance of this multipurpose undertaking that eventually would include a chain of lakes stretching 120 miles upriver. The mammoth, three-pronged mission that began at Clarks Hill and added the northernmost Hartwell

Lake and Dam in 1963, ended in 1984 with completion of the smaller Richard Russell Lake and Dam between the other two.

The year 1944 may have signified congressional authorization for the Clarks Hill Project, but efforts to harness the Savannah River had been a priority ever since the early settlers arrived in the Georgia Backcountry. Although the river was the magnet that drew people to the area, changing water levels could just as easily cause harm as provide some of the basic necessities for life. Low water from prolonged drought reduced water supplies and created hazardous conditions for watercraft using "nature's roadway" for transportation, while floods from excessive rainfall were a frequent threat to anyone living or doing business near the river. In 1840, for example, with flood waters five to ten feet deep in downtown Augusta, "Petersburg boats were poled through the streets like gondolas on Venice canals."[9]

Suggestions for solving Augusta's recurring flood problems dominated conversations among city leaders and citizens alike for decades. By 1911, however, "the 3rd flood in 24 years brought an end to talking and the beginning of action."[10] A series of lakes and dams on the upper Savannah River was considered the better solution even then, but that idea drew constant opposition because of the anticipated expense. Instead, the decision-makers chose a less costly alternative, an earthen levee that still stretches along the riverbank from Columbia County to the New Savannah lock and dam near Bush Field.

Augustans breathed a collective sigh of relief when their flood control project was completed in 1919—but not for long. Barely ten years later, yet another flood would overshadow for local residents the nation's worst-ever stock market crash in the same October 1929 month. Following days of torrential rainfall, frightened citizens rushed for higher ground as the swollen river broke through weaknesses in some sections of the levee, over the top in others, and once again inundated the city.

Despite the Flood Control Act of 1936, which authorized rebuilding the levee stronger and higher than before, it was obvious something besides earthen riverbanks was needed to prevent future devastation and potential loss of life. Nearly a decade later, with help from the federal government and supervision by the Army Corps of Engineers, two thousand construction workers began the eight-year task to construct that "better solution" and finally harness the mighty Savannah River.

Few could have known at the time how well or in how many ways that "solution" worked. Within fifty years, not only had an estimated $45 million in flood damage been prevented but, before long, the lake and surrounding amenities were attracting approximately 6 million visitors a year to what has become one of the ten most popular Corps recreation sites in the country. Nor can we forget that, like the Augusta Canal a century before, clean, low-cost energy produced by power generators at the dam soon drew new industry and greater prosperity to the region, including those mentioned at the beginning of this chapter.

Even a small, man-made lake presumes the displacement of some public or private property, but imagine the amount of land required to accommodate a 71,000-acre body of water (at full pool) plus 80,000 acres of managed property surrounding the newly created lake. Put another way, Clarks Hill Lake reaches nearly forty miles up the Savannah River from the dam and twenty-nine miles along the east-west Little River in Georgia—the boundary between Columbia and Lincoln counties—plus seventeen miles in South Carolina. So, was there a public outcry at so large an exercise of eminent domain (the taking of private property, with compensation, for the public good) by the U.S. government?

Very little. Naturally, individual property owners and lingering residents of primarily waning towns on both sides of the river expressed initial dismay at their personal loss. But after the Corps went to considerable pains to rescue architectural treasures, relocate cemeteries, and find new homes for displaced residents, it was not long before the scenic, recreation bonanza created by the lake far outweighed the loss. To the mainly rural population who lived north of the dam, or those who had never been affected by flooded streets or the need for large amounts of hydropower, it was that third, recreational purpose of the lake that soon turned disappointment into delight.

Recreation? How do we count the ways? Boating, swimming, fishing, camping, water skiing, hiking, bird watching, boat races, fishing tournaments, or simply watching the sun rise or set over the water provide endless opportunities to step away from the bustle of life and enjoy the interlocking beauty of the Creator and the ingenuity of man.

It also would be difficult to count the ways this water paradise affects the residents of Columbia County. For starters, 130 miles of the lake's 1,200-mile shoreline—measured not "as the crow flies" but around coves, curves, and points of land jutting out into the water—lie inside the boundaries of the county. Popular attractions nestled along that portion of the irregular shoreline include Mistletoe State Park, one of six state parks in the two-state area, and the county's own Wildwood Park a short distance above Pollard's Corner, the definitive landmark for all lake locations in Georgia, at the intersection of U.S. Route 221 and State Routes 47, 150, and 104.

Travel five miles past Wildwood Park and you also will find the large, well-developed Fort Gordon Recreation Area, or turn east at Pollard's Corner for Petersburg Campground, the largest of the Corps's thirteen camping areas at the lake and one of three in Columbia County. In addition to long- or short-term campgrounds and commercial marinas, plus individual home sites or established church and civic getaways in the county or nearby, there are enough day-use beaches, boat ramps, and places to picnic, fish, or swim without spending more than a few hours away from home. In short, individuals often move here, and businesses choose to locate here, because of what many call the county's greatest resource, Clarks Hill Lake.

Major highways in both states take you close to many portions of the lake in the county or beyond, while short, private roads leading to those preferred destinations shield you from the sight and sound of highway traffic. Finally, at the end of the day, a week or a long summer stay at your own "house at the lake" on that leased Corps of Engineers land, those highways return you to your home before the little ones in your midst have time to ask the proverbial, "Are we there yet?" For most residents of Columbia County, Clarks Hill Lake is only an hour or two from everywhere but, in effect, a world away.

Savannah River Site

If we were to add 50,000 acres to the land required for Clarks Hill Lake and its borderlands, we would approximate the 310-square-mile area on the South Carolina side of the river that used to be called Ellenton, Dunbarton, and about five other small towns. Since the 1950's, this area has encompassed one of the largest nuclear weapons facilities in the country, the Savannah River Site.

Residents knew "something was going on" when they spotted government vehicles roaming through their normally quiet neighborhoods in early 1950. On November 28 of that year, they learned what that "something" was. In a joint announcement by the Atomic Energy Commission and E. I. DuPont, the company that had built the plutonium production complex at Hanford, Washington, for the Manhattan Project during World War II, they were informed that a nuclear weapons facility would soon also occupy their towns. Backed by then President Harry S. Truman, who considered this most costly defense undertaking at the time "one of the highest urgency," the AEC would direct the project that DuPont would design and build.[11]

But this was the era of "the cold war" and, like most of the country, people in rural South Carolina knew the United States was in a race with the Soviet Union to develop nuclear technology, and a heightened sense of patriotism softened the blow for those who were about to lose their homes. The government's first construction project, creating the town of New Ellenton to house the displaced, plus the promise of thousands of new jobs, helped too.

And jobs there were. By June 1951, 8,000 construction workers began building the five nuclear reactors and nearly 1,000 related facilities needed to manufacture plutonium, tritium, and other ingredients for nuclear weapons. By September of the following year, that work force had risen to 38,000. Understandably, what the AEC called the Savannah River Plant (SRP), and local residents dubbed "the bomb plant," created the greatest economic impact this neighboring Georgia–South Carolina region had ever known.[12]

Included in that initial, two-year "impact" were the hastily developed housing developments, primarily in Richmond, Aiken, and Barnwell counties, and approximately fifty new service-related businesses made necessary by a sudden, 46,000 increase in the area's population. But when the bulk of the construction phase ended in 1953, those congested cottage and trailer parks closest to the plant diminished or disappeared altogether, as 11,000 engineers, plant operators, and other personnel came here to stay. "Here," for those seeking a permanent home "out in the country," helped create another, mid-twentieth-century population explosion in Columbia County.

Revolving missions at one or more of the five reactors, including that ever critical production of nuclear weapons materials, plus the University of Georgia's Savannah River Ecology Laboratory to study the effects of radiation on organisms and the environment—and additional work with NASA's deep-space exploration program—emanated from SRP for the next thirty years. Some of those early missions would end, however, as world conditions, including the demise of the Soviet Union, and future needs of the nation's nuclear program changed.

By the late 1980's, no longer would the Atomic Energy Commission or the Department of Defense (DOD) be the facility's primary sponsors, nor would DuPont continue to manage day to day operations. Westinghouse Savannah River Company replaced DuPont, the Department of Energy (DOE) replaced DOD, and the name Savannah River Plant was changed to Savannah River Site (SRS). Most importantly, from the 1990's to the present day, the mission has changed from nuclear material production to an extensive waste processing program for storing, recycling, and protecting the environment from those no longer needed weapons ingredients and spent reactor fuels.

By no means are those new or continuing missions at SRS less important than the original purpose of the site. A wealth of information and expertise has been gained from the earlier projects, and that knowledge plus the vast facility itself will be a valuable national resource for further gains in science, ecology, and nuclear power technology for years to come. In August 2007, for example, following eight years of planning and negotiation, construction began on a Mixed Oxide (MOX) Fuel Fabrication Facility to mix surplus weapons grade plutonium with uranium oxide for commercial nuclear power reactors which, in turn, are used for clean electricity generation. Plans for this 600,000-square-foot facility include a start-up date of 2016, and the mission to last until 2035 or beyond.[13]

By no means, also, will future generations of personnel assigned to SRS stop needing homes and schools, possibly a favorite fishing spot at the lake, or some of that after-hours "quality-of-life" atmosphere found here in Columbia County. Our SRS neighbors should be around for a long time to come, too.

Today the differences we mentioned between life for the first residents of Columbia County and those who live here now may not seem any greater than the contrast between a county with 9,500 people in 1950 and a population of 110,000 one decade into the twenty-first century.

Bedroom community? What bedroom community? Longtime residents and newcomers alike find it difficult to imagine the present mixture of shopping centers, subdivisions, commercial plants, and service industries as an extension of any locality but their own. Following a chapter about some of the people who aided that growth and helped create the quality of life found here, we'll end our journey through Columbia County's past with an assessment of the county today.

45

Lasting Impressions

If we were to tell the story of every man or woman whose contribution helped foster that twentieth-century growth and betterment of Columbia County, this book would never end. Thus we have selected samples from a very long list, including: an educator, a community activist, an artist, government and industry leaders, plus other headliners whose names and accomplishments are well known. Nor could we choose one person to head that list—unless it is the man most associated with those "good schools" that have attracted new residents to the county for the past six decades, and whose story appears first.

John Pierce Blanchard

It's unanimous. The person most often judged responsible for the highest-rated education system in the CSRA, and one of the best in Georgia, is John Pierce Blanchard. Always known by all three names, this son of country doctor Pierce Gordon Blanchard, was born in the Phinizy community of Columbia County in 1919, graduated from Leah High School, and after receiving his undergraduate degree from Georgia Southern and a masters in education administration from the University of Georgia, came home to teach, coach, and before long, serve as principal of the

John Pierce Blanchard, Sr., newly elected superintendent of schools, Columbia County, in his office in the courthouse, Appling, Georgia. Courtesy *Columbia County News-Times*.

Leah school. By the age of thirty, he was superintendent of all Columbia County schools.

"The strength of the school system in this county is largely because of the foundation Superintendent John Pierce Blanchard laid."[14] Mary Sanders should know. Her fifty-five-year teaching career was well underway in 1949, when Blanchard was elected school superintendent for the first of eight consecutive, unopposed terms.

No modern buildings greeted the young educator or served the needs of his teachers and students when he arrived at his new post. At the time only two consolidated schools, built twenty years earlier in Harlem and Evans, plus his own junior-senior high building in Leah existed.

Otherwise, approximately fifty small schools in the predominantly rural county housed hundreds of children with one to four teachers per school. In 1955, during Blanchard's second term as superintendent, the Evans building was destroyed by fire. What at first must have seemed like a tragedy only hastened the modernization of all Columbia County schools.

Long before it was fashionable or the law, Blanchard's concern for the county's black children was well known. Until this time, only white students were attending those few consolidated schools. By the fall of 1956, however, not only were the displaced Evans students entering new classrooms, but every school-aged child in the county began the school year at one of eight new consolidated schools. Though still segregated by race, all buildings were constructed, staffed, and equipped alike—four for black students and four for white.

"You know, he saw it coming." Mary Sanders, by then principal at one of those new schools, remembers the integration process and credits her superintendent for turning a potentially explosive transition into little more than a ripple.

For at least three years before integration became law, Blanchard took a number of steps to ease the pending crisis. He discussed the subject in teachers' conferences, integrated the summer program, and offered supplemental reading programs for all students at the four black schools. He integrated the faculty early, too, and the bus drivers, who began picking up both black and white children along their routes at the same time. Miss Sanders and others recall his aggressive recruitment of black teachers and his diplomacy in moving white teachers to different schools. Part of that diplomacy included asking each teacher to list three schools where they would most like to teach—and fulfilling his promise to try placing them in one of the desired three. By the end of the 1960's, when neighboring communities were enduring boycotts and settling their skirmishes in court, Columbia County children were already attending identical, integrated schools. This time the boundaries were geographical, nothing more.

Blanchard may not have known that building eight new schools from the ashes of one, or handling the integration crisis with color-blind foresight, would become permanent educational patterns for the years and policies to come in the county where he lived, taught, held elective office, and sent his own five sons to school. But he set the stage, using problems as stepping stones to something better, and determining each new educational approach based on its ultimate result—how the decision would benefit or deter the learning process for each child.

The "man of vision," who retired in 1980 and died in 1992, left a lasting legacy. Capable successors have built on his foundation, and monuments to his memory exist throughout the county to this day. Blanchard High School (now Columbia Middle School), the county's first secondary school for black students, was named for him, as were the Harlem High School library and the Evans High School football stadium on Cox Road. In July 2000, through the combined efforts of the Columbia County Historical Society and State Representative Bill Jackson, family members, fellow educators, and friends gathered near the Appling Board of Education office to unveil a concrete memorial to the late but far from forgotten superintendent. Representative Jackson summarized the reason for the tribute: "John Pierce Blanchard could have been a U.S. Senator, or even a Governor, but he chose not to go far from the trunk of the tree. Because of that, we are all his beneficiaries."[15]

Most of those beneficiaries are the children of Columbia County, as those who designed this monument carefully acknowledged. Blanchard's likeness dominates the front of the monument, and four of his sayings, including "The purpose of education is to expel the darkness and expose the light," are etched around the base. The words of others adorn the back: "He dedicated his life to children; Education for all children was his reward."

Josie Dozier

To read about longtime Winfield resident Josie Dozier is to wonder if hers is the story of just one woman or the name of a group of people working together as a community improvement society. But the record is clear. With the humanitarian concern of a Florence Nightingale, the activism of Susan B. Anthony, and courage of Harriet Beecher Stowe, Josie Dozier's heart and hand prints linger throughout Columbia County and the CSRA long after her death in 1993.

Born in 1906 and raised in Richmond County, the adopted daughter of Will and Garrett Hall graduated from Tubman Girls School at the age of sixteen, attended La Grange College in western Georgia for one year, and returned to Augusta to complete a two-year program at the Lawton B. Evans Training School for Teachers. By 1925 and the age of nineteen, she was immersed in what she expected to be a lifelong career. Five months later, the new teacher of grades 4–6 plus 7th-grade math and English at the Winfield School married Thomas Albert Dozier, a local farmer and member of the Columbia County Board of Education that had hired her. Consequently, after completing her first school year, the new Mrs. Dozier put her education career on hold—for 20 years. Homemaking and raising the couple's four children would become her "career" now.

In 1946 Josie did return to education, not to the regular classroom this time, but to Columbia County's newly established Visiting Teacher program. Educators had learned that more potential service men and women from Georgia were rejected for military service (4-F) during World War II than from any other state, and Josie's new "classroom" was designed to find out why. Although physical impairment is the primary cause of a 4-F classification, this new program did uncover a startling fact: All over the county, children were not in school. Josie agreed with those who fostered the new program that, if a child is not in school, there must be a reason. "Let's find that reason and eliminate it," she said.[16]

Josie spent the next six years finding and eliminating those obstacles to education throughout the county. Sometimes the reasons were traditional, such as having parents who were uneducated themselves and may not have valued the education process. Other, more practical reasons for either temporary or long-term absenteeism included keeping older children home to care for younger siblings, especially if a parent were sick or away, or helping out on the family farm. Often Josie became a symbolic part of the family, as her well-honed maternal instincts merged with her teaching skills during this early venture in "home-schooling." "I loved them to death," she said at the time, "and they loved me. . . . I did love that work."[17]

To some degree, although she was no longer employed by Columbia County or any public school system, Josie would continue to be a "teacher" for the rest of her life, sometimes in multiple venues at the same time. Her community, her local government, and her church would be her classroom now as she worked, organized, or in a variety of ways sought to meet a need. What follows may only be a partial list.

—While finding children who were unschooled during those visiting-teacher days, Josie also became aware of extreme poverty in some of the children's homes. Soon she was helping to form a welfare organization, which after a few years became the county's Department of Family and Children Services (DFCS). Related organizations also benefited from her concern for the community's health and well-being, as she perennially served on boards and committees to raise funds and awareness for the Heart Association, the American Cancer Society, the March of Dimes, and the Red Cross. Speaking of the Red Cross, besides becoming a charter member of the Columbia County chapter, she served simultaneously as area home service secretary and member of the executive council for twenty-two east-central Georgia counties.

—For about nine of her public service years, Josie once again became gainfully employed, this time as a social worker at Fort Gordon. But her various supervisors should not have been surprised when, in addition to her duties in their departments, she organized citizenship classes for the foreign spouses of soldiers stationed there. At last count, those future American citizens had come from thirty different countries.

—Meanwhile, whether she was employed or spending forty-plus hours a week in community service, Columbia County was very much her workplace. For more than fifteen years she was active in the 4-H organization, serving locally as well as for the Northeast Georgia District. At some point she also turned her home into an office, and spent nearly a year writing, reporting, and editing the county's only newspaper, the *Columbia News*. During those chief-cook-and-bottle-washer days, she increased the size of the paper from four to eight pages, and delivered a much improved product to her successor. With perhaps a little time left on her hands in 1976, she helped organize the Columbia County Historical Society.

—But even with such a full calendar, Josie demonstrated that life should never be "all work and no play" by indulging in more hobbies than most people enjoy without such a busy schedule. Her avid interest in flowers is reflected in the name she chose for her home, "Rosewood Estate," and in the greenhouse outside. She also raised vegetables and peacocks, made quilts, played the piano, and went fishing with her husband.

—Finally, all through her adult life Josie's twin priorities continued to be her family and her church. For more than fifty years she held a variety of positions at Shiloh United Methodist Church, including Sunday school teacher and superintendent, president of the missionary society, and church pianist. She also served in wider Methodist circles as Christian Social Relations secretary and assistant treasurer for the Augusta District, and as a trustee of the nearby Whiteoak Campground, a recreation center and meeting place for the denomination.

Josie Dozier's accomplishments and contributions to her community did not go unnoticed, as evidenced by the plaques, citations, and other signs of recognition that lined the walls of her home. Her proudest achievement—and greatest surprise to the lady who sought no recognition for herself—may have been earning the CSRA Woman of the Year award from a field of more than two dozen nominees in 1971. Closer to home, in 1987 and at the age of eighty-one, she received the (former sheriff) Edward Tankersley Memorial Community Service Award during a ceremony at, to no one's surprise, Winfield's Josie Dozier Community Center. At some point during the ceremony, also at no one's surprise, Josie was asked to what she attributed her long life.

"I think it's just being interested in a lot of things. If you're not interested in things and don't get involved, you grow old."[18]

Josie lived another six years, part of that time in a nursing home where, as others took care of her, she interviewed fellow residents and filled a book with their stories. Her story, the organizations she formed, and the needs she met have long outlived her.

The Pollards of Appling

"Jake loved every person and clump of dirt in this county. He didn't think there was any place on earth but here."[19]

Mattie Pollard, widowed and well past ninety by the time this interview took place, had just summarized the life of her husband of more than sixty years, G. B. ("Jake") Pollard, Sr.—merchant, farmer, political activist, and Columbia County's longtime clerk of Superior Court.

It's doubtful many people in this rural county seat ever knew that the letters "G. B." in her husband's name stood for "Griffin Buchanan." Not that it mattered. Family, neighbors, and associates alike all called him by the old family nickname, "Jake," just as they would his son, Jake, Jr., a generation later. Mattie, both Jakes, and the couple's two daughters were all born in Columbia County and, as a family, had only one address: the 1851 house next door to the Appling Courthouse, where Mattie had lived from the time she was a year old until her death ninety-seven years later.

By profession, Jake, Sr., raised timber and cattle on his extensive landholdings, and owned Appling's only combination service station and general store in the center of town. But others could work the land, care for the cattle, and manage the store, leaving him time to serve his county in a variety of appointed or elected ways, including a term as deputy sheriff, four years as county ordinary (now probate judge), and thirty-two years as clerk of Superior Court. Still, the man with seemingly unlimited energy and ability may have been better known by what he did away from the farm, the store, and the office, than by how he performed on the job. When asked to describe this "man of all trades," those who knew him best all agreed: Jake Pollard was someone who could get things done—one "thing" in particular.

Thomas Edison may have invented the incandescent light bulb in 1879, but it would take another fifty years—and the persuasive ability of Jake Pollard—before those bulbs could be turned on in Columbia County. The problem was not local contentment with the kerosene lamp. Electric power had not yet come to the rural communities of Columbia County because no one had urged the power companies to secure the proper rights-of-way to erect poles, string wires, and bring that power here. Mattie remembered when all that changed.

"Jake knew everyone, including the folks at Georgia Power Company, so one day he brought a company representative home for lunch. After the man ate our plain, country meal of turnip greens and corn bread, he listened to Jake tell him how his company would benefit if they considered running those poles and wires into our towns and connecting electricity to our homes."

Apparently that "lobbying" effort worked. To this day, Jake Pollard, Sr., is known as the man who turned on the lights in Columbia County.

Jake's efforts also were very much in evidence at Appling's Kiokee Baptist Church, where the family worshipped and gave liberally of their time and resources. His numerous involvements included chairing the building committee during construction of the 1937 building, and serving as a deacon for nearly fifty years, most of that time as chairman.

"Dad was so popular, people just trusted him," his son recalls. "He was as good as his word." Still, as he must have learned from his lifelong immersion in Christian principles both at Kiokee and at home, "men should be doers of [God's] word and not hearers only" (James 1:22). Whether it was allowing the needy to carry a frequently unpaid "tab" at his store, or establishing a bus line between Appling and Fort Gordon for soldiers who had no other means of transportation, Jake Pollard, Sr.'s deeds as well as his word were an accurate reflection of this trusted public servant.

We could begin our segment about G. B. "Jake" Pollard, Jr., by saying, "all of the above," for if ever a father served as a role model for his son or a son followed in the proverbial footsteps of his father, it would be this family's father and his namesake son.

After completing Leah High School, attending Hurst Business College, and graduating from Augusta Law School, Jake Pollard, Jr., could have stopped working part-time in his father's store, moved away from the small community where he grew up, and begun a career as an attorney. But he didn't take the bar exam, and he did not move away.

Except for leaving temporarily to serve in the U.S. Air Force during the Korean War, this native son has always lived in Appling, Georgia. The only "moving" he did was into the house he and his wife Helen built next door to his boyhood home when he returned from military service.

But there was another reason why he did not become a lawyer. By 1960, after thirty-two years as Columbia County's clerk of Superior Court, Jake, Sr., not only decided to retire from the office, but suggested that his son take his place. With public service so much a part of his family structure, the younger Jake accepted that idea—and soon was elected to the office he would hold for the next twenty-eight years. By the time he left the clerk's office to run for the State Senate in 1988, someone by the name of G. B. ("Jake") Pollard had been the county's clerk of Superior Court for sixty consecutive years.

Jake, Jr., was elected to Georgia's twenty-fourth Senate District for four terms, all but the first contest unopposed. When he left office in 1996, his colleagues issued a resolution paying tribute to his clear thinking, hard work, and strong convictions. One of those "convictions" was the reason he turned down a request to seek the position of Senate Majority Leader. Although elected as a Democrat, he thought it more important to consider each decision on its own merit, not because it was proposed by a Democrat or a Republican. Becoming Majority Leader, he believed, would have meant too much party loyalty, and he turned the suggestion down. Serving in the Georgia Senate had been honor enough. Though he also enjoyed his work as county clerk, the Senate enlarged his territory from one county to seven, the added responsibility meaning, "I could help more people." Shades of the father appearing in the son, in the Senate as well as at Kiokee Baptist where he, too, served as a deacon—forty-one years in all, thirty-eight years as chairman.

Following Jake's retirement from the Senate, friend and fellow Senator Don Cheeks of Augusta submitted a second resolution, this one to rename Appling-Harlem Road, which extends from Appling to the Columbia County line below Harlem, the "Jake Pollard, Jr., Highway." Jake turned that idea down, too—unless Senator Cheeks removed the designation "Jr." from the resolution. Reluctantly Senator Cheeks complied. Those green signs that line the highway today could be in honor of Jake, Jr., or Jake, Sr., which is what the son had in mind.

Jake Pollard, Jr., may not have brought electricity to the county, but he brought decency, servanthood, and a gentle demeanor to both the political process and the people he served. Like father, like son.

Mattie Pollard was busy during those years, too, first as a stay-at-home mom until her children were in their teens, and then as Appling's first postmaster—a generic term that, at the time, applied equally to both men and women. Because the position opened before there was a post office building in town, she performed her duties wherever she found room: a corner of Howell's Store in the center of town, a converted corn crib on the other side of the street, and finally in the still-standing, small, white building Jake built for her next door to his store in 1945. Mattie and Jake may have supplied her equipment, but the government paid rent for the building that remained the Appling Post Office even after Mattie's retirement in 1966, until a new, government-owned building was erected in 1973.

Mattie displayed other similarities with her public-servant husband and son. She too was active in their church, serving as the adult Sunday school teacher for thirty-nine years, and she also thought there was no place on earth equal to the county where she was born, raised her family, and from which, except for two brief trips to Texas and Pennsylvania, she had never been more than a few miles away.

"I've never had any desire to travel," she said, "because everything I wanted was right here. To wake up in the morning when everything is fresh and new, whether it's raining or sunny, is just invigorating. Every day you have a whole new life before you."[20]

As the previously mentioned "Pollard's Corner" suggests, there are other members of the Appling Pollard family, and that intersection of travel routes northeast of town is more than a place to stop for gas, groceries, fishing supplies, or directions to Clarks Hill Lake. These Pollards also have been known throughout the CSRA for generations, both for their humanitarian efforts and for their family-owned Pollard Lumber

Company, one of the largest industries in the history of Columbia County.

Levi ("Bud") Pollard, also known as L. A. Pollard, Jr., was Jake Pollard, Sr.'s brother and founder of the company, which began along the railroad line in Harlem in 1946. Before long, with the aid of his son Robert, Bud opened two additional branches of the company in South Georgia. But by the early 1950's Bud decided to close all three branches, seek a consolidated location, and turn the management of the company over to his son. Robert surprised his father when he suggested making that location back in Appling where most of the family lived, and where "I can go home for lunch."

Bud wondered how the business could survive away from the railroad, the primary shipping point at the time between the mill and the consumer. But Robert saw the future of the company as less dependent on the railroad and more closely tied to the emerging trucking industry. Trucks, after all, could travel on any accessible road or highway, while trains could only run on those far fewer miles of existing track.

The company did resettle in Appling, as travelers between Evans and the lake already know. Stacks of yellow pine lumber products have lined a portion of Washington Road southeast of "the corner" for as long as anyone can remember. That part of the county was formerly known as the community of "Hazen," but after Bud opened "Pollard's Corner Store" in 1954, the Georgia Department of Transportation officially renamed the area after the store, the business, and the predominant family who lived nearby. The local landmark has appeared on Georgia maps ever since.

Robert Pollard continued as company president and remained one of the CSRA's leading businessmen until his death in 1995. Most people recognized him by his connection to the lumber company and his further involvement in the banking industry. Not as many knew this quiet, unpretentious man for his humanitarian activities which, much like his cousin Jake, were learned from his father. We may never know the extent of Robert Pollard's benevolence, but there is a record of his service and generosity to Kiokee Baptist Church on the pages of Waldo Harris' 1997 book, *Georgia's First Continuing Baptist Church*.

Returning to that earlier family example, when plans were being made in 1937 for a new building for this historic church, L. A. Pollard, Sr., and Jr. (Bud), agreed jointly to purchase the necessary twelve acres of land and donate them to the church.[21] Six decades later the present building next door would occupy part of that same tract. Robert's father and grandfather also served as trustees and members of successive building committees for the church, and when the former building was enlarged in the 1960's, their families donated the elegant new steeple and accompanying chimes.

By this time Robert was serving the church in a similar capacity, including helping to raise funds for improvements to the 1937 building. But when Kiokee outgrew even this 7,500 square foot addition and a completely new building was proposed in 1994, Robert Pollard was among the benefactors who made it possible for this latest building to be occupied debt-free when services were held there for the first time on Christmas Eve the following year. Members of Robert's family also donated the land on Tubman Road, where the Daniel Marshall Historic Site was created in 1984.[22]

Shortly after Robert Pollard died, and in appreciation for his service to the community, local delegates to the state legislature—Ben Harbin, Joey Brush, and Emory Bargeron—presented a request to the Georgia House of Representatives to rename Kiokee Creek Bridge near Pollard's Corner after him. The name change quickly passed both the House and the Senate during the 1996 session. Family and friends gathered on July 11 of that year for the dedication ceremony.

Robert's sons, Robert, Jr. and Andy (Levi Anderson Pollard IV) manage the company now, aided by about a hundred employees and a continuous—renewable—supply of nearby Georgia pine.

Lynell Widener

In more than two-hundred-years of Columbia County history, Lynell Widener is the only person to hold the title of artist laureate. She also may be the only county resident included in the *Guinness Book of World*

Records. The Columbia County native, whose artistry graces the cover and numerous pages of this book, rightfully claims both honors. Today her paintings are also displayed on the walls of area banks, libraries, government offices, museums, and in many private homes.

Born in 1924 to Luther and Marie Blanchard McNair, who lived on White Oak Road near the McDuffie County line, Lynell showed an interest in capturing the beauty of her surroundings from the time she was a young child. But the day the teenager walked through the mezzanine of J. B. White's Department Store in downtown Augusta and watched studio artists adding color to black-and-white portraits, she knew what she wanted to do now that she was almost grown up.

When Lynell expressed an interest in their work, one of the studio employees invited her to try coloring some of the portraits herself. What may have been a gamble for White's turned out to be a stepping-stone for the future artist laureate. The studio was impressed enough with those early samples to hire her to work for them, and coloring portraits was Lynell's first job out of high school. Working as a free-lance photographer for the *Augusta Chronicle* at the same time heightened her interest in capturing scenic images on canvas as well as in print.

Marriage, two children, and two years in California while her husband served in the Army intervened, but when the enlistment was over, the young family returned to the area and settled across the river in South Carolina. With her children in school and their home not far from the Aiken campus of the University of South Carolina, Lynell enrolled in art classes at the university and spent more time in front of her easel at home. When divorce ended her fourteen-year marriage, Lynell continued painting while returning to the *Augusta Chronicle* to work full-time as a photographer and occasional writer. From time to time she also took art lessons from area artists, including Freeman Schoolcraft, a well-known Chicago artist who had joined the faculty of Augusta College.

A few years after she and David Widener were married, the family, which now included a son born to the new couple, moved back to Columbia County. Very soon, memories of Lynell's childhood—public buildings; familiar street scenes; Whiteoak Campground, where her family had spent summer camp-meeting weeks from the time she was a month old; and many views of the river—were transferred to canvas in the studio she fashioned out of the garage in their new home. In 1978, following an exhibit of forty paintings she had completed during the previous two years, she explained why she spent so much time dwelling on local subjects.

> When my husband and I joined the Columbia County Historical Society I became aware of the destruction of many of our county landmarks through fire and progress. That became heavy on my heart and I felt it was necessary to paint as many of these wonderful places as possible. . . . For a county with such a rich, southern heritage, it is mandatory for future generations to have a glimpse of our wonderful past."[23]

Sometime after the exhibit and at the suggestion of Superintendent of Schools John Pierce Blanchard, county officials declared Mrs. Widener the county's first—and to this date, only—artist laureate.

In addition to painting, Lynell added art students and an arts column in the *Columbia County News-Times* to her already busy schedule. Sometime in the late 1990's she also went back to school, this time taking group classes at Augusta College to try her hand at other kinds of art including pottery, ceramics, and sculpture. Vases, pottery, and a few sculptures are now displayed among dozens of paintings in her "art-gallery" home.

Today Lynell Widener paints—or sculpts—"only when I want to," but along the way she has collected other unique honors. When the Olympics came to Atlanta in 1996, her painting of a polo player—perhaps with her polo-playing husband as her model—was on display as part of the equestrian exhibit. Her most exciting achievement, however, may be what she did a year or two before that, when she joined about twenty other artists in Savannah, Georgia, to create the world's largest painting at the time: a three-football-field-long likeness of the 1993 Elvis Presley postage stamp.

Lynell's framed letter from the *Guinness Book of World Records* acknowledging her participation in that week-long effort hangs prominently in her home today—across the room from the proclamation naming her artist laureate of Columbia County fifteen years before.

On Stage and in the Sky: Oliver Hardy, Terri Gibbs, and Susan Still Kilrain

If you drive through Harlem, Georgia, or on any approaching highway today, you can't miss the signs telling you this city is the birthplace of Oliver Hardy, the shorter, "rotund" half of the early twentieth-century comedy team, Laurel and Hardy. Stan Laurel was born in England, where the taller man may also be celebrated today. But if so, the festivities there could not possibly outshine Harlem's annual Oliver Hardy Festival, which has grown from a thousand visitors on that first October Saturday in 1989 to nearly forty thousand during the same fall day twenty years later. Certainly Oliver Norvell Hardy, born to Oliver and Emily Hardy at the home of his mother's parents in 1892, is a strong contender for Harlem's favorite son.

Before the twice-widowed Oliver Hardy, Sr., married the also-widowed Emily Norvell Tant, he was a prominent Harlem or Columbia County son in his own right. The salesman and county tax collector, who later served on the Harlem Town (now city) Council, was known as "the consummate politician . . . with a warm camaraderie and other traits that would be exhibited in his son."[24] The father, however, would never know of the similarity. The fifty-one-year-old man died when his son was only ten months old.

Widowed again, Emily Hardy and her child—whose original name, Norvell, was later changed to Oliver Norvell at his request—left Harlem and moved temporarily into the hotel her husband had owned in Madison, Georgia, and where they had already spent some time. That connection, or possibly Emily's own experience, soon led to her position as manager of the Baldwin Hotel in Milledgeville, and to Oliver's introduction to traveling performers who often stayed there. And the rest, they say, is history.

Oliver was still a teenager when he became projectionist and frequent performer at the Electric Theater in Milledgeville. Later, having tried college but knowing he would rather be on stage than in class, Oliver moved to Jacksonville, Florida, and joined a small film colony there. Six years later he was in Hollywood, where, after working as a supporting actor, he joined the Hal Roach Studios and met his comedic counterpart, Stan Laurel. Over the next three decades, Laurel and Hardy made more than a hundred films together and remained friends as well as costars until Oliver's death in 1957.

Oliver Hardy never returned to Harlem; even his burial site is in Hollywood. But judging by the enthusiasm of those he left behind, memories of the funny man who still has thousands of fans in this country and in Stan Laurel's England never left Harlem. In 1989, following extensive planning by Mayor James Lewis, City Hall staff, and members of a committee to keep the actor's legacy alive, the city held its inaugural Oliver Hardy Festival. A resounding success from the beginning, the festival has grown each year in both attractions and interest, and now includes a parade, street dance, Laurel and Hardy "movie mania" and look-alike contest, more than three hundred vendors, and plenty of food and entertainment throughout the day.

In 2002, after visitors had begun arriving with Laurel and Hardy memorabilia, the city turned the old post office in the center of town into an impressive Laurel and Hardy Museum and placed those items on permanent display. Today, between festivals, guests may visit the well-stocked museum and accompanying gift shop, Tuesday–Saturday throughout the year, from ten in the morning until four in the afternoon.

Terri Gibbs may not have been born in Columbia County, but she has called Grovetown home ever since her family moved there from Miami, Florida, when she was a year old. Before long the little girl was sitting at the piano, belting out songs she had learned from her musical family, and taking initial steps toward a lifelong career in country and Christian music. All this, despite complications from her premature birth that left her totally blind.

Terri Gibbs, gospel singer

She thanks her family—two uncles who sang in a gospel quartet, a great grandfather who led "all day gospel sings" for his family and friends, and an aunt who began teaching her how to play the piano when she was just three years old. She also thanks God for her musical ability. Not surprisingly, Terri's first performances were in church, where she either sang with her cousins or played the piano while other family members did the singing. School and community talent shows, which she often won, and solo spots with local bands or traveling country music artists increased her exposure and led to an area-wide reputation as "a promising singer" when she was in high school.

Besides writing music and performing it herself, Terri spent time listening to music, all kinds: pop, early rock, country, gospel, soul, and a broad list of recordings by contemporary singers. She was especially drawn to Ray Charles, another blind singer with whom she felt a unique bond. By the time she finished high school she had narrowed her choice to country music—and set her sights on Nashville.

For eight years she submitted demos, made visits to the Country Music Capital, and continued to perform with local bands. In 1980, "with the help of a few pros" including country singer Chet Atkins, songwriter-producer Ed Penny offered her a recording contract with Music Corporation of America (MCA). After release of her first single, "Somebody's Knockin'," and further exposure during a high-profile tour with country music legend George Jones, Terri Gibbs's local reputation went nationwide.

Right away MCA released a full album of Terri's music with "Somebody's Knockin'" as the title song. The album quickly reached the Top Ten on the debut album charts, while the title song earned similar status in three categories: Country Music's Top Ten, Adult Contemporary's Top Five, and overall, a major "crossover" hit. As if that were not honor enough, in 1981 Terri received the Country Music Association's first Horizon Award for New Artist of the Year, and the prestigious New Female Vocalist of the Year award by the Academy of Country Music. Before the year was over, she had also received her first Grammy nomination.

Despite all her personal success, about five years later Terri felt a call from God to make a major shift in her career. Her main interest now was to return to those "deep gospel roots" and concentrate on the recording of gospel music. The timing could not have been better. Her album *Turn Around* became the first CD release by New Canaan Records, a division of Word Records, and earned her a second Grammy nomination. Terri became the flagship artist for that new label, which led to further award nominations and two crossover music videos.

Terri's life changed again in 1988, when she married David Daughtry and the following year gave birth to David, II. But she did not give up her career; she just continued to share her music as well as her faith through her recordings and frequent public appearances, this time with her husband, and when he was old enough, her son by her side.

Sadly, her husband died in 2008, but Terri has continued to record her music, fill the calendar with performance dates, and encourage her now twenty-year-old son as he begins a music career of his own. David Daughtry and the Pumpkin Center Boys, named for a local community in North Harlem, already has a web site, a blog, and a following. With his mother as adviser and coach, before long we can expect to hear more from this young man and "the Boys."

In summary, Terri has always hoped people would not think of her as "a blind singer," but as a singer who happens to be blind. She also hopes her music will help her audiences establish that same connection with God that is so much a part of her own life.

"My singing is now more than a performance," she says; "it's a ministry. I'm finally where I belong." (For further information, or to hear samples of Terri's music, please visit her website: www.terrigibbs.us.)

As NASA Astronaut Susan Still explained in a simultaneous interview with the *Augusta Chronicle* and WRDW (Channel 12) from the Space Shuttle *Columbia* in 1997, "It's a lot different than flying airplanes out of Daniel Field."[25]

Born in Augusta in 1961, and raised there until her parents Dr. and Mrs. Joseph Still moved to Martinez, the shuttle pilot was speaking from experience. She knew the difference between flying a small plane on short hops around the city's private airport, and leaving earth at the controls of a powerful, bus-sized aircraft for sixteen days in space. Her father, founder and director of the Joseph M. Still Burn Center in Augusta, consented to her request for flying lessons at Daniel Field when she was sixteen years old, and witnessed her first solo flight the following year. Twenty years later he would also witness his astronaut-daughter's launch into space.

With stars in her eyes by the time she graduated from high school, Susan entered Embry-Riddle Aeronautical University—located next to Florida's Daytona Beach International Airport and sixty miles north of the Kennedy Space Center—to major in aeronautical engineering. A master of science degree in aerospace engineering from the Georgia Institute of Technology followed in 1985, the same year she was commissioned an

Astronaut Susan Still Kilrain.
Courtesy National Aeronautics and Space Administration.

ensign in the United States Navy. Two years later she was designated a naval aviator and selected as a flight instructor. Further specialized training, including Test Pilot School, led to over three thousand flight hours in more than thirty different aircraft during the next ten years.

Susan reported to the Johnson Space Center as an Astronaut Candidate in 1995. After more training, and work with Vehicle Systems and Operations plus serving as a spacecraft communicator for numerous missions, now Lieutenant Commander Still was ready for a mission of her own.

Make that "missions." The now well-trained Lieutenant Commander was chosen as the second female astronaut to pilot a space shuttle, and she would have that opportunity at the controls of the *Columbia* on mission

STS-83, April 4, 1997. The Microgravity Science Laboratory Spacelab Mission was to last sixteen days. Mission Control brought the shuttle and its crew back home in four. A faulty cell in one of the shuttle's three power-generation units was thought too problematic to continue the mission. Shuttle pilot Still was commended for bringing the spacecraft safely back to earth, and for her handling of the aborted mission.

Disappointment? Only momentarily. NASA made immediate plans to re-fly both the mission and crew as soon as the power cell problem was resolved. Three months later, with her parents again watching from the family viewing area of the Kennedy Space Center, Lieutenant Commander Still, Mission Commander Jim Halsell, and the remainder of the original seven-member crew began the re-flight. This time, retitled mission STS-94 would last the full sixteen days—and provide opportunity for that earlier mentioned, in-flight interview with the *Chronicle* and the Augusta TV station. She also called her Dad from space—and her boyfriend, Navy SEAL Colin Kilrain, who would later become her husband.

In September of that year the hometown girl—and her hometown—celebrated her accomplishment together, when the Augusta-Richmond County Museum sponsored a public Susan Still Day. Several hundred people, including many children, listened as she recounted details of the mission, told how it felt to "blast off" and be weightless—"we had to keep pushing each other out of the way"[26]—and described how the earth looked from 187 miles away.

The museum had a particular interest in Astronaut Still's flight. They had given her a prehistoric Indian arrowhead to carry into space, and she returned the well-traveled relic to them during the celebration. The arrowhead, along with her flight suit from mission STS-94, the shirt she wore on that first solo flight above Daniel Field in 1979, and other artifacts are now displayed in a permanent exhibit on the ground floor of the museum.

But the now very experienced pilot, who owes her early interest in science and space to her teachers in middle school math and high school chemistry, wanted to do something to pass that excitement along to a new generation of children. With the aid of her parents, Susan sponsored the Children's Discovery Gallery on the museum's second floor. The exhibit includes an early fur trader and his dugout canoe; a replica of the 1903 Wright brothers airplane; and a simulated cockpit from the *Columbia*, complete with video and voice recording of Astronaut Still during liftoff and landing of the shuttle flight. A message on the plaque at the gallery entrance reads, "To inspire children to think, to learn, to dream, Susan L. Still."

Susan joined her fellow crew members and the rest of America in mourning the loss of *Columbia* and its newer crew in February 2003. As tragic as the incident was, she remembered that the earlier shuttle *Challenger* had blown up about the time she was beginning her journey toward becoming an astronaut. "We all know [space travel] is risky and we accept that risk. . . . As devastating as [this tragedy] is, I think every one of them would say they would do it again."[27]

Considering the coincidental naming of the shuttle and Columbia County, and knowing that a former *Columbia* Astronaut once lived among us, following the tragedy local residents signed a specially commissioned, three-by-four foot plastic sympathy card and sent it to the families of the lost *Columbia* flight crew via the Johnson Space Center in Houston. A few weeks later, the Martinez-Evans Rotary Club, along with Columbia and Metro Augusta Clean and Beautiful, planted seven Little Gem Magnolia trees at Patriots Park, one for each of the fallen *Columbia* crew.

Susan Still Kilrain retired from NASA in 2002 and from the U.S. Navy in 2005. She and her still active-duty, Navy SEAL husband live in Virginia Beach, Virginia, with their four children: Quinn Marie, Sean, Liam, and Maura.

46

THE STATE OF THE COUNTY AT THE
TWENTY-FIRST CENTURY

What a journey! From the river-island home of prehistoric nomads and the disappearing settlements of Brandon, Kioka, Wrightsboro, Cobbham, Sawdust, Berzelia, and more; to the communities of Phinizy, Leah, Appling, Winfield, Grovetown, Harlem, Evans, and Martinez that took their place, we've met pioneers, planters, statesmen, freedom fighters, educators, entertainers, politicians and entrepreneurs, the adventurer and the religious refugee, our neighbors and ourselves, an infinite mixture of humanity with one common thread—at one time or another, we all have called Columbia County, Georgia, home.

From Moses Waddell's late eighteenth-century school with a handful of students near present-day Appling, and a scattering of Quaker homeschools in nearby Wrightsboro, nearly twenty-three-thousand students now attend thirty public and a half dozen private schools across the county, with new buildings already on the drawing board.

From one Baptist church "on the banks of the Kiokee" in 1772, eighteen churches with ties to the Southern Baptist Convention are now spread throughout the county. Likewise, from the turn of the nineteenth-century circuit (connected) parishes of Shiloh, White Oak, and Dunn's

Chapel, thirteen United Methodist churches now call Columbia County home. Also, from the latter 1800's to the present day, a growing number of churches with primarily African-American congregations have established a lasting presence here. And if your worship preference is not represented by the above groups, nearly every major religious affiliation in this country and beyond is likely already a short distance from your home or seeking a Columbia County location.

From small, general stores like those once owned by Jake Pollard, Sr., and J. D. Howell in Appling, William Rountree in Evans, and Hartwell Morris, Sr., in Martinez, hardly a recognized supermarket, drug store, "big box" department store, or hardware chain has by-passed the county. Do you need a doctor, lawyer, bank, someone to fix your car or teach your child how to play the piano? All these and other services once found no closer than Augusta are here in multiples, along with an abundance of places to stay, eat, play, or be entertained.

Do you like to read, search for information, take part in a book discussion group or indulge in an afternoon of Scrabble? Until 1956, when the Evans Branch of the Augusta Regional Library opened in a former post office building near the new, consolidated Evans School, the only libraries in Columbia County were in high schools or private homes. Harlem became the site of a second county library in 1981, a year before the Warren C. Gibbs Memorial Library on Belair Road replaced that now too-small building in the center of Evans. Grovetown's Euchee Creek Library opened in 1994, followed by upgrades to the Harlem Branch in 2001 and 2003. But thanks to passage of a special option, one-cent sales tax referendum in 1999, the Harlem project was only the first phase of an increased library presence in the county. Phase two would place another, larger library in heavily populated Evans.

For nearly a decade, which began by increasing awareness of overcrowded conditions at the Gibbs Library, assessing community interest and projected use of a larger facility, and petitioning county officials to include library funding in the Special Purpose Local Option Sales Tax (SPLOST) referendum, Dr. Jefferson Hardin, chairman of the Columbia County Library Board, and his committee studied the latest trends in public library design, and visited an array of new buildings throughout the Southeast. They also sought—and received—donations for "extras" which, by then, the allotted sales tax revenue of $12.2 million would not cover. Among those donations was a $500,000 gift from Columbia County native, Jabez Sanford Hardin, Jr., founder of Sysco Food Services, Inc., in Memphis, Tennessee, and son of Jabez Sanford Hardin, Sr., Columbia County Superintendent of Schools, 1921–1948. Although Dr. Hardin and the superintendent's son were not related, their identical surnames and ensuing friendship became an encore to turning a sparse, multipurpose room at the new library into a well-equipped Performing Arts Center, an effort made possible by that generous gift from a grateful son to honor his father.

Ground-breaking for the two-story, 50,000 square-foot library took place on September 16, 2003, just behind the county's new Justice Center on Ronald Reagan Drive. Two and a half years later, with kindergarten children from Evans Elementary School taking part, county officials and library staff cut the entrance-wide ribbon and declared the newest county library open to the public. Ample parking, professional landscaping, monuments and memorials, children's playground, and a 750-seat amphitheater surround the building, while separate areas for children, adults, computer lab, meeting rooms, and shelves holding 110,000 books fill the inside.

Besides a surge in book circulation, meetings of many kinds—including book signings and discussions, guest author presentations, children's story hours, and those Sunday afternoon Scrabble games—help explain the immediate popularity of the new library. A Coffee Shop, Friends of the Library gift shop, entrance to the Performing Arts Center, and a perpetual art gallery greet you as you enter the spacious lobby, and capable librarians are available once you are inside. They, or one of three automatic checkout stations, also assist you as you leave.

In addition to libraries, Harlem and Grovetown also have their own museums. The Harlem structure concentrates on the memory of favorite son, comedian Oliver Hardy, but thanks to the vision of Rosa Lee Owens and well-known area historian Charles Lord, with the support of city leaders and residents alike, Grovetown opened its own, local history museum in early 2000. Housed in the historic, substantially renovated Fields House on Robinson Avenue, and open Friday through Sunday of each week, the attractive cottage is full of donated artifacts, memorabilia, and well-documented evidence of the city's origin and growth.

Other cultural opportunities, once located only beyond county lines, have also found a home here. Ron Jones, formerly with the Atlanta Ballet, opened a dance school in Martinez in 1985. Today that location on Fury's Ferry Road is the home of the Columbia County Ballet, where students take lessons and prepare three or more events each year. The New Nutcracker, the ballet's annual holiday production at the Performing Arts Center, is always sold out weeks in advance.

In 1997, through the combined efforts of Earl and Kathy Williams and Jacques Kearns, members and music director at the First Baptist Church of Evans, the Columbia County Choral Society began rehearsing and presenting periodic performances at the Evans Church. The approximately forty-to-fifty member group has continued to present their well-prepared seasonal, patriotic, or nostalgia-filled show-tune concerts ever since.

Although we will soon hear more about the recently formed Columbia County Symphony Orchestra, the Augusta Symphony added a Columbia County Series to its schedule several years ago, with concerts either in the Performing Arts Center or "on the ground" at the Columbia County campus of the University Hospital complex on North Belair Road. Add to this impressive list a variety of concerts by local or visiting musicians, and dramatic productions by local high schools or Stage III, a community dinner theater founded in 1998 by well-known local actors Fred and Maria Elser, and area concertgoers or theater patrons should have no problem finding something to do or someplace to go any weekend of the year. For all performing and visual artists, the latter having organized the Artists' Guild of Columbia County in 2004, Columbia County Arts, an umbrella organization with representatives from each member group, helps coordinate and keep these activities and events in the public eye.

But if you think this county has overemphasized arts, culture, and how to exercise the mind, wait until we list where and how to exercise the body. Recreation, either for children, seasoned athletes, or those who want to stay or get in shape, has almost been "priority No. 1" in Columbia County for decades.

As an outgrowth of championship athletic teams in local schools—or perhaps as a feeder, the county's Recreation Department and more than 1,300 trained volunteers annually register thousands of children and youth in football, baseball, softball, basketball, soccer, swimming, tennis, and—you name it—sports. Thanks to county commissioners and supportive citizens, who repeatedly approve budgets and special option sales taxes to fund new or improved facilities, the county has not skimped on places to swing a bat, carry a ball, or walk a track.

Six major parks—Appling, Blanchard Woods, Harlem City, Goodale in Grovetown, Riverside on Hardy McManus Road, and, one of the largest athletic complexes in Georgia, Patriots Park on Columbia Road—provide venues for a myriad of local activities and major tournaments for both regional and Southeastern competition. In 1992, when then Commission Chairman Mike Graybill addressed a celebrating crowd during dedication ceremonies for the new, hundred-acre Patriots Park, he summarized the reason behind such a youth-centered emphasis like this: "Instead of jails, we build parks."

Mr. Graybill might have added that we also build or provide access to community centers for the not-so-young; hiking, biking, fishing, and boating sites for all ages; aesthetic play and gathering locations such as the popular Savannah Rapids Park and Pavilion; environmental and educational opportunities, including Reed Creek Wetlands Park in Martinez and Heggie's Rock, the Nature Conservancy's nationally recognized sixty-acre granite outcropping and rare-plant preserve in Appling; and the bountiful pleasures and facilities at Clarks Hill Lake a short drive away.

And how could a county within a stone's throw of the prestigious Augusta National Golf Club not mention that we have golf on our side of the county line, too? Three courses—Bartram Trail, Three Oaks, and Jones Creek—are open to the public, while homeowners in the West Lake subdivision in Martinez and Riverwood Plantation in Evans enjoy their own, private course. Speaking of the Augusta National, it is no exaggeration to say that, because of the proximity, Columbia County plays host to thousands of guests when the world's greatest golfers and the sport's most avid fans rent homes, rooms, and every hotel in town during the Master's Golf Tournament, the first week in April of each year.

While we are talking about tournaments and competition, we have one more category to cover. After reading the following list, see if you agree that award-winning itself may just be Columbia County's primary "sport." From an array of champions in a variety of athletic, academic, and artistic pursuits, this top-of-the-charts sampling is what some Columbia County folks have "won" in the past decade or two.

—Just as the *Augusta Chronicle* is the oldest daily newspaper in Georgia, the *Columbia County News-Times* is the oldest weekly (or biweekly) publication in the state. Beginning as the *Columbia Advertiser* in 1880, the Harlem-based paper became the *Columbia Sentinel* in 1883 and, in 1920, the *Columbia News*. Under new management, the newspaper moved to Martinez in 1963, purchased the short-lived *Martinez-Evans Times* and created the *Columbia News-Times*. In 1997 new owner Tim Shelnut added the word "County" to the paper's name, which it remains under the current owner, Southeastern Newspapers. Since joining the Georgia Press Association in 1999, this newspaper, now located in the Publix Shopping Center on Washington Road in Evans, has won General Excellence—the highest prize in its category—in all but two of the years in which it was eligible to compete.

—Not to be outdone, the newspaper's Columbia County partner in the media, Beasley Broadcasting's premier radio station, WGAC, is bursting at the seams with awards. With its transmitter already near the corner of Washington and Davis roads since 1942, the Augusta station later moved into a small studio at the same Columbia County location. Following two more address changes in the 1990's to increasingly larger studios along South Belair Road, WGAC moved into its current, still larger location on the Jimmie Dyess Parkway in 2004.

But the station's physical expansion only parallels what has been happening inside: WGAC has won Georgia Association of Broadcasters

Radio Station of the Year Award eight years in a row. Morning Show hosts Harley Drew and Mary Liz Nolan, who have been the "alarm clock" for the entire CSRA during all those award-winning years, have acquired at least as many personal "bests" as has the station. The popular pair plus long-standing, also "best" afternoon talk-show host Austin Rhodes, along with a talented team of reporters and technical staff, no doubt account for the station's continued success.

—Although every Columbia County school is an award-winner in one category or another, each of our four high schools deserves special recognition here. (Columbia County's fifth secondary school, Grovetown High School, did not open until the fall of 2009.)

Four times, beginning in 1991, the Evans High School Band has traveled to London to participate in the Lord Mayor's New Year's Day parade. Three of those appearances, as well as a trip to New York City to perform in the Macy's 1993 Thanksgiving Day parade, were under the direction of longtime bandmaster Richard Brasco. Reid Hall, who succeeded Mr. Brasco following his retirement in 2003, directed the band's fourth London appearance in 2006.

Drama frequently comes to the forefront at Harlem High, but in 2004 director Roy Lewis and his award-winning students performed the Rodgers and Hart musical *Babes in Arms* in Edinburgh, Scotland. Selected by the American High School Theatre Festival, the Harlem drama troupe took part in Edinburgh's Fringe Festival, considered to be the largest performing arts festival in the world.

Several times since opening in 1988, Lakeside High School has been recognized nationally as well as regionally for superior academic achievement. But in 2009 Principal Jeff Carney announced that *Newsweek* ranked the school No. 309, or among the top one percent of public secondary schools in the nation.

Not to be outdone, Greenbrier High School has compiled an outstanding athletic record. Under the coaching of Athletic Director Garrett Black, the girls' softball team has won several regional championships plus a state title, and the baseball team has earned five state titles since the county's fourth high school opened thirteen years ago.

—It should come as no surprise that the schools, groups, and individuals on this list are based in communities that also earn "best of" awards. In 2005, *Money* named Evans the thirty-second best place to live in the country; and in 2009, citing quality housing, low crime rate, and ample employment opportunities, the magazine called neighboring Martinez sixty-third among those same top one hundred towns. Also, in its August 2009 edition, *Family Circle* called Evans one of the Ten Best Towns for Families in America. Reasons for the latter distinction include affordable housing, green space, job growth, and quality schools.

—And this just in: For the third time in the past four years (2006–2009), a baseball team from the Columbia County Recreation Department has won their division title in the Dixie "O" Zone World Series. This time the team of twelve-year-olds, coached by John Sandlin, traveled to Texarkana, Arkansas, defeated teams from Texas and Mississippi, and returned home with the championship trophy.

With all we have witnessed on our journey, or experienced as residents of Columbia County today, we must pause to ask a final question: What is the engine that drives all this activity, amenity, infrastructure, and organization? Is it only coincidence that one particular "mixture of humanity" decided to come here, live here, prosper, and develop what we found here? Or is there another element, another group of people we have not yet addressed in our report to whom we owe a measure of thanks for what, by all accounts, is a fine, even above-fine place to live, work, and play?

Columbia County is not Camelot—although we do have a neighborhood subdivision by that name—and Columbia Countians are not perfect. As we have learned while discussing everything from where to build a courthouse to how to manage population growth, residents often have opposing views on how those major decisions are made. Since decisions necessitate decision-makers, like every other entity or municipality, that means we also may disagree on who should be our leaders and, once in office, how they perform their job. Whatever our opinion, however, even a casual appraisal of Columbia County today proves our "engine" is running very well.

No matter how much revenue reaches the county treasury from an ever-increasing number of tax-paying property owners, businesses, and industry, sixty-four percent of that income goes directly to the school system. Of the remaining thirty-six percent, nearly half is allocated to the Department of Public Safety, leaving the remaining nineteen percent to cover all other locally funded obligations. Coupled with recent cuts in both state and federal subsidies, that our county government is still able to pay salaries and expenses, complete existing projects, and prepare for future needs is a testament to good budgetary management. That Columbia County has not raised its tax millage rate in ten years, while becoming one of only five Georgia counties to qualify for the very high bond rating of AA Plus when securing loans, is further evidence of that good management.

With support from state and congressional legislators and an active Chamber of Commerce, our commissioners, county administrator, staff, and cadre of employees deserve our thanks as well as our oversight for the meticulous way they perform their tasks. For all the attention to our schools, landscape, and elusive "quality of life," that people still choose to come here, and once here choose to remain, is also due to the quality of government they find here.

What shall we do with such a legacy? Above all, let's remember it, learn from it, improve what is necessary, imitate those who made lasting impressions on us and build on the strong foundation already laid. If we accept this challenge, when an updated story of Columbia County is written a generation or a century from now, our descendants will have even more to celebrate than we do today.

Columbia County: Born of revolution, deliberation, and grit; developed in sacrifice, conflict, and toil; sustained by knowledge, diligence, and faith. Like those who showed us the way, may we deliver this flourishing, once-fledgling settlement in the Backcountry of Georgia to those who come behind us for as long as the rivers run.

Endnotes

Introduction *PAGES xxi–xxiv*

1. Alfred, Lord Tennyson, "You Ask Me, Why"
2. Morgareidge, *Foundations of Government*, 11–14.

I. A Long, Long Time Ago *PAGES 3–30*

1. Matt. 26:11.
2. McCullar, *This Is Your Georgia* (1972), 96.
3. Bonner, *The Georgia Story*, 50.
4. Reese, *The Most Delightful Country*, 124.
5. Cashin, *The Story of Augusta*, 11.

II. From Colony to County *PAGES 31–94*

1. Coleman, *A History of Georgia*, 34.
2. Fleming, *Autobiography of a Colony*, 181–85.
3. Candler, *The Colonial Records of Georgia* 6:212.
4. Ibid., 172.
5. White, *Columbia County*, 30, 49–50.
6. Knight, *Georgia's Landmarks* 1:762.
7. *Collections of the Georgia Historical Society* 35:335–36.
8. Knight, *Georgia's Landmarks* 1:762.
9. Jones, *Memorial History of Augusta*, 45–46.
10. Hollingsworth, *Indians on the Savannah River*, 77.

11. Hooker, *Carolina Backcountry*, 240–41.
12. Presley, "Crackers of Georgia," 115.
13. Ibid., 115.
14. Baker, *Story of Wrightsboro*, 4.
15. Cashin, *Forty Years of Adversity*, 237.
16. Davis, *Quaker Records*, 110–11.
17. Knight, *Georgia's Landmarks* 1:767.
18. Harris and Mosteller, *Georgia's First Continuing Baptist Church*, 19–28.
19. Ibid., 248.
20. Fetter, "Portrait of a Patriot," 1.
21. Miller, *Great Georgians*, 69.
22. Cashin, *King's Ranger*, 9.
23. Ibid., 27.
24. Ibid., 28.
25. Cashin and Robertson, *Augusta and the American Revolution*, 6.
26. Fleming, *Autobiography of a Colony*, 117.
27. George III was the son of Princess Augusta for whom the Georgia city was named.
28. McCullar, *This Is Your Georgia* (1972), 219.
29. Coleman, *American Revolution in Georgia*, 122; 307 (note 22).
30. Ibid., 89.
31. McCullar, *This Is Your Georgia* (1972), 216.
32. Cashin and Robertson, 38.
33. Ibid., 53.
34. Jones, *Memorial History of Augusta*, 103.
35. The name of the Trading Post is also spelled "McKay," and the building called "The White House," but it is not, as many claim, the still-standing Ezekiel Harris House near the river at the western edge of Augusta.
36. Cashin and Robertson, 55.
37. McCullar, *This Is Your Georgia* (1972), 249.
38. Paul Chrastina, "Greene's Army," 10.
39. Jones, *Memorial History of Augusta*, 113.
40. Cashin and Robertson, 98 (note 205).
41. Cashin, *King's Ranger*, 134.
42. Jones, *Memorial History of Augusta*, 130.
43. Cashin, *King's Ranger*, 227–28.
44. Jones, *Memorial History of Georgia*, 133.
45. George Lamplugh, "William Few's Brownsborough Plan," 44.

III. Steps and Missteps Along Independence Way *pages 95–122*

1. Jordan and Puster, *Courthouses in Georgia*, 26.
2. Jones, *Memorial History of Augusta*, 218.
3. Pearl Baker, "The Itinerant Court House," *Columbia News* (Sept. 1968), 1.
4. Ibid.
5. Coulter, *Georgia: A Short History*, 199.
6. Foster, *James Jackson*, 106.
7. Ibid., 112.
8. Ibid., 108.
9. Ibid., 114.
10. Ibid., 116–17.
11. Ibid., 118.
12. Knight, *Reminiscences* 1:34.
13. Foster, *James Jackson*, 137.
14. Tennyson, the poem "Charge of the Light Brigade," written in celebration of a noble but disastrous effort by the British Cavalry in the Crimean War, 1854.
15. Jones, *Memorial History of Augusta*, 150.
16. King, *Georgia Voices*, 99–100.
17. Gilmer, *Sketches*, 267.
18. Jackson et al., *Georgia Studies Book*, 146.
19. Foner and Garraty, *Reader's Companion to American History*, 579.
20. Maurice Melton, "War Trail of the Red Sticks," *American History Illustrated* (Feb. 1976), 33–42, quoting an editor in *Augusta Chronicle*, 36.
21. Jackson et al., *Georgia Studies Book*, 142.
22. Ibid., 150.
23. McCullar, *This Is Your Georgia*, (1982), 136.

IV. More than Her Share of Heroes *pages 123–74*

1. Though some records say Baldwin lived in Wilkes County, careful research, including Baldwin's land grant and appointment as the U.S. Representative for Middle Georgia–Burke, Richmond, and Washington counties–reveal those records to be in error. Wilkes County was in Upper Georgia. (Abstracts of Georgia Land Plat Books A & B, 1779–1785, Book A, p. 26.)

2. Bernstein, *Reader's Companion*, 832.

3. Jones, *Memorial History of Augusta*, 135.

4. Mellichamp, *Senators From Georgia*, 50.

5. This phrase was said of Sir Thomas More, England's accomplished, yet sometimes controversial, sixteenth-century statesman, by More's contemporary, Robert Whittinton.

6. Gilmer, *Sketches,* 101.

7. King, *Georgia Voices*, 106.

8. Coulter, *Old Petersburg*, 91.

9. Ibid., 92.

10. Ibid., 98.

11. Ibid., 100.

12. McCullar, *This Is Your Georgia* (1972), 329.

13. Mooney, *William H. Crawford*, 62.

14. Knight, *Reminiscences* 2:121.

15. Mooney, *William H. Crawford*, 81.

16. Ibid., 88.

17. Ibid., 127.

18. Ibid., 207.

19. Not until 1832 were presidential nominees chosen at the major political party conventions, or the presidency determined by the popular vote of the people.

20. Mooney, *William H. Crawford*, 301.

21. Ibid., 316.

22. Ibid., 341.

23. Knight, *Reminiscences* 2:122–33.

24. Knight, *Georgia's Landmarks* 2:36.

25. Knight, *Reminiscences* 2:116.

26. Knight, *Georgia's Landmarks* 2:692.

27. Ibid., 2:693.

28. Knight, *Georgia's Landmarks* 1:479.

29. Coulter, *Old Petersburg*, 153.

30. The Bible, Elijah's contest with the Prophets of Baal, I Kings 18.

31. Coulter, *Old Petersburg*, 155.

32. Knight, *Georgia's Landmarks* 1:428.

33. Coulter, *Old Petersburg*, 155, 158.

34. Gilmer, *Sketches*, 186.

35. Knight, *Landmarks* 1:429.

36. Ibid., 430.
37. Ibid., 835.
38. Ibid., 834.
39. Material for this segment taken from Mercer Archives, supplied by the university.

V. From Depot to Courthouse: By River, Road, and Rail *PAGES 175–200*

1. Morse, *Universal Standard Encyclopedia* 19:7030.
2. Allen, *We Americans*, 172.
3. Jones, *Memorial History of Augusta,* 482.
4. Hanson, *History of the Georgia Railroad* , 9.
5. Cashin, *The Brightest Arm of the Savannah,* along with Canal Authority brochures, provided most of the material for the segment on the Augusta Canal.
6. Ibid., 112.
7. Ibid., 140.
8. This reference to John Trowbridge given by Thomas Nesbitt, wealthy Burke County planter and admirer of Trowbridge; material supplied by Trowbridge descendant Ann B. Sawyer of North Augusta, South Carolina.
9. Quote attributed to Russian author Leo Tolstoy, on page 18, Book XIV, of his historic tome, *War and Peace.*

VI. From Africa to the Backcountry of Georgia: The African-American History of Columbia County against the Backdrop of the Civil War *PAGES 201–46*

1. The subtitles in this section are phrases from familiar African-American Spirituals.
2. Thurmond, *Freedom*, 7.
3. Wood, *Reader's Companion to American History*, 1010.
4. Pastors often cited two biblical references to support this claim: Noah's curse—not God's—against his son Ham in Genesis 9; and Moses' modification of slavery, which was already a custom in their new land, in Leviticus 25:44–46.
5. Nobel E. Cunningham, Jr., *Oxford Companion to United States History* (Oxford–New York, Oxford University Press, 2001), 405.

6. The word "gerrymandering" was named for Massachusetts Governor Elbridge Gerry who in 1812 redrew the map of a new voting district favorable to his political party. Opponents, and a Boston cartoonist, thinking the shape of the new map resembled a salamander, named the political manipulation practice after him (Chantrell, *Dictionary*, 230).

7. United States Constitution, Article I, Section 2.

8. Thurmond, *Freedom*, 70–71; also Wood, *Reader's Companion*, 990–91.

9. Thurmond, 72.

10. United States Constitution, Article I, Section 9.

11. Thurmond, 148, regarding the 1829 law making it unlawful to educate Negroes, whether they were slave or free. Perpetrators could face imprisonment or a $500 fine.

12. Thurmond, 121.

13. Emma Lazarus, "The New Colossus," the inscription on the base of the Statue of Liberty, New York Harbor, 1883.

14. Thurmond, 132.

15. Despite individual preferences for other titles, the most common name for this conflict is The Civil War. There are many reasons for this decision but, ultimately, outside the Southern states, the Confederacy was never recognized as a sovereign nation either by any other country or the United States Government. Therefore, this was considered to be a war within one country, not a conflict between two. (Many sources, including Frank E. Vandiver, "Confederate States of America," in Foner and Garraty, *Reader's Companion*, 212.)

16. Williams, *Land We Lived*, 26.

17. Harris, *Plain Folk*, 16–17; Gilmer, *Sketches*, 452–53.

18. Gilmer, *Sketches*, 452–53.

19. Powell, *Triumph of Liberty*, 45.

20. James D. Mosteller, *A History of the Kiokee Baptist Church in Georgia, 1772–1952*; Waldo P. Harris, *Georgia's First Continuing Baptist Church*, a revision and expansion of Mosteller's book (College Park, Ga.: N & R Printing, Inc., 1997).

21. Harris and Mosteller, 161–62.

22. Thomas Holley: *Company F—Thomson Guards; Company K—Ramsey Volunteers;* and *Company K—Hamilton Rangers.*

23. Holley, *Company F—Thomson Guards*, quoting Captain William Johnston, Thomson Guards, Winchester, Va., Oct. 4, 1862, p. 125.

24. Holley, *Company F—Thomson Guards*, 11.

25. Holley, *Company K—Hamilton Rangers*, 95.

26. Dameron, *Benning's Brigade* 2:2.

27. Thurmond, 181.

28. James M. McPherson, "Emancipation Proclamation," in Foner and Garraty, 351–52.

29. Jackson et al., *Georgia Studies*, 194.

30. Foner, *Reconstruction*, 70.

31. Thurmond, 241.

32. Leviticus 25:8–14.

33. From President Abraham Lincoln's Second Inaugural Address, March 4, 1865.

34. Bennett, *America: The Last Best Hope* 1:390.

35. Smith, *Grant*, 422.

36. Ibid., 418.

37. Suddeth et al., *Empire Builders*, 246–47.

38. Smith, *Grant*, 422.

39. Foner, *Reconstruction*, 159.

40. Suddeth et al., *Empire Builders*, 251.

41. Foner, *Reconstruction*, 68–69.

42. Bennett, 404.

43. Foner and Garraty, "Reconstruction," in Foner and Garraty, 922.

44. General Robert E. Lee's surrender to General Ulysses S. Grant took place at Appomattox, Virginia, April 9, 1865.

45. Williams, *Land We Lived*, 59, 109.

46. Ruppersburg, *Georgia Voices*, 180.

47. Williams, *Land We Lived*, 98.

48. It was not unusual at the time for either Black or White schools to accept high school graduates, or even those with some high school education, as teachers.

49. Williams, *Land We Lived*, 50.

50. All of this information is recounted in detail by Columbia County native Joseph B. Williams in his *Land We Lived* (2005), 31, 41–44.

51. Thurmond, 273.

52. James Weldon Johnson was an educator, lawyer, general secretary of the NAACP, and author of "Lift Every Voice and Sing," the 1900 poem known today as the Black National Anthem.

53. Harris and Mosteller, *Georgia's First Continuing Baptist Church*, 123, 136.

54. Harris and Mosteller, 137; Cashin, *Old Springfield*, 14–15.

55. Harris and Mosteller, 126.

56. Ibid., 124.

57. Harris and Mosteller, 137; Cashin, *Old Springfield*, 14.

58. Cashin, *Old Springfield*, 69.

59. Seaborn, "Walnut Grove School," *Columbia County News-Times*, Nov. 25, 1987. 7–B.

60. Sharyn Kane and Richard Keeton, *In Those Days*, 73.

61. Cline, *Augusta Chronicle*, Feb. 5, 2006.

VII. CONCLUSION: AN OVERVIEW OF THE TWENTIETH CENTURY AND THE STATE OF THE COUNTY TODAY *PAGES 247–98*

1. These figures may be verified with the Georgia State Office of Planning & Budget, or the Atlanta Office of the U.S. Census Bureau.

2. Cashin, *Story of Augusta*, 221–22.

3. Ibid., 237.

4. Ibid., 269.

5. Mark Dunn, *New Georgia Encyclopedia*. Material taken from the Internet; no page number available.

6. *Augusta Chronicle*, Apr. 14, 2004. 7–A.

7. Brackett, *Augusta Chronicle*, Aug. 9, 2009. 1–E.

8. Material for this segment taken from the Army Corps of Engineers brochures and from Pavey, "Debate on Lake's Name Continues," *Augusta Chronicle*, Apr. 12, 2004, 1–A.

9. Cashin, *Story of Augusta*, 91.

10. Ibid., 210.

11. Karin Schill, *The Place Called Home: A Collection of Articles about Local History from the Augusta Chronicle*, Bill Kirby, deputy metro ed, 1997, p. 70.

12. Schill, quoting Al Hodge, president of Metro Augusta Chamber of Commerce, 71.

13. Material for this segment supplied by Pavey, "Deal in Works," *Augusta Chronicle*, June 10, 1909, 1–A; and following Internet sites: "Savannah River Site," *Wikipedia*; and "MOX Fuel Fabrication Plant Project" [South Carolina]," *Shaw Areva Mox Services*, May 4, 2009.

14. Seaborn, "Head of the Class," *Augusta Magazine*, June-July 1995. 4.

15. Preston Sparks, "Marker Honors Beloved Educator," 1.

16. Angie Lee, "Free Time Rare," *Augusta Chronicle*, Oct. 14, 1979. 4–E.

17. Peggy Cheney, *Columbia News*, Sept. 23, 1981; also included in Janette Kelley's *Our Heritage*, 58.
18. Billy Hobbs,"Dozier Receives Tankersley Service Award," *Columbia County News-Times*, Nov. 8, 1987. 1–A.
19. Seaborn, "Minutes from Everything and a World Away," *Augusta Magazine*, Sept. 1996, 21.
20. Ibid., 21, 22.
21. Harris and Mosteller, 96.
22. Ibid., 420–21.
23. Coles McKagen, "Lynell Widener," in Kelley, *Our Heritage*, p. 110.
24. Charles Lord, "Movie Star's Father Once Loomed Large," *Augusta Chronicle*, May 12, 1999. 8–C.
25. Amy Joyner, "Plenty to Do: Still Busy Aboard Columbia," *Augusta Chronicle*, July 9, 1997. 1–A.
26. Ibid.
27. Brian Neill, "Mars Tripping," *Metro Spirit* (Augusta), Jan. 29, 1904. 16.

SOURCES

Allen, Thomas B., ed. *We Americans.* Washington, D.C.: National Geographic Book Service, 1975.

American History Illustrated. Feb. 1976.

Baker, Pearl. *A Handbook of History, McDuffie County, Georgia, 1870–1970.* Thomson, Ga.: Progress-News Publishing Co., 1972.

———. "The Itinerant Courthouse," *Columbia News* (Sept. 1968).

———. *The Story of Wrightsboro, 1768–1964.* Thomson, Ga.: Wrightsboro Restoration Foundation, 1980.

Bennett, William J. "From the Age of Discovery to a World at War," *America: The Last Best Hope,* vol. 1. Nashville, Tenn.: Nelson Current, 2006.

Bernstein, Richard. *Reader's Companion to American History.* Boston: Houghton Mifflin Co., 1991.

Bonner, James C. *The Georgia Story.* Oklahoma City–Chattanooga: Harlow Publishing Corp., 1961.

Boyer, Paul S., ed. *The Oxford Companion to United States History.* Oxford–New York: Oxford University Press, 2001.

Bridges, Edison C., Harvey H. Jackson, Kenneth H. Thomas, and James N. Young. *Georgia's Signers and the Declaration of Independence.* Covington, Ga.: Cherokee Publishing Co., 1981

Brooks, Robert P. *History of Georgia.* Athens: University of Georgia Press, 1972.

Campbell, Tunis, and the Georgia Freedmen. *Freedom's Shore.* Athens: University of Georgia Press, 1986.

Candler, Allen D., ed. "Proceedings of the President and Assistants, Oct. 12, 1741, to Oct. 30, 1754," *The Colonial Records of the State of Georgia* 6 (1906).

Carter, Jimmy. *The Hornet's Nest: A Novel of the Revolutionary War.* New York: Simon & Schuster, 2003.

Cartledge, Rev. Grover Harrison. *Historical Sketches: Presbyterian Churches and Early Settlers in Northeast Georgia.* Athens, Ga., 1968. Copyright: Historical Foundation of the Presbyterian and Reformed Churches, Montreat, N.C., 1960.

Cashin, Edward J., Jr. *The Brightest Arm of the Savannah: The Augusta Canal, 1845–2000.* Augusta, Ga.: Augusta Canal Authority, 2002.

———. *Colonial Augusta: Key of the Indian Country.* Macon, Ga.: Mercer University Press, 1986.

———. *The King's Ranger. Thomas Brown and the American Revolution on the Southern Frontier.* Athens: University of Georgia Press, 1989.

———. *Old Springfield: Race and Religion in Augusta, Ga.* Augusta: Springfield Village Park Foundation, 1995.

———. *The Story of Augusta.* Spartanburg, S.C.: Reprint Co., 1991.

———. *William Bartram and the American Revolution on the Southern Frontier.* Columbia, S.C.: University of South Carolina Press, 2000.

Cashin, Edward J., Jr., and Heard Robertson. *Augusta and the American Revolution: Events in the Georgia Back Country, 1773–1783.* Printed for the Richmond County Historical Society, by the Ashantilly Press, Darien, Ga., 1975.

Chantrell, Glynnis, ed. *Oxford Dictionary of Word Histories.* Oxford-New York: Oxford University Press, 2002.

Chrastina, Paul. "Greene's Army Faces Larger British Forces," *Old News*, 13, no. 4 (Dec. 2001), 9–12.

Clements, John. *Georgia Facts: A Comprehensive Look at Georgia Today, County by County.* Dallas, Tex.: Clements Research II, Inc., 1989.

Coleman, Kenneth. *The American Revolution in Georgia, 1763–1789.* Athens: University of Georgia Press, 1958.

———. *Colonial Georgia: A History.* New York: Charles Scribner's Sons, 1976.

———. *Georgia History in Outline.* Athens: University of Georgia Press, 1960.

Coleman, Kenneth, ed., and Jackie Erney. *Famous Georgians.* Atlanta: Georgia Department of Archives and History, 1976.

Coleman, Kenneth, general ed. *A History of Georgia.* Athens: University of Georgia Press, 1977.

Cook, James F. *The Governors of Georgia, 1754–1995.* Macon, Ga.: Mercer University Press, 1995.

Coulter, Ellis Merton. *Georgia: A Short History.* Chapel Hill: University of North Carolina Press, 1960.

———. *Old Petersburg and the Broad River Valley of Georgia.* Athens: University of Georgia Press, 1965.

Crutchfield, James A. *It Happened in Georgia.* 2nd ed. Guilford, Conn.: Globe Pequot Press, 2007.

Dameron, Dave. *Benning's Brigade.* vol. 2. Westminster, Md.: Heritage Books, 2005.

Davis, Robert Scott, compiler. *Quaker Records of Georgia.* Roswell, Ga.: Augusta Genealogical Society, 1986.

Doctoro, E. L. *The March.* New York: Random House, 2005.

Dunn, Mark. "Fort Gordon," *New Georgia Encyclopedia.* http://www .georgiaencyclopedia.org/nge/Article.jsp?id=h-1321

Evans, Lawton B. *A History of Georgia.* New York–Cincinnati–Chicago: American Book Co., 1908.

Fleming, Berry, ed. *Autobiography of a Colony.* Athens: University of Georgia Press, 1957.

Fleming, Thomas. *Liberty! The American Revolution.* New York: Penguin Group, 1997.

Foner, Eric. *Reconstruction: America's Unfinished Revolution, 1863–1877.* Francis Parkman Prize Edition, History Book Club, New York, by arrangement with HarperCollins Publishers, Inc., 2005.

Foner, Eric, and John A. Garraty, eds. *The Reader's Companion to American History.* Boston: Houghton Mifflin Co., 1991.

Foster, William O. *James Jackson: Duelist and Militant Statesman, 1757–1806.* Athens: University of Georgia Press, 1960.

Gilmer, George R. *Sketches of Some of the First Settlers of Upper Georgia.* Baltimore: Genealogical Publishing Co., 1965.

Granger, Mary, ed. *Savannah River Plantations.* Savannah: Georgia Historical Society, 1947.

Hanson, Robert H. *History of the Georgia Railroad.* Johnson City, Tenn.: Overmountain Press, 1996.

Harris, J. William. *Plain Folk and Gentry in a Slave Society: White Liberty and Black Slavery in Augusta's Hinterlands*. Middletown, Conn.: Wesleyan University Press, 1985.

Harris, Joel C. *Stories of Georgia*. Spartanburg, S.C.: Reprint Co., 1972.

Harris, Waldo P., III, and James D. Mosteller. *Georgia's First Continuing Baptist Church: A History of the Kiokee Baptist Church in Georgia*. College Park, Ga.: N & R Printing, Inc., 1997.

Hatcher, George, ed. *Georgia Rivers*. Athens: University of Georgia Press, 1962.

Holley, Thomas. *Company F-Thomson Guards: Tenth Regiment Georgia Volunteers, Army of Northern Virginia, Confederate States of America*. Fernandina Beach, Fla.: Wolfe Publishing, 2000.

———. *Company K-Hamilton Rangers: 48th Georgia Infantry Regiment, Army of Northern Virginia*, Confederate States of America. Printed in the U.S.A., 2007.

———. *Company K-Ramsey Volunteers: The Sixteenth Georgia Infantry Regiment, Army of Northern Virginia, Confederate States of America*. Fernandina Beach, Fla.: Wolfe Publishing, 1995.

Hollingsworth, Dixon. *Indians on the Savannah River*. Sylvania, Ga.: Partridge Pond Press, 1976.

Hooker, Richard J., ed. *The Carolina Backcountry on the Eve of the Revolution: The Journal and Other Writings of Charles Woodmason*. Chapel Hill: University of North Carolina Press, 1953.

Inscoe, John C., ed. *Georgia in Black and White: Explorations in the Race Relations of a Southern State, 1865–1950*. Athens: University of Georgia Press, 1994.

Jackson, Edwin L., Mary E. Stakes, Lawrence R. Hepburn, and Mary A. Hepburn. *The Georgia Studies Book: Our State and the Nation*. Athens: University of Georgia Press, 1998.

Jackson, Harvey H., and Phinizy Spalding, eds. *Forty Years of Adversity.* Athens: University of Georgia Press, 1984.

Johnson, Charles J., Jr. *Mary Telfair: The Life and Legacy of a Nineteenth-Century Woman.* Savannah: Frederic C. Beil, 2002.

Jones, Charles C., Jr. *The Dead Towns of Georgia.* Atlanta: Cherokee Publishing Co., 1974.

———. *Memorial History of Augusta, Georgia: From Its Settlement in 1735 to the Close of the Eighteenth Century.* Spartanburg, S.C.: Reprint Co., 1980.

Jones, Charles Edgeworth. *Georgia in the War, 1861–1865.* Augusta, Ga.: Self-published, 1899.

Jones, Dorothy M. *Wrightsboro: 1768–1799: McDuffie County, Georgia,* 1870, for The Wrightsboro Quaker Community Foundation, Inc., Printed by The McDuffie Progress, Thomson, Ga., 1982.

Jordan, Robert H., and J. Gregg Puster. *Courthouses in Georgia, 1825–1983.* Norcross, Ga.: Harrison Co., Publishers, 1984.

Joyner, Amy. "Plenty to Do: Still Aboard Columbia," *Augusta Chronicle* May 12, 1999, 1–A.

Kane, Sharyn, and Richard Keeton. *Beneath These Waters: 11,500 Years Along the Savannah River.* 2nd ed., Funded by the U.S. Army Corps of Engineers, Savannah District, Administered by the Interagency Archeological Service Division, National Park Service–Southeast Region, Atlanta, Ga. 1994.

———. *In Those Days: African-American Life Near the Savannah River.* Funded by the U.S. Army Corps of Engineers, Savannah District, Administered by the Interagency Archeological Services Division, National Park Service–Southeast Region, Atlanta, GA, 1994.

Kelley, Janette. *Our Heritage: Personalities, 1754–1983.* Thomson, Ga.: Luckey Printing Co., 1983.

Killion, Ronald G., and Charles T. Waller. *Georgia and the Revolution.* Atlanta: Cherokee Publishing Co., 1975.

King, Spencer B., Jr. *Georgia Voices: A Documentary History to 1872.* Athens: University of Georgia Press, 1966.

Kirby, Bill, deputy metro ed. *The Place We Call Home: A Collection of Articles About Local History From the Augusta Chronicle.* Augusta, Ga., 1997.

Knight, Lucian Lamar. *Georgia's Landmarks, Memorials and Legends.* 2 vols. Atlanta: Byrd Printing Co., 1913, 1914.

———. *Reminiscences of Famous Georgians.* 2 vols. Atlanta: Franklin-Turner Co., 1907.

Lamplugh, George R. *Politics on the Periphery: Factions and Parties in Georgia, 1783–1806.* Cranbury, N.J.: Associated University Presses, Inc., 1986.

———. "William Few's Brownsboro Plan," *Richmond County Historical Society* (Winter 1973), 40–45.

Lane, Mills. *People of Georgia.* Savannah: Beehive Press, 1992.

Lee, Angie. *Augusta Chronicle,* Oct. 14, 1979.

McCommons, Mrs. Leila, and Miss Clara Stovall. *History of McDuffie County.* Tignall, Ga.: Boyd Publishing Co., 1988.

McCullar, Bernice. *This Is Your Georgia.* Montgomery, Ala.: Viewpoint Publications, Inc., 1972.

———. *This Is Your Georgia.* Edited and revised by Stanley Chambers. Montgomery, Ala.: Viewpoint Publications, Inc., 1982.

McPherson, James M. "Emancipation Proclamation and the Thirteenth Amendment," in Foner and Garraty, *Reader's Companion to American History.*

McWhiney, Grady. *Cracker Culture: Celtic Ways in the Old South*. Tuscaloosa: University of Alabama Press, 1988.

Macy, Jesse. *The Anti-slavery Crusade: A Chronicle of the Gathering Storm*. New Haven: Yale University Press, 1919.

Mellichamp, Josephine. *Senators From Georgia*. Huntsville, Ala.: Strode Publishers, Inc., 1976.

Miller, Zell. *Great Georgians, 1733–1983*. Franklin Springs, Ga.: Advocate Press, 1983.

Mooney, Chase C. *William H. Crawford, 1772–1834*. Lexington: University Press of Kentucky, 1974.

Moore, Rayburn S., ed. *Man of Letters in the Nineteenth-Century South: Selected Letters of Paul Hamilton Hayne*. Baton Rouge: Louisiana University Press, 1982.

Morgan, Edmund S. *American Slavery, American Freedom: The Ordeal of Colonial Virginia*. Francis Parkman Prize Edition, History Book Club. New York: by arrangement with W. W. Norton & Company, Inc., 2005.

Morgareidge, Kay R., ed. *Foundations of Government: The Georgia Counties*. Atlanta: Hill R. Healan, Publisher, 1976.

Morse, Joseph Laffan, ed. in chief. *The Universal Standard Encyclopedia*. New York: Standard Reference Works Publishing Co., 1956–1957.

Neill, Brian. "Mars Tripping," *The Metro Spirit*. Jan. 29, 2004. p. 16.

Newman, Joseph, directing ed. *200 Years: A Bicentennial Illustrated History of the United States*. 2 vols. Washington, D.C.: U.S. News & World Report, 1973.

Pavey, Rob. "Deal in Works," *Augusta Chronicle*, June 10, 1909, 1–A.

———. "Debate on Lake's Name Continues," *Augusta Chronicle*, Apr. 12, 2004, 1–A.

Perkerson, Medora Field. *White Columns in Georgia*. New York: Bonanza Books, 1952.

Perryman, Clinton J. *History of Lincoln County*. Self-published, 1933.

Pollard, Lester, ed. *Rosemont 104th Anniversary Booklet*. Appling, Ga.: Rosemont Baptist Association, Inc., 2006.

Powell, Jim. *The Triumph of Liberty: A 2,000–year History, Told through the Lives of Freedom's Greatest Champions*. New York: The Free Press, 2000.

Presley, Delmar E. "The Crackers of Georgia," *Georgia Historical Quarterly* 60, no. 2 (Summer 1976), 115.

Reese, Trevor, ed. *The Most Delightful Country of the Universe: The Colony of Georgia, 1717–1734*. Savannah: Beehive Press, 1972.

Ruppersburg, P. B., ed. *Georgia Voices: Non Fiction*. Athens: University of Georgia Press, 1994.

Shearer, Benjamin F., and Barbara S. Shearer. *State Names, Seals, Flags, and Symbols*. Westport, Conn.: Greenwood Press, 1994.

Smith, Gerald. *To Seek a Newer World: A History of Columbia County, Georgia*. Murfreesboro, Tenn.: Southern Heritage Press, 2001.

Smith, Jean Edward. *Grant*. New York: Simon & Schuster, 2001.

Standard, Janet Harvill. *The Wilkes County Scrapbook*. vol. A. Washington, Ga.: Wilkes County Publishing Co., 1970.

Stokes, Thomas L. *The Savannah*. Athens: University of Georgia Press, 1951.

Suddeth, Ruth Elgin, Isa Lloyd Osterhout, and George Lewis Hutcheson. *Empire Builders of Georgia*. 4th ed. Austin, Tex.: Steck Co., 1966.

Temple, Sarah Gober, and Kenneth Coleman. *Georgia Journeys, 1732–1754*. Athens: University of Georgia Press, 1961.

Thompson, C. Mildred. *Reconstruction in Georgia: Economic, Social, Political, 1865–1872*. Gloucester, Mass.: Peter Smith, 1964.

Thurmond, Michael. *Freedom: Georgia's Anti-Slavery Heritage, 1733–1865*. Atlanta: Longstreet Press, 2002.

Trueblood, Elton. *Abraham Lincoln: Theologian of American Anguish*. New York: Harper & Row, 1973.

Vandiver, Frank E. "Confederate States of America," in Foner and Garraty, *Reader's Companion to American History*. Boston: Houghton Mifflin, 1991.

White, George. *Statistics of the State of Georgia*. Savannah: W. Thorne Williams, 1849; repr., Spartanburg, S.C.: Reprint Co., 1972.

White, Michael. *Columbia County: A Study of Its Streams, Rivers, and Historic Water Mill Sites*. Augusta, Ga.: Self-published, 1998.

Wikipedia: The Free Encyclopedia.

Williams, David, Teresa Crisp Williams, and David Carlson. *Plain Folk in a Rich Man's War: Class and Dissent in Confederate Georgia*. Gainesville, Fla.: University Press of Florida, 2002.

Williams, Joseph B. *Land We Lived*. Self-published, 2005. Signature Book Printing, www.sbpbooks.com.

Wood, W. Kirk, ed. *A Northern Daughter, Southern Wife: The Civil War Reminiscences and Letters of Katharine H. Cumming, 1860–1865*. Augusta, Ga.: Richmond County Historical Society, 1976.

Woodworth, Steven El, and Kenneth J. Winkle. *Atlas of the Civil War*. New York: Oxford University Press, 2004.

INDEX

Index

Index

Index

BARBARA SEABORN was raised in New England, graduated from Gordon College in Wenham, Massachusetts, and moved to Columbia County when her military husband was stationed at Fort Gordon. A free-lance writer and musician, she has pursued both professions for most of her adult life. Currently she is a columnist for the *Columbia County News-Times*, writes music commentary for the Lorenz Corporation in Dayton, Ohio, and serves as organist at Woodlawn United Methodist Church in Augusta. She has two sons and five grandchildren.

Award-winning artist and Columbia County native, LYNELL WIDENER has painted for pleasure and by profession since she graduated from high school. In addition to taking art lessons from a variety of local artists, she has studied art at the University of South Carolina, Aiken, and at Augusta College, now Augusta State University. Her paintings are widely displayed today in local businesses and private homes. In 1979 she was declared "Artist-Laureate" of Columbia County. Her family includes three children, five grandchildren, and three great-grandchildren.